Death in the
Baltic

For Taylor,
Warm regards,

[signature]

East Prussia (Ostpreußen) 1923–1939

- East Prussia
- Poland
- Free City of Danzig
- Lithuania
- Memelland (occupied in 1923 by Lithuania)
- Latvia

Lithuania

Memel

Tauragé

Curonian Lagoon

Memel-land

Heydekrug

Tilsit

Memel River

Königsberg

Pillau

Pregal River

Insterburg

Gumbinnen

Vistula Lagoon

Braunsberg

Frauenburg

Pr. Eylau

Danzig

Elbing

Heilsberg

Angerburg

Goldap

Marienburg

Rastenburg

Suwalki

Vistula River

Marienverder

Dt. Eylau

Osterode

Allenstein

Ortelsburg

Grudziądz

Poland

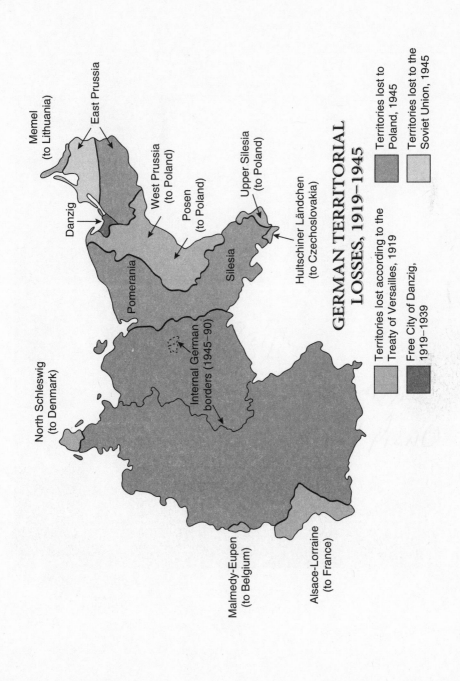

GERMAN TERRITORIAL LOSSES, 1919–1945

North Schleswig
(to Denmark)

Memel
(to Lithuania)

East Prussia

Danzig

West Prussia
(to Poland)

Posen
(to Poland)

Pomerania

Upper Silesia
(to Poland)

Silesia

Hultschiner Ländchen
(to Czechoslovakia)

Internal German
borders (1945–90)

Malmedy-Eupen
(to Belgium)

Alsace-Lorraine
(to France)

Territories lost according to the
Treaty of Versailles, 1919

Free City of Danzig,
1919–1939

Territories lost to
Poland, 1945

Territories lost to the
Soviet Union, 1945

Death in the Baltic

THE WORLD WAR II SINKING OF THE
WILHELM GUSTLOFF

CATHRYN J. PRINCE

palgrave
macmillan

First published in 2013 by PALGRAVE MACMILLAN® in the U.S.—
a division of St. Martin's Press LLC, 175 Fifth Avenue, New York, NY
10010.

Where this book is distributed in the UK, Europe and the rest of the
world, this is by Palgrave Macmillan, a division of Macmillan Publishers
Limited, registered in England, company number 785998, of Houndmills,
Basingstoke, Hampshire RG21 6XS.

Palgrave Macmillan is the global academic imprint of the above
companies and has companies and representatives throughout the world.

Palgrave® and Macmillan® are registered trademarks in the United
States, the United Kingdom, Europe and other countries.

ISBN: 978-0-230-34156-2

Library of Congress Cataloging-in-Publication Data

Prince, Cathryn J., 1969–
   Death in the Baltic : the sinking of the Wilhelm Gustloff / Cathryn J.
Prince.
      pages   cm
   Includes bibliographical references.
   ISBN-13: 978-0-230-34156-2
   ISBN-10: 0-230-34156-X
   1. Wilhelm Gustloff (Ship) 2. Shipwrecks—Baltic Sea—History—20th
century. 3. Germans—Prussia, East (Poland and Russia)—History—20th
century. 4. Refugees—Prussia, East (Poland and Russia)—History—20th
century. 5. World War, 1939–1945—Evacuation of civilians—Prussia,
East (Poland and Russia) 6. Shipwreck victims—Interviews. 7. World
War, 1939–1945—Baltic Sea. 8. World War, 1939–1945—Naval
operations—Submarine. 9. World War, 1939–1945—Naval operations,
Soviet. I. Title.
D772.3.P76   2013
940.53'161089310438—dc23
                                                     2012030182

A catalogue record of the book is available from the British Library.

Design by Letra Libre

First edition: April 2013

10 9 8 7 6 5 4 3 2 1

Printed in the United States of America.

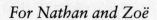

For Nathan and Zoë

CONTENTS

Eight pages of photographs appear between pages 112 and 113.

ACKNOWLEDGMENTS

lthough writing can at times be a lonely process, it is not possible to complete a book alone. I am therefore grateful for having so many people in my life who were present during the writing of this book.

Many thanks to the archivists at the United States Holocaust Memorial Museum in Washington, DC, and at the National Archives and Records Administration in College Park, Maryland. Thanks to Simon Hessdorfer of the Bundesarchiv in Bayreuth, Germany, for answering my questions from afar. Thanks to Wendy Gulley, curator at the Submarine Force Museum in New London, Connecticut. Many thanks to Marco Hedler for his valuable research assistance and to Edward Petruskevich, curator of the online Wilhelm Gustloff Museum. Thanks are also due to the many librarians and professors who pointed me in the right direction when it came to tracking down bits and pieces of history.

I am incredibly grateful to Jill D. Swenson and the entire team at Swenson Book Development. Jill, thank you for helping develop the initial book proposal, for helping me shepherd it through the writing process, and most of all, for your friendship and advice.

My deep thanks to my editor at Palgrave Macmillan, Luba Ostashevsky, for recognizing the importance of this story and giving it a home. Your insightful edits helped drive the narrative of this story and kept it on track. I'd like to also recognize Laura Lancaster and the entire team at Palgrave Macmillan, including Andrew Varhol, Victoria Wallis, Allison Frascatore, and Roberta Melville, as well as the art department for their exceptional and bold book jacket design.

My heartfelt thanks go to the survivors and their families for opening their doors to me, both literally and figuratively, for sharing their stories, photographs, diaries, and letters.

For my parents, Marvin and Norma Prince, the words "thank you" will never adequately express how much your encouragement and enthusiasm for what I do means to me.

My children, Nathan and Zoë: Perched upon my soul, you are my laughter and light.

Pierre: From the start you knew this was not going to be an easy book to write. I am blessed to have you by my side. You are my yesterday, you are my today, and you are my tomorrow.

INTRODUCTION

Sometime after the publication of my second book, and well before the idea for my third book took root, my father mentioned a startling fact. He told me about a small passage in a history trivia book that mentioned a German ship sunk at the end of the war in Europe, in January 1945, which ranked as the highest loss of life in peacetime or wartime. He said the sinking made the *Titanic* look like a fender bender.

Few people outside the military took note of the sinking and few American historians have written about it. The most information I found consisted of footnotes in World War Two histories mentioning the bare facts: that the *Wilhelm Gustloff* was sunk by a Soviet torpedo early in the morning on January 30, 1945, and that more than 9,000 refugees perished in the frigid waters of the Baltic. I had no explanation for the lack of news articles. Was it because it was something that happened to our enemy? Was it because there were no Americans aboard? As has happened before, my reporter's instincts kicked in, and I promptly began researching the *Wilhelm Gustloff*.

Looking at January 30, 1945, and the weeks, months, and years before that date allows us to gain further insight into one of the most tumultuous times in history. By hearing from a few whose stories have not yet been told, we gain a little more understanding of what millions endured.

I got the contact information for Horst Woit, who had been a 10-year-old boy aboard the *Wilhelm Gustloff* with his mother Meta, from a Canadian documentarian I found through a website. After the sinking, Horst Woit lived behind the iron curtain in Soviet-occupied East Germany for several years until immigrating to Canada in the late 1940s.

My mother and I traveled to Canada to meet Horst. Wearing a faded blue sweatshirt and jeans, Horst waited for us outside, his dog beside him. We hugged hello. It seemed a natural greeting. Nearly 70 years later, the sinking continues to haunt Horst. It is something he thinks about every day. Though the loss of life was massive, and as desperate as the conditions were that forced Horst and his mother to flee, stories like Horst's have remained largely unknown, in part because it happened in wartime to refugees and naval personnel from Nazi East Prussia. Growing up in Canada after the war, Horst told us, he read stories about the *Titanic*—what a horrific accident it had been, the grisly details of how almost 2,000 people perished in the frozen waters. In those moments he would want to yell, "Well, let me tell you about a sinking nearly five times as bad as the *Titanic*."

I knew after the first hour of our visit that Horst's story and those of the other survivors had to be told. Stories like Eva Dorn Rothschild's, who at 86 still shows the same spirit that got her kicked out of Hitler Youth when she was barely 13. Or that of Helga Reuter and her parents, Kurt and Marta. They had owned a furniture store in Königsberg until the Nazis requisitioned it and turned it into a uniform factory. Kurt and his wife did what they could to make sure the workers were well fed and clothed. I visited Helga in Las Vegas, Nevada, where she now lives in a one-room apartment in her son's house.

Black-and-white photographs of those who survived and those who died when the *Wilhelm Gustloff* sank beneath the Baltic Sea sit on my desk. They are a constant reminder of why I wrote this particular book. For nearly 70 years the survivors have lived in a world where most people are ignorant of this wartime catastrophe. By looking at this tragedy through several individual stories, another perspective of World War Two surfaces. By listening to the stories and reading the letters and diaries of those who survived and those who perished in the icy waters of the Baltic Sea on that January morning in 1945, a moment in history is resurrected.

One

"YOU HAVE TO GO
ON THIS SHIP"

To the streams of refugees who first glimpsed the ship soaring several stories out of the water, the *Wilhelm Gustloff* appeared as a harbinger of hope.

The Russian Army was closing in on East Prussia's coastline, and by January 1945 most every German—from the highest ranking officer to the mother trying to protect her child—understood that they had lost the war. The Third Reich was in free fall, on the verge of social, political and economic ruin, but to say as much amounted to treason. Indeed, displaying a defeatist attitude earned junior military officers a swift execution.[1] The teenagers who were drafted to be the face of Nazism in the Hitler Youth began to desert. If they were caught, they were forced to wear cardboard signs that read, "I am a deserter. I was a coward in the face of the enemy," before being thrown over balconies with ropes around their necks.[2] On the eastern front the German Army investigated those soldiers suspected of self-inflicted wounds, trying to gather legal proof of defeatism.[3] The Nazi leadership strained to convince the German people to ignore the shifting forces of war. Adolf Hitler broadcast daily orations rousing his people to fight to the last man.[4] Reich Minister of Propaganda Joseph Goebbels insisted that Germany could still emerge victorious. Despite the threat of retribution from the police, thousands of Germans living in the eastern part of the country—referred to as East Prussia—chose to evacuate their home cities and towns. For days they arrived in a constant stream to the port of Gotenhafen, a major naval base situated in East Prussia on the Bay of Danzig. The province also shared a border with Lithuania to the north and east, and to the west lay the Free City of Danzig, and to the south and east, Poland. These refugees were part of a late-stage effort called Operation Hannibal that was to evacuate them from the advancing Soviet Red Army.

The Baltic seaside city of Gotenhafen (now Gdynia—see appendix with list of cities and current names) had come under Nazi control in 1939 after the Third Reich invaded Poland. The Germans renamed the seaside city after the Goths, an ancient German tribe. Almost immediately the military turned the seaport into a German naval base. They expanded the base in 1940, making it an extension of the Kiel shipyard, located across the Baltic Sea near the Danish border. Until the Soviet onslaught, the Gotenhafen harbor had been largely spared from the hostilities, which made it an attractive place for heavy cruisers and battleships to lay anchor.

Days before the first bedraggled evacuees arrived in Gotenhafen, the German authorities ordered Friedrich Petersen, the *Wilhelm Gustloff*'s 63-year-old captain, to acquire fuel, prepare to take on refugees, and get ready to sail westward to the German port of Kiel. Before the war, the *Wilhelm Gustloff* had been a 25,000-ton passenger liner that took ordinary Germans on what was often their first vacation. During the war the *Gustloff* was first used as a hospital ship and then by the German navy as a U-boat training school. On that freezing January in 1945, it joined thousands of ships, large and small, in Operation Hannibal, an eleventh-hour exodus designed to transport primarily wounded military personnel and war materiel, and secondarily refugees from the eastern territories away from the fast approaching Red Army. The *Gustloff* wasn't the only ship crowding the key naval port, but at 684 feet long it was one of the largest. Along with the *Gustloff* sat a cohort of smaller liners, fishing boats, dinghies, and trawlers.

With the influx of refugees from across East Prussia, Gotenhafen's population swelled. Hundreds of thousands of people clogged the harbor, trailing their belongings. Everyone vied for boarding passes. Initially, the German authorities issued passes to wounded soldiers and sailors and to Nazi Party officials and their families only. Later, passes were given to women with children and families. The harbor thrummed with fear and anxiety. An air of lawlessness threatened the once orderly city. As a warning to others, German police shot looters and left their bodies lying on the streets or strung from lampposts.

There were people of every age; women wrapped in woolen shawls, men in fur coats, children perched on sleds. Many had been without adequate food and water for weeks. People searched for food, a ladleful of soup or a slice of bread, amid broken buildings and bomb craters. Rats ran rampant over mounds of garbage. People sought shelter in abandoned trolley cars and abandoned buildings. There were no resources to collect the piled-up corpses. Wounded soldiers arrived daily from the front lines. As the refugees abandoned their belongings, the port of Gotenhafen resembled a graveyard of overturned carts, upended sledges, discarded trunks and suitcases.

The thousands of evacuees waited sometimes days on end in these conditions. The Nazi leadership had finally allowed them to leave their homes and try to outrun the Red Army troops, which were, at that moment, surging toward the Baltic Coast.[5]

In this crowd stood a little boy of ten gripping his mother's hand. Dressed in long underwear and ski pants, his hair was yellow. Once, Horst Woit lived in Elbing, East Prussia, a German enclave on a lagoon to the Baltic Sea. The town's iron works manufactured locomotives, U-boats, and armored vehicles for the German military. The Russian Army would soon lay waste to the land.[6]

Woit was sad that he and his mother, Meta, had left their home. Home meant bread slathered with marmalade his mother had saved even during strict wartime rationing, a box of tin soldiers, and a mother who tucked him in nightly. Home comforted the young boy after his father left for the front just a year and half before. While war raged across much of Europe, his home remained largely peaceful. Then the Soviet tanks came too close and war thrust the Woits into a desperate flight for safety.

The Woits set out from their house intending to reach Schwerin, a city northwest of Berlin. That's where his mother's younger brother and his wife and son lived. The family had decided it would be the best and safest place to meet, as it was likely to fall under either British or American control. Once there, Meta would resolve whether she and her son would stay in Germany or emigrate.

Horst, an only child, was born on December 24, 1934, in the city of Insterburg. His grandparents lived in neighboring Gumbinnen and his aunt lived with her family in nearby Königsberg. His parents left Insterburg and moved to Elbing, 37 miles east of Danzig, before his second birthday. Today Horst treasures the few pictures that date from his childhood, collected after the war from relatives and friends. One of them shows Horst as a toddler, standing in front of a school. Later in the war the school was turned into a military hospital. In another black-and-white photo taken on his first day of school, a beaming six-year-old holds his first-day coronet of cookies, a family tradition.

The Woits didn't own a car. Taking the train to visit his grandparents, Heinrich and Johanna Wesse, in Gumbinnen remains one of Horst Woit's fondest childhood memories. He remembers his mother putting him on the train in Elbing with a sign hanging around his neck declaring his destination in case he forgot. After Meta took him to the train station and helped him board, Horst would settle into his seat, preferably next to a window but always under the watchful eye of the conductor. He loved watching the landscape roll past during the trip.

"By the time I got to there I had driven everybody nuts, asking all the time 'Are we there yet?'" Horst said. "My Grandpa used to pick me up at the train station; he was a great guy. I have a picture of him from the First World War on the Russian Front and one of Bismarck on parade."

Horst and his grandparents were close. Adventure filled his weekend visits. On at least two occasions his grandfather rushed the young boy to the hospital for serious scrapes and cuts. He still has the scars.

Then, in late 1944 the train trips stopped and became smaller in his mind, the same way the station in Elbing looked as the train pulled away. Soon "all one ever heard was 'the Russians are coming closer,'" Horst said. Then too, ever so quietly, worry trickled into the house. And just like that the smells and sights of lovely childhoods, of flowers, spring, birds, and bicycles disappeared.

"At the time the Second World War started I was five years old and I did not understand the real meaning; but as time went on I could not go to the school I started at—it became a hospital. Then my father was drafted into the army and my mother had to go to work. I spent a lot of time on my own, browsing the city," Woit said.[7] After Horst's school became a hospital, he went to classes in another building. The adults in his life spoke little about the war. Looking back on that time, Horst said he believes his mother, his teachers, and his grandparents were trying to protect the children.

In January 1945 Leonilla "Nellie" Minkevics Zobs and her parents, Voldemars and Zelma, also chose to flee East Prussia before the Red Army could attack. Years after the war, the Minkevicses eventually moved to Lincoln, Nebraska, nearly half a world away from the town where she grew up. Nellie and her husband, Peter Zobs, became naturalized citizens.[8] Of course, the then 24-year-old remembered the war's outbreak in 1939 and what happened in the weeks before the Soviet tanks penetrated the German lines during the winter of 1944–1945. A few years before she died, Nellie recalled the moment she left her home for the last time to walk to Gotenhafen where a boat waited to whisk her to safety.[9] Together with her father and some family friends they walked to the pier where the vessel awaited.[10] Like the thousands of other refugees boarding the *Wilhelm Gustloff*, she wore heavy winter boots and a woolen coat over her dress.

"On the roads of the Reich were not only troops hurrying toward new positions but hundreds of thousands of refugees— fleeing the frontier areas as the invaders approached, fleeing the cities as the bombers came over," she said, recounting her story decades after the event for a newspaper interview. "We thought we were so lucky to get on the *Wilhelm*. We were getting away."[11]

Eighteen-year-old Eva Dorn Rothschild regarded the *Wilhelm Gustloff* with trepidation.

"It was big. It was easy to hit. I didn't feel safe, and I had a very bad feeling," she said nearly 70 years later, sitting on her plant-filled balcony in Ascona, Switzerland. In the distance, the Alps rise protectively around Lake Maggiore.[12] Art and artifacts fill her apartment, and music from the 1930s wafts softly from inside, a reminder of her childhood when she used to go often to the theater.

Eva was a conscript in the German Navy Women's Auxiliary, and in January 1945 she had already been stationed in seaside Gotenhafen for more than a year. She served in various capacities, including in a spotlight battery and as a lookout for enemy aircraft. Wearing her dark blue uniform and cap, Eva boarded the *Gustloff* almost a full week before the other refugees. She carried a small suitcase aboard and little else. Reflecting on those years, she said she doesn't remember being scared of the Russians in the way the civilians were; her duties didn't leave much time to think.

Born in 1926, Eva grew up in Haale (Saale), Germany, about 24 miles from Leipzig, one of Europe's principal centers for music and art. She once dreamed of singing opera, not a far-fetched dream since her parents were musically gifted. Her mother, Paulina Aliza Dorn, was a classically trained opera singer; her father, Matius Brantmeyer, played the viola in a chamber ensemble. The pair, though never married, had four children—three boys and a girl. Eva was 11 years younger than her youngest brother. Hers was not an easy childhood. Her parents parted ways when she was quite young, leaving her to live with a mother more interested in shopping and luxuries than attending to Eva. Her mother had lost her job in the theater during the Depression and her father had remarried. Yet, though they were cash-strapped, Eva's mother still bought clothes and cosmetics on credit.

"She was always beautiful and always beautifully dressed. But she was also tempestuous," Eva said of her mother. During the early 1930s, Eva's mother rented out rooms in their flat to help pay off her debts and also sold their big iron stove. It wasn't enough. Paulina and her daughter had little to eat. Eva remembers carrying her tin pail to a soup kitchen to get food. Ironically, the soup kitchen volunteers cooked on the old stove that her mother had sold, so the workers usually gave Eva an extra serving or two.

"I was forced to be a grown-up very early in life," Eva said, sitting tall in her chair, gracefully holding a cup of hot coffee. Her ability to fend for herself shows itself in her elegant carriage. At 86, Eva is steel under grace.

Milda Bendrich boarded the *Wilhelm Gustloff* with her two-year-old daughter, Inge. Still tethered to the pier, the sides of the former hospital ship and U-boat training vessel rose like a sheer cliff out of the water.

Decades later, in a long, handwritten letter to Inge, Milda Bendrich explained how it was they left their home in Gotenhafen in the middle of winter and joined the mass pilgrimage to the docks. Bendrich made the trip with her daughter, her parents, Rosalie and Karl Felsch, as well as two elderly neighbors. "It was the last week in January 1945 and the coldest winter in two decades. The Soviet armies were about to engulf Gotenhafen and at long last, after weeks of being forbidden, the women, children, and the aged were given permission to leave their homes. Suddenly the Germans—old German nationals like us, Reich Germans who were posted to the front for war duties, Baltic Germans who were invited to come back to the Reich at Hitler's invitation . . . as well as refugees from areas now occupied by the Russians—realized that everyone had to flee as best they could," wrote Bendrich. "Previously leaving meant death; a bullet in the brain. Now permission was granted even to relatives of [those in the] German armed forces. People were also allowed to freely discuss the events at hand."[13]

Milda's friend knew a purser who was serving on the *Wilhelm Gustloff*. Milda hoped this contact would be enough for her to secure much-coveted passes for the ship. As one of the officers in charge of boarding papers and financial matters, the purser handed Bendrich two tickets. Emboldened, Bendrich asked if she might have four additional boarding passes. She wanted two for her parents and two for her elderly neighbors who had moved to Gotenhafen from Warsaw before the war started.

Initially the purser refused Milda's request, repeating his orders that he could only issue tickets to families with young children. As Bendrich's parents and elderly companions were retired and had no young children in their care, they didn't quite meet the Third Reich's requirements for receiving boarding passes. The

purser explained that room had to be spared for wounded soldiers, U-boat crews, naval personnel, and the young women serving in the naval auxiliary. Next, women with young children were
permitted, then families. Only after them would those traveling
alone be considered for a place aboard the large ship. Bendrich
pleaded. She simply couldn't abandon her parents and neighbors
to the Soviet Army, and, if he denied her appeal, she just might
refuse to board. For some reason unbeknown to Milda, her emotional appeal together with a brazen display of self-sacrifice and
bravado convinced the young man.

"In this way I blackmailed the purser into giving me the six
tickets I needed, and thus the blame for the fate of my parents
and these two elderly ladies rests with me," Bendrich explained to
Inge in her postwar letter.

Before the war Bendrich had lived in Warsaw, Poland. In the
1920s, she and her two brothers decided to move to East Prussia
to look for work. Milda was an English-Polish-German transla-
tor and her brother worked in shipping. At the time Gotenhafen,
a lively city, presented the perfect opportunity. Milda's parents
didn't move to the city until 1944, after life in Warsaw became
too dangerous.[14]

"My grandfather was a Baptist minister and a schoolteacher
for Baptist children. I do not know if he was still working when
the Nazis took power," Inge Bendrich Roedecker said.

Like Bendrich, the thousands of East Prussians waiting to
board the *Wilhelm Gustloff* had vacated homes, some of them in
towns where they had lived for two, three, or more generations.
The refugees hailed from deeply traditional villages in East Prussia
on slightly quaint farmlands in typical one-story farmhouses set
back from the street. They tended cherry, apple, and nut orchards.
Other East Prussians hailed from bustling cities and towns such as
Königsberg, Danzig, and Elbing. Germans had lived in East Prussia for at least 700 years. Over time the area became ethnically

and culturally mixed. There were some ethnic Poles with German names and Germans with Polish names.[15]

There were people who led compartmentalized lives, never mingling with those of other faiths and ethnicities. Religious differences marked East Prussia. The Prussian Germans adhered to the Protestant faith, the Poles to Catholicism, and the Russians followed the Orthodox Church.

Although East Prussia was technically part of the Third Reich, Berlin and the war felt distant. For example, Königsberg lay about 327 miles from Berlin, which created both a physical and emotional distance. Not every East Prussian harbored a deep-seated desire to formally reunite with greater Germany. Indeed, they wanted the protection of the German government as the Soviet Red Army advanced, but the majority of them didn't want to leave their homes.

Born in the seaside town of Schwarzort, East Prussia, Rose Rezas Petrus was a young woman of 19 when she laid eyes on the *Wilhelm Gustloff*. In 1939, with war clearly on the horizon, the Germans sent Rose, together with other ethnic Germans living on the coast, deeper into East Prussia to work.[16] Before the Soviets closed in during the winter of 1944–1945, Rose worked on a German army telephone switchboard. In the war years, young women were also trained as radio operators, telegraphers, stenographers, and workers in munitions factories. When the Soviets moved closer to the front, many of these women were sent to work digging and building antitank obstacles and supporting antiaircraft artillery crews. When survival meant fleeing west, Rose and her sister, Ursula, made their way to Gotenhafen, where the *Wilhelm Gustloff* was anchored. Ursula had been visiting from Memel when the Russians advanced so far that she couldn't return to home. (Memel was an East Prussian city which, like Schwarzort, has since been returned to Lithuania.)

Now 86 and a mother of three, Rose lives in Littleton, Colorado, in an assisted living facility. She remembers everything that happened to her before, during, and after the war. Today the Atlantic Ocean separates her from her childhood. Yet "she speaks about it every day," said her son Peter.[17] Although Rose tried desperately to wipe the experience from her mind, forgetting became a useless exercise.

As a seaman-mechanic in the Kriegsmarine, the German navy, Walter Salk had been assigned to several ships during the war. In January 1945 he served on the *Wilhelm Gustloff*. Salk would have spent much of his time below decks in the belly of the ship, doing repairs and regular maintenance to keep it running smoothly. Before coming to Gotenhafen, the young man from Essen, Germany, had served on the *T.S. Mürwik*, a torpedo boat. It was during that deployment that Salk, with his bold eyebrows and cheerful eyes, met a young canteen worker named Christa Hausen. Their friendship blossomed.

Walter came from a very close-knit family and throughout his navy service he frequently wrote his parents, Hedwig and Willi Salk. Walter's older brother, Erwin, had died the year before when his U-boat sank in the North Atlantic.[18] Knowing how much his parents worried about him, Walter shielded them from war's realities. Instead, he preferred to ask them about home and how they were faring. The Krupp's factory was located in Essen, which made it and the city a target for Allied bombs. He also, without fail, asked after his little sister, Inge.

In December 1944, the Salk family received Walter's cheery but brief Christmas letter with welcome relief. They too knew the Americans and British were getting closer to Essen. More than 200 bombing sorties left the industrial city with more rubble than brick. The intensity of the bombing raids was one reason Hedwig and Willi agreed to send Walter's sister, Inge, to Czechoslovakia as part of the Kinderlandverschickung (KLV), or "Save the Children in the Country."

The program, which started in 1940, took children from urban areas and sent them to farms and other rural places. Ostensibly its aim was to protect children between the ages of four and the early teens, from the Allied bombing. The German leadership considered these children old enough to be separated from their parents. They sent them on trains to remote, rural villages for up to six months at a time. Families had virtually no choice but to participate in the KLV. Moreover, parents weren't encouraged to visit their children and many children weren't able to communicate with their parents. The children lived in Hitler Youth supervised facilities ranging from dilapidated inns to homey alpine resorts.[19] These children worked on farms and, among other duties, were also supposed to help reeducate those Germans coming from the East. Without the guidance and care of their parents, these children were immersed in the Third Reich's canon.

While in Czechoslovakia, Inge Salk faithfully kept a diary rather than risk sending letters home. The older youth in the program and the adult leaders frequently censored their charges' mail. Inge drew lively little pictures next to her many entries. She poured her heart out between its ruled pages and light brown cover. On February 10, 1944, Inge wrote a piercing entry: "My dear brother has fallen for the Fatherland. . . . I got the letter January 30, 1944, on a Sunday before noon. The first pain was indescribable . . . but the war has made us hard . . . but you just have to find your way out of this, just because you just have to. . . . I look at a picture of him and it seems like a bad dream, but I have to endure. . . . My thoughts keep turning to the past but they just don't find Erwin."[20]

Meanwhile, Inge's other brother, Walter, wrote home as often as he could, frequently recounting the mundane, from when he had duty to how many cigarettes he received. He always asked after Inge and his grandparents. He wrote shortly after the start of 1945, on January 3, to thank his family for the "Lovely greetings and the 50 DM [deutsche marks] of which I am grateful." His last letter was dated January 14, 1945, sixteen days before the *Wilhelm Gustloff* set sail. Even with Russian Army's swift advance and the uncertainty of his fate, Walter Salk's letter was happy.

"My dear Parents! . . . everything is as always. Yesterday, some comrades and I went out. . . . I will be glad when I leave Gotenhafen . . . and get stationed somewhere else. I will let you know my new address. Now I must close, I have duty later. . . . Your son, Walter."[21]

In January 1945, Irene East and Ellen Maybee, née Tschinkur, stood before the *Wilhelm Gustloff.*

"One day they came and got you and said you have to go on this ship," Ellen Tschinkur Maybee said.[22] The two girls went to the port and waited outside in the freezing harbor to board with their mother, Serafima, and their older cousin, Evelyn Krachmanow. She had come with them since her mother was sick with tuberculosis and too ill to travel. The Tschinkurs and Evelyn carried little. The only thing Serafima brought with her was a briefcase containing important papers, some jewelry, and money.[23]

In 1939, soon after the Germans and Russians signed the Molotov-Ribbentrop pact, Kurt and Serafima Tschinkur and their daughters, Irene and Ellen, had been forced to leave Riga, Latvia. The family was just one of millions forcibly uprooted from their homes because they were Baltic Germans. Their mother, Serafima Ivanova Karsubova, had been born in Moscow. Their father, Herbert Christoph, had been born in Riga. However, somewhere on Herbert's side, a few generations back, there was German blood. Therefore, they were "returned" to the Third Reich from the Soviet Union.

Irene and Ellen connected with many cultures as they grew up. They spoke Russian and Latvian and attended a kindergarten where they learned German and English. Their relatives lived in the same elegant building where their grandparents ran a bakery. Above the door hung the guild sign—a pretzel. Today, Irene wears a miniature gold version of the pretzel sign her father once wore on his watch fob.

The Tschinkurs had not been given much notice when they were resettled: They were allowed to take only one suitcase each. So brown-haired Irene and blonde-haired Ellen left behind their 39 dolls, each one dressed in clothes their mother had sewn. Knowing they would need some sort of currency, Serafima handed Irene several sterling silver teaspoons to hide under her clothes.

"'Don't show them; don't tell them you have them in your sweater,'" Irene said, remembering her mother's warning as they waited on the dock for the boat that was coming to take them away. "The German policeman bent down. I looked up. 'I'm not supposed to tell you I have silver spoons in my pocket,'" she blurted.

For some reason the policeman didn't punish the mother or her daughters, he simply nodded and let them pass with the silver. The family also took silver soupspoons. There is only one left; Serafima and Herbert Christoph traded the rest on the black market for food during the war.

"Everything was left behind in Riga. It's what you could carry. We thought we could go back," Irene said. "We had a dog, Lobo, who only ate from father's hand. We had to put him down because he would starve otherwise."

Although the Tschinkurs were not shipped to the ice-covered taiga of a Siberian labor camp, they were removed from their home. The trauma of their expulsion would forever cling to their family, long after the war ended and long after the family settled in Canada. That they would ultimately find freedom and safety in the West was not clear on the day Irene, Ellen, and their parents stood waiting to be sent to newly reabsorbed German territory in Eastern Prussia.[24]

Like many of their fellow shipwreck survivors, Irene and her sister Ellen didn't speak of their experience for decades. Today, while sitting in her dining room—where a breakfront displays New Year's and Christmas card wishes for peace, and flickering advent candles and chocolates similar to those she enjoyed as a child—Irene says she and Ellen feel they were simply ordinary people who suffered during extraordinary times; others suffered far worse.[25] At the same time, Irene says, their story has been lost beneath the stories of the great battles and the nearly mythical figures of Adolf Hitler, Franklin D. Roosevelt, Winston Churchill, Josef Stalin, Georgy Zhukov, and Erwin Rommel. With the passage of years, it became important for Ellen and Irene to speak out about the events that took place.

Helga Reuter and her sister, Inge, hadn't slept in at least 36 hours when they finally glimpsed the ocean liner now painted gray.[26] When Helga left her home in Königsberg, she wore a fur coat, ankle-high boots with rubber overshoes, and thick woolen socks. Inge wore riding boots, too snug to allow for heavy socks. Helga also wore a pair of her father's trousers. Her mother had nipped the pants in at the waist and hemmed the cuffs. Before she left, Helga slid several family photographs in her back pocket, secured with a single button. The photographs were the only family mementos she carried. Inge had money and their identification papers sewn to the inside of her skirt. Helga had asked for money but her father told her she didn't need any; she was traveling with her sister.

Born two years apart, the sisters were as close as twins. They had left their parents in Königsberg. A majestic and imperial city—a castle and cathedral lorded over the city—the Prussian kings had appointed it as the site of their coronations. The Russians now surrounded the historic city that lay on the edge of Germany, close to Russia, Poland, and Lithuania.[27]

The sisters jostled their way past knapsacks carried by refugees to the gangplank. Inge Reuter tilted her head, the cold light bouncing off her honey-brown hair, and stared at the vessel. Its smokestack looked like a stake impaling the sky. "That is a nice ship to be torpedoed on. But it's better to drown than fall into Russian hands," Inge told Helga.

"Those were her exact words. She had the vision like my mother," Helga said, under a nimbus of white hair, her veined hands holding each other as if for comfort.[28]

Then with nothing left to say or do, the girls boarded the *Wilhelm Gustloff*, without even knowing the ship's name. They simply didn't care. They just wanted to get away.

The Reuter girls were just two among hundreds of thousands of refugees arriving in Gotenhafen when the floodgates opened. They were just two among thousands of civilians who walked up the gangplank onto the deck of the *Wilhelm Gustloff*, putting their faith in the ship's ability to get them to safety.

Two

HITLER'S HOSTAGES

LIFE IN THE EASTERN TERRITORIES

"**WAR!**" the radio blared. An accompanying choir trumpeted the words of the German national anthem, "Deutschland, Deutschland, über Alles."[1] When the German forces invaded Poland on September 1, 1939, about 10 million German speakers, former subjects of the Hapsburg monarchy, lived in East Prussia, a German enclave with Poland and Russia for neighbors. Some had lived there for generations; others had been only recently relocated there. Horst Woit and his mother, Meta, lived in Elbing in East Prussia; Helga Reuter and her sister, Inge, lived in Königsberg; Irene and Ellen Tschinkur and their cousin Evi were in Gotenhafen. While the late 1930s were economically hard for the eastern parts of the Reich, they were largely untouched by the political upheavals that marked the Nazis' rise to power and affected their countrymen in the western part of Germany.

Many of these families lived in towns and cities that were ethnically and linguistically mixed. When in 1939 Germany annexed parts of Poland and incorporated them into the rest of East

Prussia, the Nazi leaders were surprised to discover some ethnic Poles who spoke only German and some Germans who spoke only Polish.

Just weeks before the invasion, Adolf Hitler and Josef Stalin had forged an uneasy truce. On August 23, 1939, German foreign minister Joachim von Ribbentrop and Soviet foreign minister Vyacheslav Molotov signed a pact that included a plan detailing how the two nations would dismember Poland. This pact, known officially as the Treaty of Non-Aggression, also directed the dislocation and expulsion of ethnic Germans from Russian lands. The Soviets were keen to extend their state west while the Germans were determined to extend their state east. Under the Molotov-Ribbentrop Pact, Stalin could virtually consume Estonia, Latvia, and Lithuania as well as push Russia's border 200 miles farther west. Hence, the Soviet Union incorporated the Baltic States, Bessarabia, and North Bukovina, and also recovered some territories that once belonged to the tsarist empire. The Baltic States had been Russian from the time of Peter the Great until World War One.

Officially the Molotov-Ribbentrop Pact was supposed to prevent hostilities between the Germans and the Russians. In a secret protocol both parties agreed to "spheres of influence." However, many civilians, like Helga Reuter and her family, had good reason to question the validity of the agreement. In late 1939 and early 1940 Helga's uncle was serving in the German merchant marine. While stationed in Leningrad, Russia, he wrote home, warning his family in Königsberg of how the Soviets were arming themselves in spite of the treaty. "He said please do not believe the safety contract," Reuter said. "He had seen the harbor full of war equipment. They were preparing for war."[2]

Reuter's uncle was correct. Laurence Steinhardt, the American ambassador to the Soviet Union, duly noted the "extensive secret mobilization" taking place in the Soviet Union in 1939. "Large numbers of recruits still in civilian clothes and reservists up to the present age of 50 are known to be departing from Moscow. Tanks and trucks believed to be conveying ammunition have been seen in the city. Horses rarely observed in Moscow together with a considerable quantity of fodder are in evidence. This extensive mobilization is being conducted with great secrecy."[3] Steinhardt correctly appraised the situation. The Soviets were prepared to occupy part of eastern Poland and were also bracing themselves against a future German invasion.

German troops and mechanized units overran Poland on September 1, annexing the country in a few short weeks. Two days later, on September 3, England and France declared war on Germany. Neither nation, however, fully engaged the Third Reich until the Battle of France began in 1940. Poland's Foreign Minister Jozef Beck said that "official circles in London and Paris state that British and French planes hesitate to bomb German railways, other communications, power plants and war industry centers because of potential effect on American public opinion."[4] Beck understood the American public did not want to enter the war. President Franklin Delano Roosevelt responded to news of the invasion with a telegram appealing to Germany to refrain from bombing civilians. "I am therefore addressing this urgent appeal to every government which may be engaged in hostilities publicly to affirm its determination that its armed forces shall in no event, and under no circumstances, undertake the bombardment from the air of civilian populations or of unfortified cities, upon the understanding that these same rules of warfare will be scrupulously observed by all of their opponents."[5]

The Tschinkurs, originally from Riga, Latvia, were resettled in the "Home to the Reich" campaign. Thousands of ethnic Germans were moved west with whatever possessions they could carry in 1940 and 1941 after the Molotov-Ribbentrop pact was signed. To achieve this, Nazi negotiators presented their case to the respective governments of Latvia and Estonia. Regarding ethnic Germans

living in other Soviet lands, such as in Russia or Ukraine, the Nazis negotiated with officials from the NKVD, the Soviet internal
secret police. The German envoys accomplished the population
swap in part by convincing ethnic Germans that they were moving to paradise. Instead, many of the newly returned immediately
were assigned to one of about 1,500 holding camps. There the
Nazi authorities assessed their hair and eye color and other traits,
such as nose and head shape, to see who among the new arrivals
most closely resembled the Aryan ideal. They wanted to weed out
those resettlers they considered having genetically inferior foreign
elements; namely Jews and those not of purely German origin.[6]
The German authorities made a ceremonial effort to welcome
the Baltic Germans to their new home in East Prussia: "We greet
our Baltic folk comrades who are now returning home into the
Greater German Reich of Adolf Hitler."[7] Although the Germans
looked at the Slavs as potential underlings, they still invested in
the East; they viewed the land as ripe for colonization and settle-
ment, the *lebensraum,* or living space, touted by Hitler as being
Germany's right.

After the Tschinkurs arrived in East Prussia, they were first
sent to Stettin to a dormitory style building called "Baltic Home."
From inside this institutional setting, authorities sorted out the
Baltic people, parceling them off to different towns and cities, all
of which now bore German names. The Tschinkurs would have
been subjected to a certain amount of reeducation including acceptance of Nazi ideology and culture. Members of Hitler Youth
often helped process the newly arrived Baltic Germans.[8]

After several weeks the Tschinkurs were sent to Poznan, a city
on the Warta River in what was formerly west central Poland.
Herbert Christoph and Serafima soon decided to leave for Gotenhafen so they could be closer to the water. Back in Riga Herbert
Christoph had belonged to a sailing club, and being near the water was a small comfort to the newly displaced family. Most of

Irene and Ellen's family stayed in Poznan, including her aunt and beloved cousins Wilhelm and Evelyn, whose nickname was Evi. In Gotenhafen the Tschinkurs lived in a nice apartment building overlooking some shops and their father ran the bakery there. "We probably took over somebody's home," Irene Tschinkur admits.

In spite of the upheaval, families like the Woits, Tschinkurs, and Reuters still had some years of relative peace remaining before the violence and fear of the mid-1940s arrived. East Prussian children had to join Hitler Youth and schoolteachers increasingly focused on imparting students with knowledge about the front and what it meant to be a good citizen of the Reich. People became increasingly wary about what they said in public and with whom they spoke. Gestapo agents seemed omnipresent. Still, most East Prussians escaped the direct effects of the Nazi regime for a bit longer than those who lived in Germany proper.

"The strange thing is that East Prussia was divided by Poland after World War One. But until the Russians got there, we felt disconnected from Hitler and what was happening," Helga Reuter said. Almost 70 years after the ship's sinking, Helga recounts what it was like to come of age during the Nazi era. She recently moved from Arizona to live with her son, David Knickerbocker, in Las Vegas. The desert areas she has lived in bear no resemblance to the East Prussian city where she grew up.

In picturesque, cosmopolitan, seaside Königsberg, Helga Reuter and her sisters, Inge and Ursula, attended a private school together with Jewish, Lutheran, and Calvinist children. Helga never paid much attention to her classmates' religions until Germany's Nazi Party imposed draconian laws on the city's Jewish population. It meant reading *Mein Kampf* in school and hearing, repeatedly, "Comradeship," a story by a Hitler Youth member named Hans Wolf. The story extolled the idea that a child in Nazi Germany could only thrive through sacrifice and loyalty to the Führer.[9]

Helga remembers the English teacher who wore a dreadful brown tweed skirt who had to stop teaching them English because England was at war with Germany and opposed to Nazi values. She remembers time out from academics to track Germany's conquests on a map pinned to the classroom wall, as well as endless rallies, parades, speeches, and rituals. And she recalls playmates who were there one day and gone the next.

"One day, my friend said, 'Please don't come with me. I cannot visit you either.' She was Jewish. This is what it was like to grow up in Hitler's Germany," Helga said, her cerulean eyes narrowing at the memory.[10]

In 1939, as Helga Reuter struggled to adapt to her disappearing childhood, the Nazis slaughtered thousands of people living in central Poland. Mobile killing squads comprised of the German SS and Einsatzgruppen (special task forces) rounded up victims and drove them on foot or in trucks to secluded sites. There the victims were forced to strip before being shot. Corpses were burned in large pits.

Anthony J. Drexel Biddle Jr., the American ambassador to Poland, sent news home of the civilian killings. Biddle supplied one of the earliest reports about Nazi atrocities. In his observations the Germans functioned "to terrorize the civilian population and to reduce the number of child-bearing Poles irrespective of category."[11]

West of the Molotov-Ribbentrop line, the Einsatzgruppen pounced on the populace. In Bydgoszcz, a village over the border, the German military killed an estimated 10,500 Poles in retaliation for anti-German riots. Reinhard Heydrich, Heinrich Himmler's right-hand man, organized the murderous task force using members from the security police and Sicherheitsdienst (SD) intelligence service of the SS. Blond, tall, and with a narrow face, Heydrich had been appointed to the post in 1933. During one operation alone the Einsatzgruppen murdered 61,000 Poles.[12]

East of the Molotov-Ribbentrop line, the Soviets also annexed territory and for the next several years murdered those they deemed a threat to their political ideals. The Soviets were similarly brutal throughout western Russia, Ukraine, Belarus, and the Baltic States. The Soviet government under Joseph Stalin implemented a strategy to send the affluent and intellectuals to Siberian gulags, where millions were subject to reeducation camps and forced labor in brutal conditions. In this way, the Soviet authorities hoped to rid the population of those who in their eyes undermined the Communist Party.

Born in Lodz, Poland, Ruth Weintraub Kent was one of six children. Her father died before the onset of the war. Of her immediate family, she lost everyone but two brothers.

"We were in the country when Hitler declared war on Poland. We wanted to come back to go to school . . . we were not able to get any transportation. There were no buses, no streetcars, and no trucks. Not even a horse and carriage. Everything was mobilized for the war effort," Ruth Weintraub said of the immediate hours and days following the Nazi invasion. "When we came back from the country, a lot of soldiers were coming down our street. Although our streets were not very wide, it seemed like masses of soldiers were marching through our streets. And we could see tanks. It was a frightening experience."[13]

Nazi storm troopers swept through Polish cities arresting, assaulting, and executing anyone deemed an enemy of the Reich. The list included Polish citizens, communists, and Jews. Upon its invasion of Poland, the Germans arrested and imprisoned Polish men of fighting age first in Auschwitz and then in other concentration camps.

After the Third Reich occupied the Polish provinces, it created various *Reichsgaue,* or administrative subdivisions of those territories. Regional provincial leaders called gauleiters headed each Reichsgau. The gauleiters helped supervise the removal of Polish citizens to make room for ethnic Germans arriving from the Baltic and other regions of the Reich.[14] The Nazi Party imported people into Poland and East Prussia as colonists to augment the labor force.

Thus began an intensive Germanization of the region. On October 7, 1939, Adolf Hitler appointed Heinrich Himmler commissioner for the Consolidation of the German Race. The one-time chicken farmer assumed the job of eliminating those that the Third Reich deemed racially and politically inferior. Himmler had served as chief of the Munich police from 1933 until 1936 when he was appointed head of all the German police.[15]

Extreme violence descended upon East Prussia. The violence was directed not only at Jews and Poles, but also set its sights on a mosaic of people from vastly different ethnic backgrounds and religious faiths. Lawyers, clergy, and teachers were deported and killed. Arrests and deportations came with little or no warning, most often at night. Families were often separated. Polish citizens left behind dear possessions—a wedding album, a grandmother's teapot, a favorite doll. "I had the clothing I was wearing and nothing more. Hungry and cold, I sat down on the bench, it was very cold, and then came the grief and sadness that I had known in my life. I was nineteen years old then, and I didn't know then the world of poverty that fell upon me," wrote Stanislaw Jaskolski, an ethnic Polish civilian, about his arrest in East Prussia.[16]

Germans had actually begun gathering information on Jews and Polish intelligentsia living in East Prussia before the war started. The Nazis scouted locations for a concentration camp long before the first shot hit Westerplatte, a peninsula near Gotenhafen on the Baltic Sea. They chose Stutthof, a small village just about 22 miles from the fairy tale–looking city of Danzig. Occupying wet, muddy land, the camp was along the Danzig-Elbing highway on the road to the Krynica Morska resort on the Baltic Sea. Prisoners built the camp, which originally operated as a civilian internment camp under the direction of the Danzig police chief. The first inmates arrived on September 2, 1939—150 Polish citizens were imprisoned in Konzentrationslager or KZ Stutthof concentration camp.

The number of inmates in Stutthof swelled to 15,000 by September 15. In 1941 Stutthof became a holding center for political prisoners. By the time the Russians liberated the camp in 1944, prisoners from 26 European countries, in addition to the United States and Turkey, had passed through its barbed-wire gates.[17]

Many of the prisoners in Stutthof worked at the munitions factories of Deutsche Auskustungswerke, or DAW, in Gotenhafen, Elbing, and other Baltic towns. The Nazi concentration camps spawned subcamps at an exponential rate. Stutthof had 150 subcamps along the Baltic coast near towns and villages, including Elbing, Gotenhafen, Thorn, and Königsberg. As of 1944, camps occupied nearly every region of the Third Reich, though some camps held only 10 prisoners. "When the train stopped and we were told to get out and it was already light, and you could see the sign where in large letters was written Stutthof," recalled Stutthof survivor Stanislaw Jaskolski. "On all sides stood SS men dressed in black military uniforms, with skull and crossbones on their caps and Ukrainians who served Hitler."[18]

Like Dachau and Auschwitz-Birkenau, the East Prussian camp of Stutthof became an extermination center where Nazis gassed, shot, and worked prisoners to death. Camp doctors administered lethal injections to more than 60,000 prisoners. The camp doctor reserved the right of selection for the gas chamber. It was in Stutthof that Rudolf Spanner experimented with various methods to render human fat into soap, leather, and book covers. Inside the soap factory "they hauled the bodies, they tore off the skin for another different use and the body was cooked in a huge kettle," wrote Jaskolski.[19] Every day special commandos pushed carts brimming with corpses to the camp's crematorium; the corpses burned day and night.[20] Stutthof resembled an open graveyard where the only difference between the living and the dead was that the living occasionally moved.[21]

After more than a month in Auschwitz, Ruth Weintraub, the girl from Lodz, was transported to Stutthof. Inmates like Ruth and Stanislaw were used as forced labor in brickyards and private enterprises such as the Focke-Wulf airplane factory.[22] They were just a few miles from where the Woits, Reuters, and Tschinkurs lived.

In Königsberg the Reuter furniture factory and showroom shared the block with another business. The Nazis closed the Jewish-owned business and nailed a large sign above the shop's windows that read *Feinde,* or Enemy.

Two years before the war, in 1937, the German authorities had ordered the Reuters to relinquish their furniture factory to the Reich. The German authorities turned it into a uniform factory and the Reuters had to knock to be let into their building. While Helga doesn't know for certain, it's possible that Polish, Russian, and French prisoners, incarcerated in one of KZ Stutthof's 150 subcamps, worked in the Reuter factory.[23]

Though East Prussian civilians were far away from Berlin, they shared in certain sacrifices from the start, namely food rationing and the conscription of men into the Nazi forces.

"Fortunately, we grew our own food, chicken and rabbit. So we had no problem with food shortages," Helga said.[24] Her father, Kurt, would try to feed the prisoners surreptitiously. Every day two soups simmered on the stove, and Kurt snuck chicken and rabbit into the soup for the workers. They were fortunate to have some meat, because as the war progressed butter, sausage—any kind of meat—became scarcer and scarcer, Helga recalled.

"The Germans found out and called him to the police station. He was called there once or twice a month. Each time my mother wondered if he would come home. The police said he was too friendly with the POWs."

The Reuters continued to resist in small ways. Helga's father often referred to Adolf Hitler as a German communist. Every Sunday the Reuters visited with their neighbors for the chance to trade news and sip hot cups of ersatz coffee. Helga remembers her parents suspected that their cook tried to curry favor with the German authorities by informing on them. The Reuters became less carefree in their conversations, but they continued to tune into a Hungarian radio station for information. This was dangerous; listening to outside news warranted the death penalty. The Reich newspapers and magazines reported news of the front only when that news portrayed Nazi Germany in a positive light. Reports extolled the Wehrmacht (the German armed forces) and the Volkssturm (Home Guard), but the broadcasts never mentioned the Third Reich's retreats and surrenders.[25]

As the war progressed, Berlin's influence on East Prussian life intensified. By 1939 an estimated 82 percent, or 7.3 million, of German children aged ten and older belonged to Hitler Youth.[26] Helga Reuter was one of those children.

Helga remembers the day her notification to join Hitler Youth arrived in the family's letterbox at their house on General Litzman Street. Her parents were hesitant but they felt compelled to enroll her.

"At first it was lovely. We made toys for Christmas; we went on picnics," Helga said. "It was fun. But suddenly it turned into drilling. I did not like it." Soon Helga feigned sickness on meeting days, wanting to avoid the group's ever-escalating militarism. She didn't want to train to join the military. She didn't want to attend the formal meetings in the required starched white shirt, navy skirt, and black neckerchief. She bristled at joining the straight-marching lines of boys and girls. Her father, however tempted he was to disobey the rules, worried about appearing to the neighbors as if he were snubbing the Nazi Party. Kurt Reuter paid the girls' dues and told his daughters Helga and Inge to attend meetings. It was too dangerous to let them risk being branded as outsiders.

Helga said the group's teachings regarding Jewish children bothered her. Growing up in Königsberg with its reputation for tolerance, Helga had never thought much about religious or ethnic differences. The city had a relatively small Jewish population; a little more than 3,000 Jews called it home when the Nazis assumed power in 1933. The Reuters worked with, associated with, and studied with Jewish people. As the war continued, Helga and her family knew it was dangerous to talk with Jews, even those who had been friends and colleagues. All around the streets were being emptied. "In my family Jewish was a religion, nothing more. My father's doctor was Jewish. Once my father saw his doctor cleaning the streets and asked him what he was doing. 'Please go away and don't talk to me. Go, go,' the doctor said. That is when our eyes really opened up. My sister's friends suddenly weren't coming around. They were just picked up." Police reveled in publicly humiliating Jews and it was forbidden for non-Jews to associate with Jews.[27]

Soon after that incident with his physician, Helga Reuter said her father started warning his three girls every day about the seemingly omniscient Gestapo. Each morning Kurt Reuter told his daughters to pay attention, whether they were riding the streetcar, sitting in school, or walking down one of Königsberg's sidewalks. Criticizing the government, talking with Jews or others, often meant arrest. He worried the Gestapo might arrest the sisters, or him and his wife, if they spied them in friendly conversation with fellow countrymen now considered subhuman enemies of the state. Kurt Reuter was right to fear his neighbors. Many denunciations came from people harboring the slightest jealousy or wanting to be seen in favorable light.

Irene and Ellen Tschinkur slowly adjusted to life in Gotenhafen, a large, bustling naval port on the Bay of Danzig. When
they lived in Latvia their father belonged to a sailing club and
they naturally gravitated to the port town, and the family often
lingered at the waterfront, looking at the sea. In Gotenhafen, the
harbor, once a place of recreation, was now overtaken by the military. Although the two sisters said they hardly noticed the naval
ships and German sailors when they walked by the waterfront,
they remember that a feeling of dread lingered: The Third Reich
mystified and scared them.[28]

Just outside of town, their first apartment in Gotenhafen was
"situated near a hill where Ellen and I would go and pick flowers
and where we saw soldiers training German shepherds in a clear-
ing," Irene said. "One day Ellen and I, we stumbled on a meadow.
There were soldiers there, training German shepherds. I felt we
shouldn't be there. We quickly went away."

The close encounter with the German shepherds unnerved
Irene. She took Ellen's hand and quickly ran down the hill, clutching freshly picked flowers between their fingers.

Once Irene and Ellen and their parents settled in Gotenhafen,
they faced a new reality. Because they were *volksdeutsch,* they
were being schooled in what was considered the proper ways of
the Reich. On one of Irene's first days of school the teacher asked
her to recite a poem. Irene stood before her new classmates and
nervously performed a little ditty about a bunny. As soon as she
finished the teacher barked at Irene. He motioned for her to stand
in front of his desk, hands turned up. The teacher caned her palms.

"I had said the poem in Russian. Only German was allowed
from this point," Irene said.

On another afternoon in school, teachers led Irene and her
classmates out of the building to a sidewalk on one of the city's
main streets. The teachers pressed small, stiff Nazi flags into their
hands and told the children to wave and smile at the soldiers and

officials marching in lockstep down the street. "There was a beautiful car, an open landeau. A man in a brownish or greenish uniform stood up in it. It was Hitler. He went by in his beautiful car. I couldn't have cared less," Irene recounts.

But the neighbors cared who waved, who attended marches, and whether children joined Hitler Youth, and there was always the danger of being snitched on for not attending. Upon turning ten years old Irene was supposed to join the Hitler Youth. Her father Herbert Christoph refused to send her, not caring to hear Irene learn to say "Heil Hitler" or sing national hymns or perfect a stiff-armed salute. The Tschinkurs were also not especially political. However, the next year, when Irene turned 11, "an SS man came to our apartment door and asked why I was not in the youth group. Dad had no excuse—so I went and had a good time. Dad had no good reason to give. It was August 1944," Irene said. Thus, Irene joined what would eventually be an organization to which more than 60 percent of children aged 10 to 18 belonged.[29]

Busy with school, piano lessons, and ballet, Irene doesn't remember having to learn Nazi songs in the first year of Hitler Youth, only what she called "just pretty outdoor songs." She remembers spending a lot of time outdoors, doing calisthenics on the beach and throwing a medicine ball. Sometimes her group went raspberry leaf picking for tea. Other afternoons they did crafts; they knitted squares of colored wool and pieced them together for lap blankets for sick people. Irene said they learned how to make little farm animals, sheds, and barns out of wood. They painted the little toys and gave them as Christmas gifts for poor children. "All that to me was fun. What would happen later on I wouldn't know. I think as the girls and boys got older, there must have been more indoctrination of something sinister perhaps. I'm glad I didn't go there," Irene said, adding that her father's discomfort with the organization never lessened. He knew that as the children grew older, what they learned and did in the organization changed. It was that part of the Hitler Youth he didn't want his daughters to participate in.

The sinister part of Hitler Youth didn't surface until children reached the age of 14. Children in the older groups were exposed to *gleichschaltung,* or "bringing into line." This stage of Hitler Youth injected teenagers with Nazi social and political thought in order to get them to conform to Nazi ideology. Though neither Irene nor any of the children in the *Jungvolk* might have realized it, the lyrics to those pretty songs often contained Nazi propaganda. Yet, most children at that age didn't understand the deeper meaning to the songs. Rather, they enjoyed the infectious rhymes and melodies.

Irene only stayed in Bund Deutscher Mädel, BDM, or League of German Girls, for five months before she and her family fled the oncoming Soviet army.

The intense Germanization was designed to assimilate children like Irene and Ellen to life inside Nazi Germany as quickly as possible. German was the official language now; the use of Latvian, Russian, or Polish in public was clearly forbidden. No longer were they to read books, see films, or visit exhibitions that contained anything the Nazi regime might consider even remotely anti-German. The German authorities were determined to smother and suppress every ounce of their old life beneath a parade of racial and political doctrine.

The port of Gotenhafen filled with Kriegsmarine and U-boat sailors training on the *Wilhelm Gustloff.* Though they heard Adolf Hitler's fevered radio broadcasts and reports of Stutthof and its nearby subcamps, Irene and Ellen's parents spoke little of the war in front of their children.

Horst Woit, a grammar school student in Elbing, East Prussia when the war started, remembers buildings draped in Nazi banners and flags hanging from lampposts. Sitting on a sofa in the basement of his lakeside home in Canada, nearly 70 years later, Horst said he remembers hearing Hitler's speeches on the radio. Yet, it was more background noise than anything else for the young boy. Aside from the fanfare and pomp of marching soldiers and older children dressed in the crisp khaki of a Hitler Youth uniform, the war and Adolf Hitler seemed remote for a young boy more concerned with making friends and eating sticky marmalade sandwiches. Horst's mother didn't talk about the war. His father, long gone to the front, never wrote home.

Eva Dorn hated Hitler Youth. She liked the required skirt and blouse all the girls wore because they were the first new clothes she'd had in years. However, she quickly grew to hate what the skirt and blouse represented.[30]

"I was ten years old when I decided not to be a Nazi," Eva said, a feisty smile playing across her face at the decades-old memory.

One weekend in 1936 Eva's Hitler Youth group went camping and hiking near the Baltic Sea. The girls were to spend the night in the tower section of a youth hostel. Each girl received a mat and a blanket. The next morning Eva awoke before the other girls. She asked her group leader permission to go downstairs to the bathroom. The older girl forbade Eva, telling her that she couldn't go until the entire group was ready. "I had to go, so I went in the corner. Can you imagine? I was humiliated. I knew then I couldn't be a part of any group that wouldn't let me take care of myself," Eva said.

The next incident came three years later during her group's weekly Tuesday meeting. Eva, then 13, was asked to lead the meeting since their regular leader was sick. Eva looked out the classroom window and saw a carousel in the marketplace. The sun shone. "I told the group, 'Why should we sit here? It's so beautiful outside. Let's go to the fair.' We did and had fun," she said. The next afternoon the group's leaders summoned the teenager. They threw Eva out of the Hitler Youth and told her she would be banned from ever joining the Nazi Party and would never amount to anything. "I was so happy, I couldn't care less," Eva Dorn said.

Eva's views of Hitler differed vastly from her brothers'. Her two half-brothers had joined the German army and they died on the Eastern Front. Her full brother was a believer; he joined the SS. One afternoon when her parents were still together, the doorbell of their apartment rang. "It was the black shirt being delivered. My mother was furious. Only then did I realize she was against the Nazis," Eva said, avoiding further discussion about her brother and his wartime activities.

In 1938 the Jews of Haale (Saale) were forced to wear yellow stars to identify them. Eva remembers an incident when she was riding the streetcar to school. At one stop, a Jewish couple got on. "If there was one thing my mother taught me it was manners. So I said to the couple, 'Please sit down.' They said, 'We are not allowed to.'" When Eva returned to her seat the other passengers berated her. "'Don't you see that they are Jews?'" Eva stared out the window. Jews had started to leave Haale. Many of them had worked in the theater with her parents. One farewell stood out; before a musician from their theater group departed for Palestine, he gave Eva an orange, a rare treat during the war.

On June 22, 1941, Germany abrogated the non-aggression pact and invaded Russia. "Stalin must be regarded as a cold-blooded blackmailer; he would, if expedient, repudiate any written treaty at any time. Britain's aim for some time to come will be to set Russian strength in motion against us," Hitler told his commanders-in-chief.[31]

Adolf Hitler, the house-painter-turned-tyrant, declared his intent to turn the Soviet Union into a wasteland. Given the code name Operation Barbarossa, German soldiers marching toward Moscow had carte blanche to use violence against Russian civilians. "The Russians must perish that we may live."[32] As in Poland, the Nazi Party policy included subjugation through dehumanization. It encouraged famine, torture, and execution. A song at the time set this idea to music:

> *The ancient brittle bones of the world tremble.*
> *Before the Red war.*
> *We have broken its slavery,*
> *For us it was a mighty victory.*
> *We will march on,*
> *Even if everything sinks into dust,*
> *Because today Germany belongs to us*
> *And tomorrow the whole world.*[33]

The command allowed German soldiers to shoot any civilians seeming to resist, without precisely defining what they meant by resistance. They shot men with cropped hair, deciding anyone with a crew cut was a Soviet soldier. They shot Asiatic Soviets and summarily executed female soldiers, reasoning that armed women mocked German notions of military propriety.[34] Soldiers snapped photos of their grisly work.

Three weeks after the invasion, 20 million Soviet citizens lived under German rule and thousands of Soviet soldiers lay in mass graves.

On June 22, 1944, three years after the German invasion of the Soviet Union, the Russian army launched Operation Bagration, named for Prince Peter Bagration, a Russian hero of 1812. The Soviets pushed forward with overwhelming force; they gave no quarter. The Red Army directed its first attacks against the key German strong points of Vitebsk, Mogilev, Osha, and Bobruisk. Stalin and his military commanders warned soldiers that their counterattack would be grueling, particularly in East Prussia. Stalin told his commanders the Germans would fight for East Prussia to the end. "We could get bogged down there," Stalin said.[35]

The Red Army marched toward Berlin with revenge on their minds. Soviets called the Germans "fascist monsters" who destroyed their cities and homes. Soviet troops, from lowly privates to higher-ranking officers, thought the worst Germans hailed from East Prussia.

Many Soviet soldiers knew people who had suffered under German occupation. They were quick to visit violence on German civilians. Reprisals took all forms, particularly physical. The famous chronicler of Soviet gulags, Alexander Solzhenitsyn, who served as a captain in the Russian army during the war, later wrote that every soldier knew German girls were fair game to be raped and shot.[36] His long poem "Prussian Nights" contains this section "Zweiundzwanzig Horingstrasse" ("Twenty Two Horingstrasse"):

> It's not been burned, just looted, rifled.
> A moaning, by the walls half muffled: the
>   mother's wounded, still alive.
> The little daughter's on the mattress, Dead.
>   How many have been on it?
> A platoon, a company perhaps?
> A girl's been turned into a woman, A
>   woman turned into a corpse.
> It all comes down to simple phrases:
> Do not forget! Do not forgive! Blood for
>   blood! A tooth for a tooth!
> The mother begs, "Kill me, Soldier!"[37]

Anti-German propaganda incited the Red Army. One leaflet distributed to Russian soldiers read: "Kill. Nothing in Germany is guiltless, neither the living nor the yet unborn. Follow the words of Comrade Stalin and crush forever the fascist beast in its den.

Break the racial pride of the German woman. Take her as your legitimate booty."[38] Some German women chose suicide.

Russian soldiers seized German men and women for forced labor in Siberia. As they pressed forward, the soldiers grabbed weapons, ammunition, food, fuel, livestock, and boots left by retreating Germans. The Soviet troops plundered so that they could send provisions home. They were allowed to send two packages a month, each weighing up to 18 pounds. Officers could send twice as much.

To the Russian invaders, the German's wartime standard of living, particularly in the eastern territories, seemed frivolously luxurious. The cultivated land and neat houses seemed to look at Soviet soldiers with reproach. Raging, the Red Army burnt to a crisp entire towns, such as Stolp, Zoppot, and Insterburg. Throughout East Prussia, from Königsberg to Elbing, the people were terrified.

In January 1943, barely six months after Germany bombed Stalingrad and advanced into its rubble, somber music accompanied the announcement that the Red Army had wrested the city from German control. Even so, the Nazi authorities tried to persuade people that a final victory was imminent.[39] The German public didn't know that the remains of the 90,000-men-strong German Sixth Army had surrendered. Rather, Hitler, obsessed with portraying the Reich as forever on the verge of triumph, ordered the press to report the siege's end as a "sublime example of heroism."[40] The surrender of Stalingrad became one more instance of martyrdom on the part of the German soldier. Those with access to outside radios and newspapers knew the truth; Hitler's armies had been defeated.[41] The fall of Stalingrad marked the turning point of the war, the beginning of Germany's defeat.

That same year Eva Dorn had begun her third semester studying music at University of Leipzig. She wasn't surprised when the draft notice arrived. Germany had declared total war. The German military gave her a choice between working in an armaments factory or the joining the Women's Naval Auxiliary. Her mother suggested she choose the Navy so she could at least have fresh air. The day after her birthday, Eva left for training at Flensburg, a German naval base near Kiel on the Baltic Sea. Eva was soon posted to Gotenhafen in East Prussia. There she quietly challenged the rules, wearing lipstick, not giving a full "Heil Hitler" salute when she passed superior officers, and always keeping a pair of high heels in her possession. Eva worked hard, making herself useful beyond her regular duties on the spotlight battery and identifying aircraft. She often worked in the kitchen and infirmary.

By February 26, 1944, the Red Army had recaptured 75 percent of occupied Russian lands and the Allies celebrated news of the Russian advance as one more step toward victory.[42] News of the Russian offensive also excited Americans in Stalag Luft III, a prisoner-of-war camp in Sagan. Inside the camp, on January 27, 1944, the 10,000 Americans cheered when they heard the Russians were less than 20 miles to the east and coming on strong.[43]

Meanwhile Helga Reuter's 21-year-old cousin, Jurgen, a soldier in the Wehrmacht, was killed outside Leningrad. The Russians carved a swastika into his chest. "We got told lies about Leningrad. The Russians had begun to break through after Leningrad. Our soldiers went in and saw that people had been murdered and raped and nailed to a barn . . . nailed to a barn," Helga said, referring to East Prussians living in the path of the Russian advance. "This scared us to hell. They said the same thing could happen to us. We were planning to leave. We didn't know where—just to the West. As if the West held milk and honey."

In East Prussia, Gauleiter Erich Koch insisted victory was nigh, adhering to Minister of Propaganda Joseph Goebbels's maxim that when one tells a lie often enough, the lie becomes true. Born on June 19, 1896, Koch likened himself to a medieval Teutonic knight. He boasted that his *gau* (province) represented

a vanguard of Germanic ideals, ready to stand against marauding Russians.[44] He banned any talk of flight. Having joined the
Nazi Party in 1922, Koch had served as gauleiter since 1938, ad-
ministering the region from the Baltic to the Black Sea. He also
controlled the region's Gestapo and uniformed police battalions.
Koch had earlier served without distinction as a soldier in World
War One. In spite of Koch's declaration that East Prussia fight and
die together, he, his wife, and his secretary fled Königsberg long
before civilians like the Tschinkurs, Rezases, and Reuters. He did
so after vilifying soldiers in the Wehrmacht who tried to retreat.
Koch went to Pillau and tried to make a show of helping to organize Operation Hannibal.

Koch ordered the Volkssturm (Home Guard) to mobilize boys
as young as 13. Adolf Hitler had called up the Volkssturm in late
1944, selling the idea of it as a similar organization to the Land-
sturm, which had fought against the French a century before. At
the start it was a volunteer force, but soon men and boys had no
choice. Hitler Youth were sent to bolster this home guard, with
16- and 17-year-olds manning machine guns. The youngsters had
poor training, wore threadbare uniforms, and were armed only
with French long rifles from 1914 that froze in the cold. The Russians slaughtered these adolescents. Reports spread of dead youth
lying in ditches with their ears cut off and gouged-out eyes.[45]

Horst Woit of Elbing remembered the Volkssturm as just one
more part of Germany's strategy of self-defense. This notion of
sacrifice for the fatherland weighed heavily on many civilians. The
German forces relied on the idea that the 80,000-strong Volkssturm and enlisted men wouldn't shy away from a *heldentod* (heroic death).

As the Russian army approached the East Prussian border,
Erich Koch ordered hundreds of thousands of inhabitants and
prisoners of war to build fortified camps and dig antitank ditches.
Heinrich Himmler said he didn't care if 10,000 Russian women

died of exhaustion digging antitank ditches for the German army, so long as the ditches were dug.[46]

In addition to the East Prussian civilians, concentration camp inmates were also compelled to dig. Dora Love, who survived three years in the Stutthof extermination camp, worked on the ditches. "They were horrors—four and a half meters deep. I doubt that it ever stopped a single Soviet tank—it was meant for the Soviet tanks but the work was for us."[47]

On January 12, 1945, about 3 million Russians attacked close to 1 million Germans on a 400-mile front that extended from the Baltic Sea to middle of the Poland.[48] In the north the Third White Russian Front advanced toward Königsberg in East Prussia. The Second White Russian Front advanced toward Danzig. The First White Russian Front moved toward Poznan. The First Ukrainian Front moved in from the south.

Though Hitler prohibited it, some German army divisions started retreating further west.[49] News of the German army retreat reached East Prussian locales, including Königsberg, Elbing, and Gotenhafen.

Adolf Hitler's policies kept civilians ignorant of the Soviet advance and prohibited evacuations. Hitler told East Prussians that he intended to keep every square inch of territory. In mid-July 1944 he told the Germans he would hold the Baltic States at all costs. For Hitler, the war was about more than domination; it represented a test of will for the German people. If they lost, they had only themselves to blame. "If the German people should collapse under the present burden, I would weep no tear after it. It would deserve its fate," Adolf Hitler told the audience during his last Reichstag speech.[50]

Nearly three years after Adolf Hitler had launched Operation Barbarossa, the Russians penetrated the German lines. When news of the breakthrough reached Moscow, celebratory gunfire crackled the air in lieu of fireworks. The Russians moved forward relentlessly, weakening the Germans daily.[51]

"The radio was sending only good news about how hard they were fighting," Horst Woit said, remembering those years. "But nobody was allowed to flee because that would cause capitulation. In the east we did not hear much about the western front. The store windows had propaganda of Russian killing Germans; gruesome."

In January 1945 Red Army tanks crunched through the snow of East Prussia, obliterating nearly everything in their path. On January 11 and 12, 1945, ten armies of the First Ukrainian Front dealt the first blow of the Soviet offensive on the Vistula. On January 13, the Third Belorussian Front bombarded East Prussia with 120,000 rounds. As Stalin's soldiers raced to form a new front, tanks and men crushed machine gun positions, mortar-firing points, and mine clusters. The Soviet army now paid back the German brutality in kind. Soldiers in the Wehrmacht who were captured and killed by the Russians were found with ears, tongues, noses, and genitalia cut off.

"In Prussia we had a pretty good life until the fall of 1944, when we had some air attacks," Horst Woit said. "In general, Germans were not afraid of the English and Americans. Of the Russians? That is another story and for good reason."

That reason was Nemmersdorf, a small village located 155 miles east of Danzig, in the district of Gumbinnen, near where Horst's grandparents lived. On October 16, 1944, Soviet forces had entered the town. Soldiers moved through the night, burning homes and torturing civilians. The massacre followed the Red Army's capture of two other East Prussian districts: Goldap and Gumbinnen.[52]

Afterward, the mere mention of the village's name distressed civilians. The authorities used it to persuade civilians that staying and fighting remained their only option. "This, this, my fellow countrymen, is what awaits you if you surrender! We will never surrender! You must fight to the last drop of blood!" said Joseph Goebbels in a speech.[53] Goebbels invited international observers to tour the village; he took photos to use in newsreels to scare people. Yes, people were outraged, but his propaganda backfired. Seeing the aftermath let people know what they could expect should the Soviets come to their home. East Prussians wondered whether they could rely on the German forces. More than ever, civilians wanted to leave after hearing about this massacre. When the fighting started, residents living in the city of Königsberg, a mere 60 miles away from the front, shuddered under the artillery.

The East Prussians were desperate to leave before the new year; the Nazi Party strictly forbade such an exodus upon pain of death. "The Nazis would have killed my father for deserting his own business. Stores downtown and furniture factories behind our house and garden had been watched from both sides," Helga Reuter said. The Reuters had a cruel example of this edict. In early January the Gestapo shot the Reuters' neighbor for trying to flee.

Even when the Nazi authorities granted permission for the mass flight, some East Prussian civilians stayed, thinking suicide might be a choice against the marauding Red Army. During the war, the US Office for Strategic Services kept an outpost in Stockholm, Sweden. On December 8, 1944, this report was transmitted: "The feelings of the Germans are very mixed—Germans can still be found who believe in German victory by means of 'new weapons,' but it would appear as if, on the whole, the Germans believe the war is lost. The terror reports, issued by the German propaganda, of the behavior of the Russians towards German prisoners of war and civilians, has, however, had its effect, and the Germans with whom I have spoken had decided to fight to the last in the conviction that life in a defeated Germany would be unbearable."[54]

Irene and Ellen Tschinkur's parents knew that if the Russians reached Gotenhafen, the naval port on the Baltic Sea, it would be catastrophic. They also knew the town officials hadn't yet planned how to evacuate the population. City officials did not issue any instructions on where to go or how to get there.

On January 12, 1945, the Red Army stood on the banks of the Oder River, the last natural barrier between Moscow and Berlin. Nine days later, on January 21, 1945, Soviets tanks moved into the town of Elbing and shelled the town from the armored vehicles.

Twelve days later, on January 26, the Russians reached the Frisches Haff, a shallow lagoon linking Elbing to Königsberg.[55] Civilians feared the Red Army, seeking revenge, would show no mercy on a population whose military had unleashed carnage upon them less than a year before.

Three

OPERATION HANNIBAL AND THE CROWN OF THE FLEET, THE *WILHELM GUSTLOFF*

Toward the end of 1944 Admiral Karl Dönitz knew civilians in Eastern Prussia were in danger. The Third Reich was on the verge of collapse. Adolf Hitler finally allowed East Prussians to evacuate at the end of January 1945. While civilians welcomed the news, some saw it as too late. Had the Führer agreed to declare all of East Prussia as vital to military operations in the autumn of 1944, as some in his military command wanted, many more civilians would have been able to flee over land. Nevertheless, by January 1945 the Russian army had captured most of the eastern territories from their German foes. Fleeing over land was impossible.

After the war, the Allies indicted Admiral Karl Dönitz as a major war criminal. He faced several charges: conspiracy to commit crimes against peace and crimes against humanity; planning, initiating, and waging wars of aggression; and crimes against the laws of war. The Allies found him guilty on the last two counts. After his release from Spandau Prison in 1956, Dönitz lived in relative obscurity in Aumühle, a small town in northern Germany. The admiral never apologized for his role in World War Two, and he never tired of answering correspondence. Eventually he penned his memoir, *Ten Years and Twenty Days*. In it, Dönitz details how he orchestrated the largest, and perhaps most successful, civilian evacuation during a war: Operation Hannibal. His book strives to put his wartime actions in a positive light; the one-time naval commander-in-chief said that by the end of 1944 he no longer gave credence to the idea of fighting until the Third Reich imploded. Instead, Dönitz wanted to focus on moving as many naval personnel as possible to bolster troop strength as well as ensure the safe passage of millions of people.

Devoted to duty, Admiral Karl Dönitz was loyal to the Nazi regime, yet he disagreed with Hitler's refusal to allow East Prussians to flee. He viewed the "salvation of the German eastern population as the one essential task which our armed forces still had to perform. If to our sorrow we could not protect the homes of our eastern fellow countrymen, we could not leave them in the lurch and the least we could do was to ensure that they escaped with their bare lives."[1]

As Operation Hannibal got underway, more than one million German soldiers fought to keep control of the Baltic coast, but it was clear they wouldn't be able to hold out against the Soviets. Dönitz understood that the Reich needed to transport "by sea men, munitions and stores to our eastern land forces and the evacuation from there of wounded, refugees and Army formations."[2] During the latter half of 1944, the Soviet armed forces either threatened or had already captured German dockyards in the eastern end of the Baltic Sea. The U-boats could no longer mount large-scale operations. Dönitz redirected their efforts toward defending the eastern front and rescuing German nationals from the Russian armies. Getting East Prussian civilians out via boats from the major Baltic ports such as Danzig, Pillau, and

Gotenhafen remained the only options. The refugees would board boats in these ports and the German navy would sail them across the Baltic to Kiel. This town in western Germany neighbored the large naval base of Flensburg, near the Danish border.

Evacuating civilians from the eastern provinces constituted a major military effort. Nearly every remaining surface ship in the German fleet participated in Operation Hannibal. Between January 23 and May 8, 1945, more than 800 ships ferried thousands of refugees and troops from Courland (in German, Kurland), Latvia, as well as from East and West Prussia, and later from Pomerania and parts of Mecklenburg, to points west. Aside from the large Baltic ports, countless numbers of people tried their luck from smaller ports and fishing villages. The German merchant marine had orders to join the effort to help evacuate 1 million military personnel and close to 2 million civilians. From the end of January through the middle of March, the German navy supervised numerous transports of refugees as well as some military personnel across the Baltic Sea to Kiel. The first boats carried U-boat trainees and replacement crew predominantly as well as families of soldiers and members of the Women's Naval Auxiliary. One of the officers, Wilhelmina Reitsch, oversaw the evacuation of nearly 4,000 women in the Naval Auxiliary, including 400 who would be assigned to the *Wilhelm Gustloff* along with the civilian refugees.[3] As the Russians neared, Reitsch noted that many of the ships took an increasing number of civilians on board, outnumbering military personnel.[4]

During the planning stages of Operation Hannibal, Admiral Karl Dönitz delegated much of the work to Vice Admiral Conrad Englehardt, who supervised the naval shipping department, which headed sea transports, and reported directly to him. Dönitz, however, decided who among the hundreds and thousands of soldiers and sailors would be permitted to evacuate the eastern front and who among them had to stay and fight the Soviets. While he wanted to help the refugees, he stipulated that Operation Hannibal must never suspend naval operations in favor of rescuing civilians. Dönitz also cautioned Adolf Hitler to make sure the evacuation didn't affect the transfer of fighting forces from Courland and from Norway.

This mass exodus took place during intense Soviet bombing and submarine attacks. The Soviet air force's constant attacks stopped the German navy from mobilizing during daylight out of Pillau, Danzig, or Gotenhafen. But the bombings did not deter refugees from flooding these harbors. Ultimately, in the number of people transported, Operation Hannibal exceeded Dunkirk, the 1940 evacuation from France of nearly 350,000 Allied soldiers in about 850 boats.

Challenges beset Operation Hannibal from the start. For one, Germany now faced chronic fuel and ship shortages. Damaged rail tracks made it virtually impossible to supply troops. Miners had long ago been conscripted into the army, so coal wasn't easily attainable. Only a three-week supply of coal remained for sea transport tasks, and only a ten-day supply remained for rail transport to move troops to the front.[5] Fuel was at its lowest levels since the war began.[6] The military leadership reserved coal supplies for military operations but agreed to spare some naval vessels to help in the mass exodus.[7] Hitler pledged his support to Dönitz to stop the Soviet navy from entering the Baltic Sea. Hitler's modest reassurances came largely because he had a great deal of personal respect for Dönitz.[8] The feeling was mutual. Admiral Dönitz often praised Hitler's character, applauding his "unswerving confidence," and calling anyone who doubted the Third Reich "stupid."[9]

Shortages of food and medicine also affected the refugees. It was common for the elderly or the very young to die on board the refugee ships.[10] Hitler ordered refugee ships to load up food and medicine in Kiel and bring it back to the Baltic ports. This was nearly impossible since the entire Reich experienced food shortages.

When fuel shortages threatened to halt Operation Hannibal, Dönitz engaged in creative thinking so he wouldn't have to abandon his plan to evacuate refugees and service members. He decided to still make sure the navy did everything possible to evacuate the refugees on oil-burning vessels, which could be spared from other operations, albeit temporarily. He knew there were 900 noncommissioned officers and 600 men already stationed in the naval base in Gotenhafen undergoing submarine training. The admiral proposed the men be used on land to help defend the medieval city of Danzig. This would free up space on boats for more civilians and offer more protection of the cities.

Hitler, however, knew these 1,500 mariners had no hope of changing the situation on land. So on January 21, Dönitz gave the order for officers to redeploy student submariners and military weapons and equipment to help mitigate the growing refugee crisis. The evacuations had to be carried out under constant attack from British, American, and Russian aircraft. Russian submarines and light coastal forces threatened the German ships as they navigated in heavily mined waters.[11]

Of all the ships to participate in Operation Hannibal, the *Wilhelm Gustloff* was the largest and most symbolic. To the Nazis, the 684-foot-long, gleaming white ship was a dream come true; a floating symbol of their ideology. The ship was named for Wilhelm Gustloff, the 41-year-old assassinated head of the Nazi Party in Switzerland.

In February 1936, David Frankfurter, a young Yugoslav Jew and student had knocked on the door of Gustloff's apartment in Davos, Switzerland. He pretended he had an urgent message to deliver to the party chief. Gustloff's wife, Hedwig, invited the student inside their home. Once inside, Frankfurter shot Gustloff in the head five times.[12] The assassination of one of his staunchest

supporters deeply angered Adolf Hitler. He stopped short of calling for direct reprisals against Jews partly because he wanted to
avoid any controversy while the Third Reich was preparing for
the Summer Olympics.[13] When the games ended and the international delegations and press departed from Munich, the anti-
Semitic and anti-Bolshevik actions started anew.[14]

Reich Minister of Propaganda Joseph Goebbels seized on the
moment to make Gustloff a martyr to the Nazi cause. Goebbels
knew the Swiss party head, a firm believer in Nazi doctrine, had
dedicated himself to spreading Nazi ideology throughout the German Swiss population. Gustloff had diligently gathered information about anti-Nazi Germans living in the neutral country that
could be harnessed for propaganda purposes. A known entity in
Switzerland, the Swiss government had banned Wilhelm Gustloff's Nazi newspaper *Der Reichdeutsche*. Yet, outside of Switzerland few Germans knew of Wilhelm Gustloff. That changed after
the assassination. David Frankfurter, convicted of murder, served
9 years of his 18-year sentence in a Swiss prison.[15]

Meanwhile, Adolf Hitler and his denizens made sure Gustloff's funeral equaled, if not surpassed, that of the former president of Germany, Field Marshal Paul Von Hindenburg, who had
died in 1934. A World War One veteran, Hindenburg had originally opposed Hitler; nonetheless, he had appointed him chancel-
lor in 1933.

Adolf Hitler presided over Wilhelm Gustloff's February 12,
1936 funeral in Schwerin, Germany. Propaganda Minister Joseph
Goebbels and Reichsführer Heinrich Himmler, head of the SS,
were among the Nazi leadership present. About 3,000 people lined
a cobblestone street in this northern lakeside city. As the funeral
procession passed the speakers' platform, their arms extended in
stiff-armed Heil-Hitler salutes. Hitler's eulogy included a vicious
rant on Jews: "Behind every murder stood the same power which
is responsible for this murder; behind these harmless insignificant

fellow countrymen who were instigated and incited to crime stands the hate-filled power of our Jewish foe, a foe to whom we had done no harm, but who nonetheless sought to subjugate our German people and make of it its slave—the foe who is responsible for all the misfortune that fell upon us in 1918, for all the misfortune which plagued Germany in the years that followed," Hitler raged.[16]

A rough granite monolith marks Gustloff's grave. Gustloff's name is deeply etched into the unpolished, charcoal gray stone. A lightning bolt carved into the stone and blackened with time is the marker's only other design.

Just one year after his assassination, Nazi Germany paid homage to the man Hitler called "an immortal for all time."[17] The Third Reich built the *Wilhelm Gustloff,* a 25-million-reichsmark flagship for Nazi Germany's "Strength Through Joy" (*Kraft durch Freude* or KdF) fleet. The ship was the Reich's pride and joy.

In the mid-1930s Nazi Germany rolled out a large-scale social program to deliver recreation to the *volk*. The KdF was an arm of the DAF, the National Socialist party's replacement for labor unions. The Deutsche Arbeitsfront (German Labor Front or DAF) was set up in 1933 after the Reichstag abolished all trade unions in Germany. Under National Socialism, workers were compelled to join the DAF and pay dues in exchange for various social programs and job security, but DAF's real purpose was to control labor unrest and strikes and to compel loyalty. Both the DAF and its subsidiary KdF were directed by Robert Ley.

A Nazi politician, Ley had served two years with an artillery unit during World War One. In 1917 the French shot down his aircraft over France. The then 27-year-old found himself a prisoner of war. The experience rattled Ley; he developed a stammer and became a heavy drinker. He returned from the war, received a doctorate in chemistry, and worked for IG Farben, one of Germany's largest industrial companies. Ley moved through the ranks of the Nazi Party and often toured factories and KdF facilities with Himmler.

In November 1933 Ley helped establish the KdF as a way to offer benefits and recreational amenities to the German working class and their families. The KdF program took a militant approach to fun. It prescribed, in detail, correct methods, time, and content of leisure allowed so that workers' productivity would be enhanced.[18] The KdF staged operas and concerts in factories. Workers had access to free physical education and gymnastics.[19] The KdF also offered coaching for football, tennis, and sailing. Across the Third Reich KdF chapters organized celebrations honoring Adolf Hitler's birthday and hosted harvest festivals. After the 1938 Anschluss with Austria, the KdF promoted the Strength Through Joy slogan, promising that all the KdF's activities would now be available to Austrians loyal to the Reich.[20]

In the Reich every Aryan citizen had the right to a vacation: The KdF's 1936 slogan "Enjoy Your Lives!" cheered people after a decade of economic depression. Until the late 1930s, most German citizens had never ventured outside their country. Only the wealthy traveled abroad. The DAF, through the KdF, subsidized holidays in resorts across Germany and in so-called safe countries such as Italy. It showed ordinary citizens what life could be like if they worked hard and followed Nazi policies. The program's cruises and train trips promised to give millions of Germans the chance to see the fjords of Norway or to visit Berlin. The *Gustloff* could comfortably transport nearly 1,500 passengers at a time on cruises through the Mediterranean and to Africa.[21] Throughout 1938, the liner brought middle-class leisure activities to the masses, giving the appearance of blurring class divisions.

Adolf Hitler wanted his cruise liners to rival British, French, and American ships. Unlike his enemies' cruise ships, passengers traveling on KdF liners had full run of the ship. First class and third class simply didn't exist. Rather the boats were a floating celebration of the Nazi Party faithful, all of whom were treated to luxury and glamour. The *Wilhelm Gustloff* boasted nearly 54,000 square feet of deck space with a gymnasium and swimming pool. A large, glass-enclosed promenade wrapped around the ship. Inside the deck were lounge chairs for passengers to relax. Passengers dined off white porcelain plates decorated with green or red stripes around the rim; they used sterling silver cutlery engraved with an eagle and swastika. From the sun deck to the cinema and everywhere in between, passengers relaxed and played.

In the first years of these cruises, passengers wrote about how some of the travelers were a tad discomfited with this style of leisure. Having to dress up for dinner frazzled a few nerves. Initially, many of those aboard the KdF cruises were unaccustomed to such grand displays of elegance and formality. They reluctantly entered community rooms to play cards or listen to concerts.[22] Publicity photos from this period show smiling, tanned German workers sunning themselves, reading, and dozing on the ship's various recreation decks.

The Strength Through Joy (KdF) enshrined the idea of community before individual. Germans had faith in such slogans as "Ein Volk! Ein Reich! Ein Fürher!" ("One People, One Empire, One Leader"). Propaganda was the glue to stick together the German nationalist community. If Adolf Hitler became the Third Reich's symbol of national unity, the KdF program provided the bread and circuses for the masses.[23]

Even more than the fun, boats such as the *Wilhelm Gustloff* showcased the power and force of Nazi Germany.[24] Blohm & Voss, the Hamburg shipyard that had also built the ill-fated battleship *Bismarck,* designed and built all the ships in the KdF fleet. The *Gustloff* had 22 lifeboats and 12 transverse bulkheads, which made 13 watertight compartments. Many of its portholes were made of armored glass to withstand bad weather and bullets. The *Gustloff* and all the other liners in the fleet were designed to be "absolutely secure." After the *Titanic* sank in 1912, no one dared call the gleaming white vessel, or any other ship, unsinkable.

Adolf Hitler launched the 25,484-ton liner from the seaside city of Hamburg on May 5, 1937. On the day of the *Wilhelm Gustloff*'s christening, Gustloff's widow, Hedwig, broke a champagne bottle across the ship's bow. Cheers and applause thundered. Flags and banners rippled in the breeze. Hundreds of German workers and party officials bid the ship adieu and bon voyage.[25] Hundreds of passengers watched the shoreline slip away as the ship sailed down the Elbe River on its way to the Madeira Islands of Portugal, just off the Moroccan coast. Captain Karl Lübbe, smartly dressed in the double-breasted coat of a naval officer, was in command. A year later on the *Gustloff*'s first recreational trip, the liner had a compliment of 400 crewmembers to serve more than 1,400 passengers. Just one day into the trip, Captain Lübbe, 58, died of a heart attack.[26] After a memorial service, the crew took his body ashore in Dover, England. That evening, the dinner menu for April 23 was marked "Mourning Captain Lübbe." A new captain came aboard; he was Captain Friedrich Peterson. The 63-year-old captain, who came from the Merchant Navy, seemed to have little patience for other viewpoints. His quarrelsome nature wouldn't bode well for the *Gustloff*.

In 1937, before the Anschluss with Austria and before Germany invaded Poland, Adolf Hitler used the *Wilhelm Gustloff* to win hearts and minds. Between April 3 and April 4, 1938, the *Gustloff* rescued the 1,826-ton English cargo ship *Pegaway* after a furious spring storm caused it to flounder 20 miles off the Dutch island of Terschelling. The *Gustloff* had only recently completed her first sea trials. After receiving a distress call around 4 A.M. from the *Pegaway*, Captain Lübbe ordered the *Gustloff* to head straight to the ship, damaged from a heavy storm. In so doing, he left behind the other three KdF ships he was with: the *Der*

Deutsche, Oceana, and *Sierra Cordoba.* The *Gustloff* pulled 19 members of the *Pegaway*'s crew aboard.

Local and international newspapers praised Captain Lübbe's efforts. In Australia, the *Sydney Morning Herald* reported that the *Wilhelm Gustloff* received a silver plaque in recognition of rescuing the *Pegaway* crew when "it foundered about 25 miles north-west of Leterschelling Light on April 4th during a gale of hurricane force and mountainous seas." The article mentioned how the *Gustloff* crew treated the crew with "the utmost kindness by all onboard and while in Hamburg they were supplied with clothing and pocket money and were helped in other ways."[27] Naturally Minister of Propaganda Joseph Goebbels and the entire Nazi propaganda ministry seized upon this opportunity to depict the Third Reich as a humanitarian regime.

During a propaganda mission on April 10, 1938, the *Gustloff* sailed up the Thames River to serve as a floating polling station for an estimated 2,000 Germans living in England who wished to vote for the Anschluss with Austria.[28] Around noontime crew members from the *Wilhelm Gustloff* picked up voters waiting at London's Tilbury Docks. This was reported in a two-page photo spread in the US edition of *Life* magazine. "Germans From England—'JA' [Yes] on a Special Trip Out to Sea" showed how nearly 2,000 Germans and Austrians living in England were taken by the Germans 50 miles to sea to vote on the German plebiscite of Anschluss. "Of England's 34,000 Germans and Austrians, mostly house servants, the first 2,000 non-Jewish applicants were accepted. They turned in a 99.4% Ja as compared with greater Germany's 99.08% Ja the same day."

Passengers were treated to concerts, celebrations, and free beer. The menu for April 9, the day before ballots were cast, bore a special message for diners: "Your Thanks For Voting Yes."

The *Wilhelm Gustloff* captivated the foreign press. Several articles speculated whether there was more to the ship than sundecks and cinema. In the United States the *New York Times* noted the ship's antiaircraft guns and questioned whether the *Gustloff* might eventually be deployed as an aircraft carrier. The article described how aerial photos of the ship "have aroused considerable speculation here whether these craft with their long upper deck, obstructed only by a funnel, could quickly be converted into aircraft carriers. The *Wilhelm Gustloff,* of 25,000 tons gross, is about 700 feet long and has a deck area of 53,800 square feet, claimed to be larger than any vessels of this size."[29] A shipping expert quoted in the article said the boat's deck could easily be lengthened to form a flying deck. It also didn't get overlooked that the ship could—and did—become a troop transport.

In May 1939 the *Wilhelm Gustloff,* together with the *Robert Ley, Deutsche Stuttgard, Sierra Cordo,* and *Oceana* took part in transporting the Luftwaffe's Condor Legion from Spain. Franco's Nationalists were sending the men home after successfully defeating Republican forces in the Spanish Civil War. The *Gustloff* unloaded medical supplies and took home 1,405 men. Of course the boat's travels involved more than public relations. It continued to offer cruises to the masses. During the winter of 1938–1939 the ship sailed to Genoa, Naples, and Palermo before depositing her passengers ashore in Venice, Italy. That March, Adolf Hitler inspected the *Wilhelm Gustloff,* but he never sailed on the ship. The ship's last peacetime cruise was early summer 1939 when she sailed to Norway and Sweden.

In September 1939, soon after Germany invaded Poland, the German military pressed the *Gustloff* back into service. Classified as Hospital Ship D, it became a floating hospital for the sick and wounded. Surgeons operated on patients in former cabins, and the glassed-in promenade deck became a solarium for the wounded. Heavily bandaged soldiers and sailors recuperated on stretchers and in chairs. This new mission required the ship and crew to follow strict international laws governing the sea.

A wide, green band encircled the white ship's hull and the floor of its decks, sides, and stack bore a red cross symbol. The ship could carry neither defensive nor offensive weapons. During the Polish campaign, the *Wilhelm Gustloff* took 685 wounded soldiers from Danzig. It also helped in relief operations for the thousands of Baltic Germans who were being brought into the official Reich under the enormous resettlement plan agreed upon in 1939.

The *Gustloff* was a floating hospital until 1940. Then, when the British blockaded the German coastline, the *Gustloff* housed U-boat crewmen undergoing training, and it remained tethered to a pier in Gotenhafen, a German navy stronghold. For the next four years the *Gustloff* served as an accommodation ship for U-boat trainees, first with the 1st Submarine Training Division and then the 2nd Submarine Training Division. Its shiny white surface was concealed under a coat of gray paint, and uniformed sailors replaced bathing beauties, shuffleboard enthusiasts, and military wounded. Submariners trained in tanks on board and learned survival skills in the swimming pool.

In November 1944, Captain Paul Vollrath, a veteran of the German navy, was posted to the 2nd Submarine Training Division in Gotenhafen.[30] The *Wilhelm Gustloff* and the *Hansa* comprised this unit. "More suitable ships for the purpose they were used for during the war could not have been found. They had everything, which otherwise would have had to be built ashore; they were self-contained units, accommodation, administration, catering, light, heating, everything was available and what is more, men, fit for sea service, did not have to be employed to keep the ships running," Vollrath wrote in his postwar memoir.[31]

The crew consisted of a merchant marine crew, who at this stage in the war were deemed unfit for active duty for either health reasons or age. A fair number of Croatian merchant seamen also served as deck crew aboard both the *Wilhelm Gustloff* and the

Hansa. The ships were tethered to opposite piers in a part of Gotenhafen harbor set aside for training crews.

In November 1944 the war in the east still seemed far away to Captain Vollrath, who wrote that "the thought that one day we may have to abandon Gdynia [Gotenhafen] looked like high treason to me."[32] Just one month later, in December, all training for the 2nd Submarine Training Division ceased. Rather than training new seamen, staff and old submarine crews were armed with spades and shovels. They were dispatched to Gotenhafen's outer suburbs to dig antitank trenches per the command of Erich Koch, the administrator of East Prussia.

Officers like Vollrath were distant from and immune to the politics and debates of the naval leadership. Captain Paul Vollrath didn't feel any sense of urgency. He viewed their change of mission as a normal wartime precaution. Confusion was par for the military's course. However, years later, when he considered that time again, Vollrath realized just how isolated he and others serving in East Prussia were from the true state of the war.

"We still believed that final victory would not be far off (so much for the power of propaganda), but in spite of our eager faith we heard at the time that Russian troops had broken through the German lines and Russian tanks had been roaming at will far behind the German lines," Vollrath wrote.[33] He noted that it had become common to see distraught refugees, who were fleeing Soviet atrocities in the eastern territories, descend on Gotenhafen. No longer could he ignore the stories of rape, murder, and arson. "Their looks and the state in which they arrived obviously spoke of a severe urgency," Vollrath wrote.[34]

This constant arrival of refugees spurred Admiral Karl Dönitz to forge ahead with Operation Hannibal. That meant changing the training and deployment schedule for hundreds of naval personnel. Captain Vollrath was yanked from the U-boat training course on the *Gustloff* in early January 1945 and instead posted to the 22nd Submarine Training Flotilla, which was part of the 2nd Submarine Training Division. Now he was billeted to the U–351, a training submarine.

Barely a week passed before Vollrath received orders to prepare to depart Gotenhafen. The harbor city joined Königsberg and Pillau on the list of fortress cities to be evacuated. Adolf Hitler had considered Pillau essential to Königsberg's protection. Throughout the long war Hitler allowed his fighting men to withdraw only in the face of utter destruction such as at Stalingrad. By January 25, 1945, it was clear that Königsberg, Pillau, and the other cities along the coast were in danger of succumbing to the Russian army.

With the Soviets threatening the entire Baltic Coast, Captain Vollrath received orders to report as a second officer aboard the *Wilhelm Gustloff*. Vollrath's previous service in the merchant marine suited him for this post. He feared losing a fifth ship. He'd already lost four ships during the war; three in the Mediterranean Sea and one in the English Channel off Boulogne; mines, bombs, and gunfire nearly took another off the coast of Le Havre, France.

Vollrath wasn't one to believe in premonitions or wax philosophical. The captain just realized that given the ferocity of the war, it was naïve to think he would get through the entire war unharmed and that no ship he served on would be lost or damaged. Vollrath didn't think he was being unfairly tested. "In any case I prepared for the worst as I did not like to be taken by surprise or worse still with my pants down. Cigarettes, a bottle of Half and Half, a popular spirit made by Mampe at that time, a flash lamp, a knife and a Mauser pistol I got ready," Vollrath wrote.[35]

In 1937 the Germans built the 684-foot-long *Wilhelm Gustloff* to prove the power of the Reich. For a few years it sailed atop the warmer waters of the Mediterranean, a more forgiving climate. Then Germany invaded Poland and the shimmering ship was confined in the Baltic Sea where ice often glazed its deck.

The *Wilhelm Gustloff* was just one of hundreds of vessels, from large cruise liners to smaller fishing boats, attempting to leave the frozen Gulf of Danzig in January 1945. Aside from the *Gustloff*, several other large passenger liners participated in Operation Hannibal carrying thousands of men, women and children: *Cap Arcona, Robert Ley, Hamburg, Hansa,* and *Deutschland.* There were smaller ships too, including the *Potsdam, Pretoria, Berlin, General Steuben, Monte Rosa, Antonio Delfino,* and *Winrich von Kniprode.* These boats were between 10,000 tons and 20,000 tons.

Most people killed during Operation Hannibal, which lasted from January through May 1945, were civilians. Aside from the *Gustloff,* the *Goya* went down between April 16 and 17, 1945, drowning close to 7,000, and the *Steuben* was attacked and sunk between February 9 and 10, drowning about 3,500. Soviet submarines sank each of these ships. This evacuation from the Baltic Sea region also involved those trying to evacuate over land. Because of the inherent chaos of war, no one knows exactly how many tried, how many died, or how many survived. However, those tragedies, which claimed thousands of lives at a time, came after the *Wilhelm Gustloff* tried to cross the Baltic Sea on a cold, dark winter night.

In January 1945 the *Wilhelm Gustloff,* the crown jewel of the German cruise liners, waited in Danzig harbor for clearance to sail. A convoy of other vessels, all under military escort, was to leave with the *Wilhelm Gustloff.* The ships were all bound for Kiel, Germany, about 289 nautical miles, or 332 statute miles, away.

Four

"WE KNEW WE HAD TO GET OUT"

On the morning of January 26, 1945, ten-year-old Horst Woit sat in his cozy kitchen for the last time.

"On this Saturday everything was what we called normal. Mom had made me breakfast. Most likely it was rye bread with marmalade and warm milk; what to eat in those days was not great," Woit said. "Then hell broke loose. Some young boy in a Hitler Youth uniform knocked on the door and told us the Russian tanks have entered the city Elbing and we have permission to flee. As most people knew this would happen sooner or later, Mom had a suitcase already packed with the exception of sandwiches."[1]

The pair dressed in thick layers for the long walk. They piled on long underwear, ski pants, multiple sweaters, and coats. They wore heavy boots that after a while made Horst's legs tire with each step. Just before they left the ten-year-old boy slid his uncle's eight-inch long, black jackknife into his pocket. Outside the snow covered the ground.

"The knife I took out of my uncle's trunk and hid in my ski pants was the only object I had. Mom did not know about it; I do not remember what she had in that little suitcase either, and I hated the long underwear because it was scratchy. I hated it with a passion," he said.[2]

Until this day Horst Woit had lived a relatively normal life in Elbing, a small city located in the northern part of East Prussia. It had a shallow port on the Elbing River, which flows into the Vistula Lagoon, which in turn emptied into the Baltic Sea. The city once belonged to the Hanseatic League, the thirteenth-century trade association that allowed commerce with England, Flanders, France, and the Netherlands. The port lay about 6 miles away from Horst's home, a long walk for a small boy in any circumstances, but on this frigid day it was a matter of life and death for Horst and his mother.

For days Russian tanks and soldiers had nipped at Elbing's heels. On the day Horst and Meta Woit left Elbing, Russian troops entered the city to confront the 100,000 German soldiers stationed there. The battle didn't ignite into full force until after they left. When it did, it lasted two weeks and ended with the Germans' surrender. Between February and May of 1945 the Soviets virtually destroyed Elbing with its thirteenth-century Gothic architecture. Horst remembers scores of refugees like himself, fleeing with their possessions. The Woits, like so many of their neighbors, had lost faith in the ability of the German army to protect them. They had waited to receive official permission. Helga's neighbor had tried to leave before official permission was granted; the Germans shot him.

Radio broadcasts still aired Hitler's directives to "lash out in all directions with fists and claws to gain control of the storm sweeping over our eastern borders."[3] The men who were left were either the very elderly or very young. They were ordered to stand firm, the ailing and sick commanded to fight to the last ounce of their strength. As Irene Tschinkur recalls, her father, Herbert Christoph, wasn't drafted because he ran a large bakery that employed many people. "He had to stay behind to keep producing bread to feed all those people who had come into Gotenhafen from the eastern parts. Before Mom, Ellen, Evi, and I left, I saw a lot of army trucks roll into the yard to pick up bread—I suppose for the front," Irene remembered.[4]

Some German citizens in the eastern territories stubbornly held out, choosing to stay on their farms or with their businesses. They believed in the Third Reich's power to stop the Soviet invaders. Others stayed, hoping the Red Army would show them mercy.

For the most part, women led children and the elderly to safety since so many men were fighting, or wounded, or dead. Many boys over the age of 12 were also gone; the Nazi military had sent them either to the front or to operate antiaircraft guns. In some instances former prisoners who had been sent to work on farms in East Prussia helped their German "hosts" prepare to leave. These prisoners helped properly pack wagons and close up homes. They helped dress children for the long and cold journey, and they stayed with the families through artillery fire, hunger, and the dangerous walk over breaking ice. Hoping to make their way to American or British lines, their fates became inextricably linked with these families.[5]

Horst's mother, her friend Hildegard, and Hildegard's eight-year-old daughter Christa decided to leave Elbing together. The two mothers felt they had a better chance traveling in a small group amid the refugees. The heavy suitcases slowed them considerably; it took them two hours to walk the distance to the Elbing River. Horst kept his head down against the cold as they walked. Meta and Horst trudged over the frozen Frisches Haff (the Vistula Lagoon), while the cold wind dipped and swirled, forcing them to bend like saplings in a storm. Gritty dirt blew across the ice. Icy winds swept the land, and snowdrifts rose higher and faster, at times blotting out the roads and trails from view. In some places wooden stakes marked the route to show refugees where to safely cross the ice. Where there were no markers, people followed a trail of broken carts, wagons, and discarded belongings. It had been an uncommonly cold stretch of weather with temperatures hovering at or below zero degrees Fahrenheit; wind gusts caused temperatures to dive as low as minus 25 degrees Celsius (minus 13 degrees Fahrenheit) at times. The refugees feared frostbite. People wore fur coats, gloves, mittens, boots, hats pulled low, shawls and scarves; it wasn't always enough.

All across East Prussia, fleeing civilians pulled sleds heaped with everything from crockery and linens to clothing and carpets. Sharp winds lashed convoys. Wheel ruts scored the icy ground and hundreds of tramping feet, both human and horse, left their mark. Masses of refugees and retreating German army vehicles jammed the narrow roads. Sometimes people had to wait for hours in one spot just to move a few more feet forward. There were also prisoners of war and retreating troops. Refugees saw withdrawing troops dig antitank trenches with their helmets because they no longer had shovels. Later witnesses to the treks described the hundreds of thousands of East Prussians as a piteous stream. Stories of Soviet atrocities drove the refugees forward.

"Russian tanks opened fire on us and drove over refugee columns crushing livestock and people beneath treads with no more thought than someone would swat a fly," Woit said.[6] Russian air force planes strafed the Frisches Haff as the refugees fled; the ice cracked under the weight of horse-drawn carts and bodies plunged beneath. Women abandoned their babies, some dead, some gravely ill, to the snow and ice. Many mothers could no longer carry their children after they died. On roads, they left their babies in the deep snow, away from the automobiles and farm wagons.[7]

Frisches Haff (the Vistula Lagoon) is a shallow body of water running alongside the Baltic Sea. It starts about 25 miles east of Danzig and runs northeast to Königsberg along the southern coast of Samland and the port of Pillau. It is less than 60 miles long.

Woit's father had once taken him sledding on this very lagoon. In the days after Horst left, the situation for refugees making their way to the ports grew ever more dire. There were people who had started their journey to the Baltic coast from towns farther east than Elbing. By this point many who were too weak to walk were becoming part of the snowy landscape. Along the way refugees passed stray livestock, ransacked houses, and corpses, some with their skulls bashed, some with their dresses pulled up, all signs that the Soviet army had passed. These were not the hot-blooded atrocities that occurred when fighting units come under hostile fire or experience an onslaught of casualties. Rather, these were cold-blooded, planned actions against people considered lower than animals. A premeditated viciousness never seen on such a large scale in the west marked the eastern front.

Horst remembers that the frozen land felt like ice needles stabbing into the soles of his feet. Irene and Ellen remember eyeing the sky warily, on the lookout for Russian aircraft. Helga remembers hearing stories of children flattened by Russian tanks. The terror of what the Russian soldiers might do propelled them toward the Baltic coast.[8] Refugees of all ages passed along this frozen route, clutching their belongings, each suitcase, each trundle carrying a lifetime inside: a doll, a wedding picture, family photos. Most took only bare essentials with them, but some took things like baby carriages, mirrors, and flowerpots.

As for the German army, though the retreat was in some cases disorderly, they tried to make sure not to leave behind anything that the Russians could find useful. The military didn't want to leave a thing for the enemy, not a pound of bread or a drop of oil. Everything had to be given to the army, from livestock and grain reserves to fuel and nonferrous metals. If it couldn't be transported, it was to be destroyed.[9] German soldiers blew up bridges, railway junctions, telegraph and telephone wires. However, because the Wehrmacht was on the defensive, their retreat was sometimes as chaotic as the flight of the refugees. In spite of that, German soldiers had almost nothing with them as they retreated; they had no winter clothes, food, or ammunition, and still much equipment was left behind.[10]

With few exceptions, the German army was no longer solely fighting on foreign soil in January 1945. This was new to a military machine that even when it surrendered in the past, as it had during World War One, it did so standing on foreign soil. Now foreign troops stood upon German soil.

After a day the Woits and Hildegard and Cristina reached Pillau, about 30 miles northeast of Elbing. Meta Woit knew she and her son were going to get on a transport ship. Eventually she planned to join the rest of her family in Schwerin.

Under cold and cloudy skies the two mothers and two children, along with 30 other people, climbed aboard a 24-foot cutter that was headed on the Vistula River to Danzig. Arriving in the port of Danzig, they boarded another small boat, which sailed to Gotenhafen. Because Meta and Hildegard were traveling with children, and because they were one of the first evacuees to arrive, they easily received boarding passes for the *Wilhelm Gustloff*.

Horst remembers being impressed by the crowds and the numerous ships. While their little group waited to board the ship, they saw scores of wounded troops arriving in Gotenhafen from the front lines. They joined the thousands of others awaiting evacuation.[11]

Horst remembers reveling in stories about the great Elbing castle built by the Teutonic knights. During the war, and though Horst doesn't recall this, the town supported the Nazi Party. He didn't know about the three subcamps of Stutthof—Elbing, Elbing (Org. Todt), and Schinau. He doesn't recall "confrontations with prisoners."[12] He was also just young enough to escape Nazi indoctrination since Hitler Youth membership didn't start until age ten. Thinking back on his childhood, Horst remembers looking forward to Sundays when soldiers would parade through Elbing's old town and the band played. Most of Elbing's men, his father included, were fighting on the eastern front. Horst and his mother never heard from him during the war.

Although the Woits had only peripheral contact with Hitler Youth until the beginning of January, he remembers seeing them all across town. While most children like Horst led quite ordinary lives, the Hitler Youth infiltrated much of daily life by the late autumn of 1940.[13] Members of Hitler Youth collected streetcar tickets and stood in as workers in munitions factories to replace men sent to the front. They manned antiaircraft guns and dug trenches at the borders of towns and cities. At the end of the war, boys as young as 12 years old were pressed into service on the front. Girls in the Bund Deutscher Mädel (BDM, League of German Girls) worked as nurses' aides and streetcar conductors. They helped ethnic German farmers settle in annexed Polish territories and even helped with evictions. They also chaperoned Baltic Germans newly arrived to East Prussia.[14]

Meanwhile in Königsberg, the Reuter family coped with the war years in their own way.

"We had a lovely childhood, but the teenager time? Forget about it," said Helga Reuter Knickerbocker, who was born in 1927 to Kurt Reuter and Marta Walloch.[15] The Reuters owned a furniture factory in Königsberg that had dozens of showrooms, each more well appointed than the last, with walnut dining room tables, satin smooth console tables, and elegantly framed mirrors. Helga and her older sisters—Ingeborg, or Inge as she was nicknamed, and Ursula—lived in a spacious home on the same property as the factory. Inge, born in 1921, "was beautiful—outside and such goodness inside. We were so very close."

Being older than Horst, Helga Reuter had to join Hitler Youth. As part of the Hitler Youth, Helga remembers going door-to-door collecting recyclables and gathering paper, scrap iron, rags, and bones. For years Nazi Germany had been "carrying on a desperate campaign to remedy her acute shortage of raw materials. . . . Kitchen remains are collected, made into fodder for cattle. Old newspapers may no longer be used for kindling fires, sardine cans no longer have individual openers (saving 2,000 tons of iron a year), men's shirts are made two inches shorter."[16]

Shortages of clothing, food, and fuel meant families across East Prussia depended on ration cards. The Reuters felt fortunate to have a small but bountiful vegetable garden and to raise chickens and rabbits. The family depended on their ration cards for daily staples such as flour, sugar, and butter. They also were allowed milk, available to families with children under 18. However, Helga didn't like milk, so her mother could cook with the precious liquid.

Before the war the upper-middle-class family employed a cook and housekeeper. They also had a chauffeur until her sister Ursula turned 18 and, to the delight of her father, she could drive. The Reuters were rich, but Helga said the hired help had been mostly because her father suffered from limited eyesight. Helga's mother, Marta, acted as his eyes; she was always by his side, never wanting or willing to leave him.

Helga's parents and grandparents had long called East Prussia home. According to family lore, Helga's great-great grandparents, who had been Lutheran, had moved to Königsberg, the capital of East Prussia, from Austria to escape tensions between the Calvinists and the Lutherans. Her mother's parents died when Helga was four. While Helga doesn't remember either of them, she grew up hearing about how they indulged her. When her parents weren't busy working in their furniture showroom, they too indulged the three daughters. Each summer Helga's parents took the girls to a resort town on the Baltic Sea. There the Reuter family delighted in time spent on the shores of the crystalline, cobalt waters. She and her sister swam, sometimes in the smooth inner waters of the lagoons; sometimes they braved the strong Baltic waves.

Before the *Wilhelm Gustloff*, Helga remembers the Baltic Sea as a beautiful place for fun. "The Baltic Sea was so beautiful," Helga said. "The sand was very light and fine; there was no pollution. But even when we had a hot summer, the Baltic Sea was still so cold."

Yet in January 1945 seashore excursions only existed in the postcard of memory. Ice now covered Königsberg Bay, although in some places it wasn't thick enough to support the unending procession of heavily laden wagons. The ice often cracked beneath horses and people, sending them to their deaths. Refugees leaving Königsberg had to navigate about 15 miles of this bay to reach the fishing port of Pillau, located across a strait from the northeastern tip of a sandy strip of land called Frische Nehrung. Some people made this crossing in six to eight hours; others took days to cross the ice. Blocked roads rendered cars useless. Since the lagoon was frozen, rescue ships couldn't enter the inner waters and get to the refugees sooner. The evacuees had no choice but to hazard a trip over the lagoon.

Once the authorities lifted the restriction on leaving, Milda Bendrich hurried to gather her belongings, including baby blankets and a change of clothes. Then she closed her home forever.

"On about January 27 I had a very early morning visit from a friend, a Marine Oberleutant," Milda Bendrich wrote her daughter Inge many years after the war ended.[17] "He came to us to ask if and how we intended to flee. There was no "if" for me, as I had heard enough about the Polish revenge on the Germans who chose to remain in Poland. The "how" I imagined would be by train. Now I learned that the train line ended in Pommern and the refugees were forced to walk the rest of the journey through the snow. I had been offered by my friends, a family by the name of

Sika, to join them in fleeing to Sudetengau. I declined and they left Gotenhafen."

Milda's parents, ethnic German refugees from central Poland, helped the new mother pack. Together they gathered clothing, linens, crockery, and books. In her letter, Milda noted the precise measurements of how she loaded suitcases and packets on "a 1.8-meter long sledge, the luggage reached 1.7 meters high." She estimated the height of the sledge because it was just taller than her father, she wrote Inge. Together the five adults pushed and pulled the sledge to the train station. The wind whipped their hair, sending snow into their eyes. A mile-long path separated them from the station. Milda and her parents and their neighbors kept getting stuck in the deep snow. The caravan of refugees planned on taking the train to Ochtersum/Hildesheim in Germany.

"You, Inge, were the only one who enjoyed this trip, as you were comfortably positioned and sheltered from the rough wind in a gap between the luggage as if you were sitting in a lounge chair," Milda Bendrich wrote in a letter to her daughter. The only thing Milda Bendrich ever saw again from her home was a tattered carton full of wool remnants and an old dressing gown.[18] The package didn't arrive until well after the war. Inge still marvels that someone had taken the time to pack the box and track her mother down.

From the autumn of 1944 on, European and American newspapers published various versions of this headline: "Berliners are receiving the first visible warning that the Red Army stands before the frontiers of the Reich."[19] In Berlin, Germany's beating heart, headlines like these caused alarm.[20] However, as several historians have noted, by 1944 it was clear Germany would lose the war.

Yet, before German officials allowed civilians to leave, Nazi administrators were already escaping from East Prussia, in part to set up a base of secure operations on the other side of the Baltic

Sea, far from Berlin.[21] The United States watched this unfold from its Office of Strategic Service station across the Baltic Sea. In September 1944 it reported that Germans have two choices: They could either endure the complete disintegration of the Nazi Party or take a chance for rebuilding their nation on a sound basis. The OSS reported that many in the upper levels of Nazi leadership were trying to drag out the war in order to escape to neutral lands where they might challenge the postwar situation using vast sums of hidden money.[22]

The OSS Stockholm station debated how best to exploit these weaknesses. The summer before refugees embarked on the *Wilhelm Gustloff*, OSS operatives brainstormed on ways to drive a deeper wedge between the Nazi party and the civilians it was forcing to stay in vulnerable lands. The Allies, particularly the Americans, wanted to use the civilians' growing alarm at the Russian advance as well as any perceptions of privileged treatment given to soldier's wives and dependents.[23] Inequality between the German people and their party leaders ran rampant. The military continued to force young boys into the Volkssturm home guard or militia. These unfortunate conscripts had no enthusiasm and many failed to fight. Meanwhile, Gauleiter Erich Koch, the provincial governor in charge of East Prussia, sent his family out of harm's way. He did this in spite of telling people that "No true German would allow himself even the thought that East Prussia might fall into Russian hands."[24] He followed the lead of Adolf Hitler. In December 1944, the Soviet troops threatened Wolf's Lair, the massive East Prussian field headquarters near Rastenberg, and so the Führer retreated to Berlin. The OSS wanted to publicize any "irrational military orders, which may encourage desertion or surrender or lead to a relaxation of discipline with detail."[25] Helga Reuter certainly considered the advice given to women and children to be most irrational. "They told me and my sister to stay behind and throw boiling water at invading Russian soldiers," she said, the corners of her mouth tilting upward ever so slightly at the absurdity of the suggestion.

With its grand cathedral and large historic city center, Königsberg became one of what Nazi authorities designated as a fortress city. Fourteen forts surrounded the major East Prussian city. Starting in mid-January more than 700 fighters hunkered inside each stone-walled fort. Civilians joined them. If they had no armaments, they were supposed to help the defense using homemade weapons. Civilians, virtual hostages in these locations, often endured incessant artillery fire from surrounding Soviet forces. Women, children, and those who escaped conscription in the Volkssturm died alongside soldiers. These cities were to be defended at all cost. "Our opponents must know that every kilometer that they want to advance into our country will cost them rivers of blood," Reichsführer Heinrich Himmler said in October 1944.[26] Fires raged across the city.

Before Erich Koch fled, he ordered hundreds of thousands of inhabitants and Russian prisoners of war to fortify the city. They had to build more tank traps, foxholes, gun emplacements, ditches, and bolstered cellars to prepare for street-to-street and house-to-house combat.[27] Koch had started the earthworks when the Russians began their 1944 offensive. Koch prohibited civilians from leaving even as war came closer and even as the Soviet army began shelling Königsberg. The thunderous artillery was so strong, it rattled people from the inside out. Königsberg wouldn't fall until April 9, and until it did, the German military and political leadership cleaved to the idea that so long as the old city remained in German hands, then Germany still held East Prussia.[28]

On January 20 the Soviet army took Tilsit, located on the south bank of the Nerman River. Between January 21 and 22 the Red Army marched into Allenstein and stormed into Insterburg. Four days later, on January 26, the Red Army arrived on the Baltic coast, surrounding the German Fourth Army on the Frisches

Haff, the lagoon extending south from Königsberg. Russian guns trained on Königsberg.[29]

In the Reuter house, Helga's parents decided she and Inge would be safer in Berlin with their married sister, Ursula. The girls would have to flee alone. Helga's father would have been killed for deserting, so her mother stayed by his side. "My parents never argued in front of us, but she, my Mom, used to dream. She didn't want us to go; she said, 'Over my dead body.' But he, my father, banged his fist on the table. He wanted his girls to get to safety," Helga said.

Kurt Reuter, who was not drafted because of his poor eyesight, was right in fearing the worst. Earlier that morning, Helga and Inge happened to be talking in Inge's room. They sat on a window seat, occasionally looking down at the street. They weren't talking about anything serious, just idle chatter to take their minds off the situation, Helga said. A shot cracked through the girls' talk. Their heads snapped toward the window. On the street below, a group of women huddled. Then the sisters saw an SS soldier dragging a young girl toward their factory driveway. Helga and Inge watched the scene unfold. An SS officer raised his arm and pointed the pistol. Helga and Inge sprinted down the stairs and ran outside. The thin young woman, still warm, lay on the cold pavement; strips of gray fabric wrapped her otherwise bare feet. A shredded gray army blanket swaddled her body.

"Now we knew we had to get out. We were scared," Helga said.

It was immediately decided that Helga, Inge, and their aunt, Ruth Walloch, would take the train from Königsberg. In his barn, their uncle Erick Reuter had left behind a pair of brown horses, Hans and Farmosa, and a wooden wagon after he was drafted into the Wehrmacht. Erick had also owned several cows that were taken by the German army stationed in Königsberg. Helga's father kept the horses in the factory garage, which had long since been emptied of delivery trucks. A son of a neighboring Polish farmer cared for the horses. And so the three young women mounted the horses and, with the Polish boy, they headed to the train station. Aside from their overstuffed knapsacks, they carried chicken and rabbit meat wrapped in cloth.

Helga remembers she quickly grew tired of riding and walking, but that in frigid temperatures it was the only way to keep warm. Not that she felt cold. She remembers she was so anxious she didn't feel the bracing air upon her face. She and Inge knew if they rested or sat upon a sledge or wagon for even a few minutes they risked frostbite.

As fuel shortages increased, transportation became chaotic, and the general health among the German home population declined.[30] When Helga and Inge reached the train station they realized they'd be lucky to board. The Königsberg train station resembled a zoo. Hordes of people jockeyed for position. There were no working toilets, no available food, and no water. Soldiers pushed ahead of civilians. Refugees remember vicious fights to secure seats on trains. Some people couldn't shove or beat their way on board and instead sat on top of cars or tried to hang on between cars. The trains reeked of excrement and urine. There was no medical attention. Some passengers who died en route were thrown out of open berths into the snow. Other refugees, chilled to the marrow, recalled how the SS doled out warm clothes. Historians later documented that these clothes were taken from Jews who had been deported to concentration camps.[31]

In January 1945, the Reich's transport system was fast coming to a standstill. Electricity and gas supplies were rapidly dwindling, telecommunication systems were breaking. At the Königsberg train station, the Reuter sisters and their aunt never had to try their luck because the train never left the station. Allied bombers had destroyed a railroad bridge just down the track. Helga remembers how she, Inge, and Ruth waited for hours in the crowded station before they were finally able to piece together the story. The word was the Germans had reduced the bridge to rubble so the Soviets might not pass. Forced to turn back, the Reuter sisters found their parents, Kurt and Marta, still at home. In fact, the last refugee train had pulled out of Königsberg on January 22, days before the three women arrived.

It was practice at the time to quarter soldiers with families. Wilhelm Krantz, a German officer quartered with the Reuters, lost two sons in the war. One served in the Luftwaffe and was shot down over Russia. His other son served on a U-boat and died in the North Atlantic. Krantz didn't hide his hatred for Hitler from the Reuters. After Helga, Inge, and Ruth came back, he advised them to leave by another route. He did this although official permission had yet to be granted to civilians. Helga and Inge were lucky to receive assistance since most people who were still in Königsberg, or anywhere in East Prussia, didn't get help from the military.[32] The German Fourth Army, which was in the vicinity of Königsberg, pushed ahead of civilians and frequently ordered them off the roads to make way for them.

That night, about eight officers knocked on the Reuters' door asking for quarter. They looked calm. They told the Reuters their truck had broken down and asked if they could stay until it could be fixed.

Marta Reuter, Helga's mother, brewed ersatz coffee, a chalky liquid made out of corn. Later that evening the officers readied to leave. They helped the three girls into the back of the newly repaired truck and off they drove toward Elbing.

The group heard the fighting; the Red Army was nearly upon them. The soldiers, the Reuter sisters, and their aunt reached Elbing, which was about 60 miles away from their home. They tried to travel over land, but they were stopped in Elbing by the same chomping Russian tanks Horst had heard.

"I saw three Russian tanks on the hill. They saw the group of us on the autobahn. We jumped into a ditch to escape the shooting," Helga recounted. "We just made it. The Russians killed nearly everybody. But it was nighttime and they couldn't see much."

It had taken nearly 36 hours for the band of refugees to reach Elbing. It took only two hours for the truck to return to Königsberg and the house on General Litzman Strasse. The driver showed no caution.

The next day, a soldier offered to take the Reuter girls to Pillau, the harbor opening from Frisches Haff to the Baltic Sea. Frisches Haff still remained the most direct route from Königsberg. This little harbor of Pillau, from which 441,000 refugees fled, was the main staging point for Operation Hannibal. Even now, Nazi propaganda continued full force. Authorities told civilians that hundreds of new tanks had been unloaded at Pillau and that the Germans were moving north to save them. The refugees were promised they would be "Home in time for the spring sowing." They were told it was all part of Führer's intricate plan "to let the Russians in, the more surely to destroy them."[33]

Again Helga, Inge, and their Aunt Ruth hitched a ride in the back of a truck. The three lay still. SS officers stopped the truck shortly before it reached the harbor. The sisters and their aunt huddled under the benches, using the soldiers' legs and gear as cover. They heard the soldiers come to the back of the truck. Helga's heart pounded as the soldiers scanned the open bed with their flashlights. The soldiers didn't see them hiding.

Along the way the sisters and their aunt had passed soldiers, Waffen SS, and uniformed police. Many of those troops stopped refugees on the roadside, searching them for their identity papers. Often the police stopped older men and teenage boys and shoved them onto trucks to be conscripted into the Volksstrum. Most would only last until their bodies gave out or were felled by a Russian bullet. Meanwhile, the refugees raced to pass the German engineers tasked with destroying the sheets of thick ice covering the rivers to impede the Russians' advance. The German navy deployed icebreakers to open the way so that three new torpedo boats could pass from Elbing to Pillau without falling into Soviet hands.[34]

It took Helga, Inge, and Ruth some time to find a boat and captain willing to transport them to Gotenhafen. Finally they found passage aboard a small tugboat, the *Elbing IV*. Russian fire had damaged the sturdy little boat; its waterlines were broken and some of the wood was splintered. In high seas, water seeped in. They had to return to Pillau to find another boat to Gotenhafen.

The sight of the harbor shocked the Reuter sisters and their aunt. Almost 70 years later Helga remembers that an overpowering stench pervaded the port. Rats ran over mounds of garbage. There were reports of people butchering and eating wayward livestock.

East Prussians used all means of transportation, including wagons, carts, carriages, horses, even cows, to flee the advancing Russian forces. Some people hitched inverted tables to horses, riding on these makeshift sleds with their belongings. Horse hooves slipped on the ice, wagons crashed and splintered. Flight routes constantly changed due to weather and fighting. Although some people walked as many as 50 miles a day, it took weeks for others to traverse the land and frozen harbors. All the while they faced Russian attacks from soldiers, tanks, and airplanes. People dove into snow to hide while the bullets punched through the ice.

Another route to Gotenhafen wound through the Frisches Nehrung, the narrow land spit on the northern side of the Vistula Lagoon. From there one could travel westward to Danzig. Hundreds of thousands of civilians tried that route; snowstorms claimed thousands of them. By the end of January, when the refugees arrived in Gotenhafen, the city of 3 million people had swelled by another million. A system of housing authorities and reception districts, called *Aufnahmekrasse,* aided the influx of refugees. The authorities wanted to keep people from sleeping in the streets. It was a futile effort; at the end of January 1945 the refugee population overwhelmed the housing authorities and districts. It was difficult to find food and shelter with so many people.

Back at the fishing port town of Pillau, the Reuter sisters and their aunt boarded a torpedo boat. On board the three shared a bowl of hot split pea soup that Inge had gotten from the galley. They warmed their hands on the bowl. Pillau, a small coastal town, normally had a population of 5,000; now more than 40,000 people crowded its streets. Indeed, as the Soviet army advanced, people were pushed further west. In the harbor towns along the Baltic Sea, from Königsberg to Elbing, the population swelled. Knees, elbows, and rucksacks banged into each other on the boats usually used to shuttle to large ships in outer harbors. The boat the Reuters took traveled about 11 knots per hour over choppy water. Seasick, Inge stood near the rail the whole time.

By the time Horst, Helga, and Irene and Ellen reached Gotenhafen by separate routes, their homelands had virtually vanished. Many towns and cities lay in ruins. The Soviets now controlled East Prussia, Silesia, and the parts of Poland previously under German rule. In Gotenhafen ships crowded the harbor. Ocean liners and fishing boats, dinghies and trawlers: anything that floated and could carry people was docked in the port.

Allied propaganda leaflets dropped from airplanes on the retreating German troops tried to lure German officers and soldiers to desert and inform civilians that the end of the war was near. The message was simple: The German people should rise up and renounce Nazism.[35] "At all fronts the enemy is advancing while we are unable to offer serious resistance to him. . . . In the East entire armies are dissolving or are hopelessly hemmed in."[36] Other bits of propaganda implored German officers and civilians to lay down their arms. It highlighted the ferocity of the Russian advance and the callousness of their own Fatherland: "Meanwhile the Cossacks and the hordes of foreign workers are turned loose on our women and children. Germany is bombed into rubble and ashes and no one will build it up again."[37]

Irene and Ellen Tschinkur never discussed the politics of war with their parents. Everyone was busy surviving. Their nighttime ritual meant never going to sleep without first putting their coats and heavy shoes next to their beds; screaming air raid sirens and runs to bomb shelters regularly interrupted dreams.

"We had dog tags with our name and blood type on them in a little leather case that we wore all during the war. And we had gas masks that smelled terrible; we had them all the time. We were told never to pick up anything on the street—anything that looked interesting, shiny," Ellen said.

When darkness settled over the house at day's end, the family lowered the heavy blackout curtains. One of their dearest possessions, somehow saved from home, is a snapshot of Irene, Ellen, and Evi. The lens captured the three girls, all wearing enormous bows in their hair. In it they are seen lighting their advent candles, encircled with a chocolate-decorated wreath. The blackout curtains sit tight against the large windows. Allied bombers flew overhead and illuminated the night sky. But those thick curtains couldn't protect the littlest Tschinkur. In 1943 the Allied bombing of Gotenhafen intensified. One night, while their little baby sister Dorit slept in her crib a bomb blew out all the windows and French doors. Broken glass fell into the room and the baby died from a brain injury. Another time Irene remembers going to the market with her mother and seeing a hand lying next to a bomb crater.

Then the day came for the Tschinkur sisters and their mother to leave. It was decided that Evelyn, their favorite cousin who

lived in Poznan, would accompany Serafima, Irene, and Ellen. Evi
was a few years older than Irene, and she looked up to Evi and
wanted to be with her all the time. Evi's mother was sick with tuberculosis and too weak to make the trip. Their father, too old for
the draft and thus far not selected for the Home Guard because
his job running the bakery was deemed essential, decided to stay
behind and vowed to meet them as soon as possible. All Serafima
took with her was a briefcase packed with jewels and money.

In January 1945 the Allies bombed Gotenhafen more frequently and Eva Dorn remembers how the light of Russian artillery made the distant sky glow red. She never interacted with
civilians now that she served on a navy base. However, Eva recalled going to the city's hospital to help after one bombing. She
saw people burned so badly only their eyes seemed alive.

Eva Dorn had extra duties in the Women's Naval Auxiliary
once the pace of the Russian advance picked up. They were coming closer every day and her spotlight battery was ordered to dig
antitank trenches.

"Then we were given a choice—to go on a ship or stay and
fight for the Fatherland. I'm not a hero," Eva said, explaining
how she ended up on the *Wilhelm Gustloff*.

𝔄s hundreds upon thousands of East Prussian civilians made
their way to ports on the sea, so too did concentration camp
inmates from Stutthof. In January 1945 the Nazis started evacuating the concentration camps. Auschwitz-Birkenau was the
first death camp to be evacuated; others quickly followed. Camp
guards forced the inmates out and marched them further west;
some of these marches lasted four months. The Nazis wanted to
relocate prisoners to camps further west and deeper inside Germany to prevent the Allies from learning about their extermination program.

There were nearly 50,000 prisoners left in the Stutthof camp, most of them Jews. About 5,000 prisoners were marched to the Baltic Sea, forced into the water and machine-gunned down to drown. The rest were forced to march west. The march passed through towns, and when locals saw them, they sometimes threw bread at the starving, risking their lives as well as the prisoners'. The prisoners marched until their legs could no longer move. When they fell a guard either shot the prisoner or beat the prisoner with his rifle, then he kicked the body to the roadside. About 2,000 prisoners died on the way. The Soviets cut off the forced march of the barely surviving prisoners in Lauenberg in eastern Germany, and the SS forced the inmates back to Stutthof where thousands more died.[38]

"Then they evacuated our camp and we started walking," said camp survivor Ruth Weintraub. "If you couldn't keep up with the speed, a German would just shoot them right there or club you."[39] Near Danzig they came to a barn where they rested; there were perhaps 300 left of 1,000. "We didn't even realize we were sleeping on dead bodies," Ruth continued. When morning came she and her fellow inmates saw Russian tanks, and the Russian soldiers began throwing food at them.

Prisoners suffered from scurvy and other diseases related to vitamin deficiencies. They had skin problems, diarrhea, lung and heart disease, and frostbite. Most wore tattered rags for clothes. They wrapped their legs and feet in mud-covered cloth strips or straw. Stutthof prisoners walked wearing makeshift clogs and thin blankets.

Stutthof survivor Stanislaw Jaskolski described his march: "Then came the day the twentieth of January 1945, the year we stood for the last roll call. It was very cold, minus 4 F to minus 22 F, snow was a blizzard and snow drifts. And then they read to us that we were going to be evacuated and that no one was allowed to rush away from the road or he would be killed. They gave us shirts for the road (trip), long johns, a blanket for two, half a loaf of bread and half margarine."[40] Jaskolski continued, "When we were brought to the road to Gdansk/Danzig we looked at how so many of us remained in hell, how [in spite of] the crematorium and gas chamber, gallows, in spite of the frost and sadness, we were doing good. We marched the whole day and we arrived at the prisoner ships from Zatoke Gdanske to the Kaszub side."

From January through March 1945 inmates of state prisons in the eastern territories were also being marched toward penal institutions in central and western Germany. They were in better physical shape than the concentration camps' inmates, but they had few clothes or shoes, and little to no food. Many of these prisoners also perished from cold, exhaustion, or starvation along the way. Guards and SS executed those prisoners who couldn't keep up. Other prisoners were "methodically massacred" when the Russians broke through the East Prussian lines.[41]

In 1945, when young children like Helga, Inge, and Horst left, they couldn't know that gone were train rides to grandparents or traditional first day of school cookie coronets. When parents like Meta and Milda decided to go, they sensed life would never return to the one they knew, that this was not but a brief hiccup. Perhaps they could keep their promises and reunite with the rest of the family when the world quieted.

Yet, for now the population embraced the notion of a German maxim: "Lieber ein Ende mit Schrecken als ein Schrecken ohne Ende"—"An end with horror is better than a horror without end."[42]

Per Admiral Karl Dönitz's orders, Rear Admiral Conrad Englehardt was fine-tuning Operation Hannibal. The first boats had sailed from Gotenhafen to Kiel without incident. In Gotenhafen German naval officers helped to ensure the evacuation of

sick and wounded troops. Civilian or merchant marine counterparts helped oversee the evacuation as well. Every day hundreds
of thousands of East Prussians arrived in the Baltic port. The Russians were advancing quickly overland. By the time the refugees
reached Gotenhafen, the Red Army was just outside Königsberg.

Five

SAVING A SCUTTLED REPUTATION

On the night of January 25, 1945, Alexander Ivanovich Marinesko caroused in a tavern of ill repute, reaching for another drink, and yet another. Normally, Marinesko favored drinking alone. Tonight was different. A Swedish woman whom he had met during a recent New Year's Eve party in Hanko, Finland, perched on a barstool beside Marinesko.[1] Heavy drinking and women had become a tonic for the dark-haired, temperamental, Soviet submarine commander. In photographs from that time period, the sailor's eyes appear to gleam with equal parts charm and swagger, and his full lips looked capable of breaking out into a sneer at any given moment.

Of course, plain displays of contempt for authority were a dangerous game to play in Stalin's Soviet Union. Reports indicate that while Marinesko's crews loved him, his high command didn't hold the captain in high esteem. They found him to be impulsive and frequently sharp-tongued.[2] His scorn earned him the suspicion of the NKVD, the Soviet internal secret police, who wondered whether the 32-year-old commander might be a counterrevolutionary in Soviet military disguise. The NKVD wielded tremendous power: its officers spied on foreigners and on its own citizens, and administered the slave-labor camps known as gu-lags.[3] The secret police also executed thousands of political pris-oners and helped organize mass deportations of Ukrainians and other non-Russians from the Baltic States. So it's no wonder the NKVD caught up with the young commander Marinesko, who was completely drunk and seemingly unfit for duty this winter night in 1945. It was a given that the NKVD kept tabs on key military personnel to enforce the Communist Party's political will. Those under constant scrutiny included generals, the infantry, ad-mirals, and captains in the navy.

That night, as the hard-boiled Marinesko was drinking with his lady friend, a group of NKVD agents came to summon him. His superiors sought the submarine commander so they could dis-cuss strategy. The submarine commander had no choice but to ac-company them forthwith. He couldn't simply shrug off this order to come in for questioning.[4]

Alexander Marinesko had a lot to be worried about. The state security apparatus fully intended to court-martial him as a de-serter. Marinesko had not only failed to report for duty on New Year's Eve 1944, but he also had broken the fraternization rule. Soviet soldiers were strictly prohibited from befriending foreign-ers, lest they be accused of helping foreign agents. The pretty Swedish woman he had bedded on New Year's Eve was a clear transgression. Marinesko engaged in what the NKVD and Com-munist Party considered anti-Soviet behavior: overt drunkenness and barely concealed disrespect for his superiors. The fate likely awaiting Marinesko was to be sent to a camp on the frozen tun-dra. In winter, temperatures in this far eastern Siberian gulag reg-ularly dipped to between minus 19 and minus 38 degrees Celsius (between minus 2 and minus 36 degrees Fahrenheit). About 30 percent of Kolyma gulag's prisoners died each year.[5]

Yet, in 1945 seasoned submarine commanders were hard to find. The Communist Party purges of the 1930s had decimated the navy's officer ranks; on June 11, 1937, many senior leaders of the Russian military were arrested and charged with treason, tried and executed. Among them was the marshal of the Soviet Union, M. N. Tukhachevsky, considered to be innovative and capable.[6] Thus by the end of 1944 the Red Army and the Soviet navy no longer had a pool of experienced soldiers and sailors from which to choose. Instead, they had to rely on poorly trained replacements. Marinesko, considered a maverick by his superiors, was one of the few submariners who could handle the rapidly changing situation in the Baltic Sea. Marinesko's crew had complete confidence in his abilities. Marinesko was granted a reprieve but remained under scrutiny. This time, the Baltic Fleet Admiral V. F. Tributs intervened and ordered the party apparatus not to waste resources court-martialing the wayward commander. To clear his name he needed to make a significant kill.[7]

When the war started in 1939, the Soviet navy boasted the largest submarine force in the world with more than 168 boats. More than two-thirds of those boats were anchored in European waters. Most of the vessels were less than 10 years old. By September 1, 1939, about one-third of the 55 Soviet submarines were stationed in the Baltic.[8] Stalin ordered more than 300 submarines built between 1934 and 1943. By June 22, 1941, when Germany abrogated the Molotov-Ribbentrop pact by invading the Soviet Union, Russia had 215 submarines in service and 100 more on the factory line.

In the late 1920s the Soviet navy had begun building a new class of submarines modeled after British boats, with technical assistance from Germany. In the 1930s the Soviet navy introduced another class of larger and faster submarines that were armed with torpedo tubes. By 1941 the Soviet Union had about 200 boats in its navy distributed among four fleets: the Northern, the Baltic, the Black Sea, and the Pacific. Many of the ships and submarines were poorly maintained. They patrolled the Baltic and Black Seas and brought supplies to the Red Army.[9]

The Soviet Union drafted most of its submarine officers from the ranks of the merchant marines, which helped control transportation along some of the world's most extensive coastline and helped protect the navy. If they had mettle and proved their qualifications, the sailors served one tour as executive officers on a submarine before assuming their own command. Even still, finding officers with adequate experience proved a continuous challenge for Soviet leaders.

Two formidable enemies conspired to keep the Soviet navy in check during the early years of the war: the German navy and the weather. German U-boats engaged in a ruthless campaign against military and civilian targets alike. Reliant on their underwater strategy, the Germans began working on a secret program for a new U-boat in 1943. This new U-boat would be larger, faster, and equipped with the most current radar. It was designed to guard the Germans position of strength on the sea.[10]

The Baltic Sea was vital to both the Reich and the Soviet Union. When Germany invaded Russia by land in the summer of 1941, only 10 of the Russian Baltic Fleet's 69 submarines actively patrolled the seas. German U-boats kept the rest of the Baltic Fleet prisoners within their bases. The Reich used the sea's shipping lanes to support the infantry with supplies, deliver fuel for its aircraft, and transport tanks and stockpiles of armaments. The Russians wanted control of the Baltic Sea to protect its coast.

From September 8, 1941 through January 27, 1944, during the nearly 900-day siege of Leningrad, much of Russia's submarine fleet was stuck in the Gulf of Finland; the German navy was able to keep the Soviet boats penned in. Landlocked, many submariners grew restless. Some cast their lot with besieged residents, wrote Victor Korzh, a captain who served aboard a Soviet submarine during World War Two.[11] Malnutrition also took its toll on submarine crews; they lost their stamina and will to fight. In addition, morale declined when the key naval bases of Libava, Riga, and Tallinn were lost to ice and Germans in 1941. It wasn't until August 1944 that the Soviet navy reached Riga and reestablished its presence in the Baltic Sea.

In 1942 the main port of the Soviet navy at Sevastopol, Ukraine, fell to German forces. This forced the Baltic Fleet to deploy ships out of Poti, a Georgian port on the Black Sea, and Taupse, a port in the eastern Black Sea. This made it difficult for the Soviets to attack German ships. The German air force also deterred submarine attacks. Like birds of prey, the Luftwaffe picked off Soviet subs when they surfaced—until June 1944 when the Soviets finally achieved air superiority. In spite of these odds, the Baltic submarine force established a reputation for ruthlessness during one of its first missions.

The fact that submarine commanders were needed protected Marinesko. Still, when the NKVD agents summoned him that night at the bar, Marinesko realized he needed to make a significant kill. He needed something that would redeem his military career. Sinking several German boats, or even one sizable German ship, would eventually elevate him in the eyes of his countrymen and raise the spirits of his beleaguered nation.[12]

Alexander I. Marinesko was born in 1913 in Odessa, a port on the northwest shore of the Black Sea. His father was a Romanian sailor and his mother Ukrainian.[13] Ever since the Tartars settled Odessa in the early 1200s it has been a major seaport, and a warm water seaport at that. French and Italian influences are apparent in the city's architecture and wide tree-lined avenues. It was a city of many nationalities and many tongues. Ukraine, one of the four original Soviet states in 1922, always retained a strong sense of nationalist and cultural identity. And it was identity that obsessed Marinesko, from how authorities perceived him to how he perceived himself. It became Marinesko's lifelong quest to shed his Ukrainian skin and become fully Russian.

Living and playing near the docks in Odessa schooled Marinesko in a variety of languages, and eventually he could speak a sort of patois combining the saltier notes of Russian, Ukrainian, Romanian, Greek, Bulgarian, and even Yiddish. Fluent in Russian, Marinesko changed the spelling of his last name from Marinesku to Marinesko, which shows he sought a more solid Russian identity. He likely believed that the 'u' ending made him Ukrainian, and because he so desperately wanted to rise through the ranks, he'd need to be more Russian. He zealously worked to rise in the Soviet fleet and prove he was as Soviet as any Russian.[14]

Marinesko wanted to belong to the class of power elites. He was determined to get his share. So, before the war, the young man enlisted, knowing the military offered the best path to success.

Joining the navy and then volunteering for submarine duty suited hardcore men on all sides of the war. Submarines were crowded and the air inside was heavy with moisture, but some men relished the close camaraderie and generally high morale in the submarine service. Their mission was often more intense and, being under the sea, they had less to fear from the German Luftwaffe.[15] During World War Two, submarines were designed and operated as weapons systems; comfort never entered the equation. Each space was accounted for; even the officers' mess doubled as a sick bay if needed. There was little variety in their daily menu; beet borscht, canned beef, and herring were ladled onto plates again and again.[16] The sailors looked forward to an occasional shot of vodka.[17] The men slept on bunks as narrow as pantry shelves. The noise of engines, various loud horns, and other equipment constantly rattled the inside of the vessel. They learned to sleep when they could, tuning out the unceasing noise. One submariner wrote how he "closed his eyes after the last spoonful of pudding."[18]

Young men dominated the world of submarines in the 1940s. The United Kingdom deemed 35 years of age too old for a submarine commander and in the United States most submarine commanders were in their early 30s. In Germany, as the war progressed, the average age dropped to under 25. Age differences aside, most of the members of this elite club were nonconformists. In his mid-20s when he joined, Marinesko fit right in.

In 1941, the Soviet Navy commissioned the *S-13* into the Baltic Fleet under the command of Captain Pavel Malantyenko. The *S-13*, was of the Stalinet, or S-class submarines. With its narrow body it looked more like a cigarillo than a cigar. Daily life aboard the *S-13* was loud, crowded, and pungent. The air reeked of oil and the sweat of 46 crew members. Although fans drove fresh air into and throughout the boat, moisture clung to the walls. They were ready to avenge the Motherland.

Soviet submarines like the *S-13* relied primarily on air reconnaissance to track enemy boats. When Russian airplanes spotted an enemy boat, they would radio that information to a submarine operating in the vicinity. The submarine then cruised into position, armed its torpedoes, and fired. On occasion a submarine spotted a lone enemy ship as it sailed on the surface of the water. When this happened, it reported sighting the target, dove, and fired.

Like many of his fellow sailors, Marinesko first whetted his appetite for submarine life in the Soviet merchant marine, followed by service in the Black Sea Fleet. He was assigned to the Baltic Fleet on a new, small coastal-type of submarine, the *M–96*, in 1939, but the boat wasn't ready for service until mid-1941. He received a gold watch to mark the occasion of being in charge of a vessel said to be the best in the Baltic Fleet. After Germany

invaded the Soviet Union in June 1941, the Baltic Fleet high command had ordered the *M–96* to the Caspian Sea to serve as a
training boat, and Marinesko was to take the sub to Leningrad
for refitting. It never reached its destination. Germany's blockade
of Leningrad at the time prevented the *M–96* from entering the
waters in the vicinity of Leningrad. On February 12, 1942, a German artillery shell hit the *M–96*. It took nearly half a year to fix
the damage.[19] Far from the action, the bored, impatient, reckless
Marinesko began to drink.

Six months later, on August 14, 1942, Marinesko and crew
were finally on patrol near the Finnish coast. The young commander was comfortable operating in shallow waters, a skill that
would serve him well when he attacked the *Gustloff.* He sighted
the German heavy artillery barge *Schwerer Artillerie-Träger,
SAT–4,* nicknamed Helena. Marinesko launched a torpedo and
reported a hit. After the war, the Soviet Union's Baltic Fleet raised
the wreck and discovered Marinesko hadn't hit as large a ship as
he had reported.[20]

A couple of months later, in October, Marinesko's superiors
ordered him to attack a German ship and capture an Enigma cod-
ing machine. Marinesko and his crew had to drop a commando
detachment on the coast of Narva Bay, in the south of Finland.
The mission failed; half of the commandos didn't return, and
those that did came back empty-handed. Still, Marinesko received
the Order of Lenin, a prestigious military recognition, and was
promoted to a higher rank.

This pattern of rising and falling from grace marked Alexander
Marinesko's career. A change in command would change everything for Marinesko.

On October 15, 1942, two Finnish submarine chasers spied
the *S-13* while it was charging its batteries on the surface of
the Baltic Sea. The Russian submarine, still under Captain Pavel

Malantyenko's command, dove to escape. It hit the sea floor. The impact severely damaged the submarine's rudder and destroyed its steering gear. Defying the odds, the *S-13* escaped and made it back to Kronstadt, the naval base off Leningrad's coast. The Soviet naval leadership relieved Malantyenko, and gave the sub's command to Alexander Marinesko early in 1943. Once again he would captain the latest Soviet model submarine, the only one of 13 type S (Stalinets) that would survive the war.[21]

He picked up the repaired *S-13* in Hanko, Finland, and his first mission with the sub occurred in October 1944. He took position near the Hela peninsula in the Baltic Sea, a place where Nazi naval communication lines snaked through the water like electric eels. On one patrol, Marinesko's keen eye spotted the small transport ship *Siegfried*, and he fired four torpedoes. Not one reached its target. He surfaced the submarine and opened fire with his cannons. Marinesko reported 15 hits and a sunken ship. A torpedo from the *S-13* did hit the *Siegfried* but didn't sink it. In fact, the *Siegfried* reached Danzig.[22]

This tendency to embellish his naval exploits would come to haunt Marinesko. But on the night of January 29, 1945, Marinesko prepared for combat. His submarine was fitted with torpedoes, grenades, and antiaircraft armaments. The *S-13* and its crew were ready for two months at sea. Alexander Marinesko had received reports that the Soviet army was on a major offensive in East Prussia, pushing back the Germans daily. He was advised to be on the lookout for German sea transports. The crew was on high alert but they didn't know the details of the situation. Aside from Marinesko, no more than five other crew members, including the radio operator, would have known what was in the dispatches.[23]

In November Alexander Marinesko was ordered to move the sub from Hanko, Finland, to Turku, located on the southwest coast of Finland. The narrow channel between the two harbors was infested with mines. The *S-13* normally carried a complement of 12 torpedoes; it took only 4 on this mission. In case something happened and the submarine sank, the Soviet navy wouldn't lose all those weapons. The boat could only move between 2 knots and 4 knots per hour. After arriving, Marinesko got orders to sink anything German. He decided to head for Gotenhafen, home of the *Wilhelm Gustloff* and the center of Operation Hannibal. The German navy was concentrated there and until now the Soviet navy had avoided this part of the Baltic Sea. Marinesko didn't ask permission to do this. He simply acted with the signature decisiveness that his crew relied upon.

As the last rope slid from the *Wilhelm Gustloff* in Gotenhafen, Captain Alexander Marinesko patiently waited at Stolpe Bank, off what is now the Polish coast. The bank, 24 miles long and 10 miles wide, runs east-west. Knowing there were enemy ships in the vicinity, Marinesko seized the initiative. It had been three weeks without a single worthy target in sight.[24]

Around 8 P.M. the first officer on the *S-13* submarine saw the lights of the *Gustloff* loom into sight. Marinesko ordered the submarine to follow the once-grand ocean liner for some distance before repositioning his boat and slipping into his strategic position.[25]

Like their enemy, Soviet officers and soldiers were taught that the more Germans they killed, the better, and it mattered not one whit whether those on board were soldiers or women and children. In their eyes everyone was complicit in this war.

Aerial surveillance showed the thousands of refugees crowding the various Baltic seaports. Russian air force pilots regularly strafed refugee columns, so the Soviets knew that East Prussians were trying to evade the Soviet armed forces.

Marinesko would have carefully calculated whether he would, from his initial waiting position, be able to carry out the task.

"The Captain of the sub must always strive persistently to destroy the enemy. Only when it is impossible to use weapons may the attack be limited to a demonstration in order to contain the enemy."[26] He'd also have made doubly sure to avoid getting closer to other Soviet submarines; to do so would have risked revealing his presence to the enemy.[27]

The waters around the gravel-rich Stolpe Bank reached just under 100 feet deep at most, making this a chancy attack in shallow water. Yet it presented Marinesko's first opportunity to demonstrate his prowess in almost a month. He knew if he returned to port without a kill, he could very well end up in Siberia. Observing the *Wilhelm Gustloff,* Marinesko probably couldn't fathom why the former KdF cruise liner wasn't maintaining a zigzag pattern. He also likely wondered why the ship's navigation lights were illuminated. A veteran submarine captain, Marinesko would determine his position of attack based on whether the *Gustloff* moved in a zigzag pattern or straight ahead.[28]

As he lurked in the water tracking his target, Marinesko might have thought about the rules of engagement employed by his German enemy. By November 1939 it was clear the Germans were going to ignore international law regarding sea warfare.

"Rescue no one and take no one with you. Have no care for ships or boats. Weather conditions and the proximity of land are of no account. Care only for your own boat and strive to achieve the next success as soon as possible! We must be hard in this war. The enemy started the war in order to destroy us, therefore nothing else matters," said Admiral Karl Dönitz during the Nuremberg Trials.[29]

Soviet submarines similarly regarded any German ship a viable target. Ostensibly submarine captains were to carefully study the silhouettes of enemy ships and were supposed to enter the measurements of enemy ships they might encounter during patrol into their maneuvering tables.[30] In that way, on the basis of precise estimates, commanders such as Marinesko "could strike blows against the enemy in a brave, audacious, and unexpected manner."[31]

When Alexander Marinesko first spotted the *Gustloff*, he was sailing on its ocean side. As the *S-13* neared the *Gustloff*, Marinesko increased his speed and circled the ship. He carefully slid his sub between the Baltic coast and the ship and cruised parallel to it. Now less than 5,000 yards away, the *S-13* was closing on the *Gustloff*.

For any ship in the Baltic, this was a risky maneuver because the waters are so shallow. Marinesko knew plenty of submarines had previously been caught in antisubmarine netting or because the shallow waters prevented submarines from diving. In addition, between 1941 and 1944, Finland had been on the side of Germany. During that time, the Germans and the Finns had completed more than 100 mine-laying operations in the Baltic Sea to jam up the Soviet navy.

Four torpedoes waited in the *S-13*'s torpedo tubes. Each torpedo was painted with an epitaph: "For the Motherland," "For Stalin," "For the Soviet People," and "For Leningrad."[32] Torpedoes can blast holes up to 20 feet wide or more in a typical ship's hull, which is made of steel an inch or less thick.

For most, if not all, of World War Two, Soviet submariners fired only a single torpedo, or perhaps two at most, at a target.[33] It wasn't until about 1944 that they shifted to volley firing, launching torpedoes in succession with a six-to-ten-second interval and at a constant lead angle. By that time the fan method, or salvo firing, was introduced, which that meant a submarine could discharge several torpedoes at once.

Unbeknownst to those aboard the *Wilhelm Gustloff*, the *S-13* had been following it for more than two hours before Alexander Marinesko ordered his crew to fire the torpedoes. The submarine captain was now less than 2,000 yards from his target. The *S-13*'s engines were about to max out; its tower broke through the surface of the water. The tower hatch was closed, but if it had to dive quickly, the torpedoes might explode.

According to some reports, German ships in the area had detected the *S-13* and even dropped depth charges at it. Submarines are actually vulnerable to sinking. Their low profile makes it hard for other ships to see them when they are on the surface; they can be accidently rammed and sunk if the ship goes unseen or can't change course. Only if the craft doesn't split apart on the way down can the crew stand a chance for rescue. If the water isn't too deep, and if rescuers can get there before oxygen runs out, sometimes the submariners can be saved.[34] Submarines are supposed to be able to withstand extremely high pressure when submerged. Nonetheless, its inner pressure hull may be vulnerable to collision damage. That means a submarine can actually crack under what seems to be a light impact with another vessel.[35]

Marinesko, diligent under the waves, borderline brash on the surface, saved his ship. And that is why Marinesko's crews loved him even when the high command didn't.

Marinesko's maneuver on January 30 was a decidedly risky attack in shallow water. It was also the first time Marinesko had launched an attack in almost a month. He looked forward to a clean kill. Yet, he knew when the moment came to order his crew to fire the torpedoes, he had to remain cool, steady, and even aloof. He knew if he returned to port without a kill he could very well end up in Siberia.

So the sailor from Odessa slid his submarine along the port side of the *Gustloff*. The boat went unnoticed. Four torpedoes were positioned and ready to strike. He was a heartbeat away from becoming a hero.

Six

BATTLE FOR THE BALTIC

𝔄ny submarine sailing in the Baltic Sea theater of operations during World War Two faced demanding and hazardous conditions. The shallow waters were tough to navigate. Once submarines attack, they must dive at least 200 to 300 feet deep: There are few places of such depth in the Baltic.

Because Hitler's strategy was to keep the Soviet fleet trapped in the Gulf of Finland, the German navy relied on an array of antisubmarine defenses.[1] One tactic was to lace the Gulf of Finland's coastline with mines and nets. Another was to sow tens of thousands of mines throughout the gulf's waters. The German navy patrolled these waters with torpedo boats, surface boats that were used to lay the mines, to escort larger warships, and to surface-patrol. From above, the Luftwaffe surveyed the routes and patrol areas favored by Soviet submarines.[2] While the war between Germany and Russia was primarily fought on land, the battle for the Baltic shaped the land war. Until 1943 Germany controlled the Baltic Sea and laid more than 60,000 mines.

The combination of these tactics devastated the Soviet navy, sinking or damaging its submarines and many of its surface ships. Throughout the first few years of hostilities, the German navy enjoyed virtually free reign on and below the Baltic Sea. The U-boats sank enemy ships and interrupted sea traffic in the Baltic Sea just as it did in the Atlantic Ocean and North Sea. Moreover, the German Kriegsmarine's control of the Baltic Sea meant the navy could keep the Wehrmacht fighting on the eastern front well supplied.

Admiral Karl Dönitz always wore his U-boat diamond-studded war badge and his World War One Iron Cross pinned to his dark blue uniform. Deeply involved in the daily operations of the German navy, Dönitz could be something of a micromanager. The admiral doggedly pursued his goal to protect the key ports of Gotenhafen, Danzig, and Kiel. His perseverance paid off: "It is important that we retain possession of the Baltic Sea, the waters in the Baltic and Norway," he told Hitler and the rest of the naval leadership. He cited economic reasons, but it was also for military reasons.[3]

Dönitz hailed from Grünaw-bei-Berein, and like his predecessor, commander-in-chief of the navy, Erich Raeder, he too had served in the German Imperial Navy. In 1916 he entered the submarine service and commanded *U–68*. At the end of World War One his boat suffered from mechanical problems that forced him to surface in the middle of a convoy after sinking a large ship. The British captured Dönitz and held him prisoner until 1919.[4]

Upon release, Dönitz promptly returned to his navy career. He advocated a strong submarine force. In 1935, after the Anglo-German Naval Treaty was inked and the 1919 Versailles Treaty restrictions lifted, Dönitz once again had a command, this time of a U-boat flotilla. He spent time as rear admiral in charge of all U-boat operations. Then, on October 1, 1939, just a month after the Third Reich invaded Poland, Adolf Hitler promoted Admiral Karl Dönitz to Rear Admiral. His command was that of Befehlshaber der Unterseeboote (Commander of the Submarines).

Alexander Marinesko understood the challenge he faced when he assumed command of the Soviet submarine *S-13* in 1942. The young officer from Odessa surely knew of the U-boats' ruthless campaign against civilian and neutral ships: An early incident in the war alerted him to its extent. On September 3, 1939, just two days after the Reich invaded Poland, Captain Fritz-Julius Lemp of the *U-30* patrolled the northwestern sector of the Irish Sea. There he spotted the S.S. *Athenia* 200 miles west of the Hebrides and fired on the British luxury liner without warning.[5] The unescorted ship carried 1,418 passengers and crew on board, most of whom were Jewish refugees. Of all the passengers and crew, 300 were US citizens. Lemp's attack killed 118 people: 69 were women, 16 were children, and 22 were American citizens.[6] Thus, Captain Lemp fired the first shots of the Battle of the Atlantic. Lemp later received the Knight's Cross of the Iron Cross, Nazi Germany's highest military honor for bravery under fire.

The Germans were mindful that the unprovoked sinking of the *Athenia* would likely be compared to the World War One sinking of the passenger ship the RMS *Lusitania,* a British ship. The Nazis decided to cover up Lemp's actions. They believed denying any involvement in the sinking was the best damage control. The Nazis also feared the sinking could draw the United States into the war, a development they wished to avoid this early on in the conflict as they didn't want to engage on multiple fronts so soon. Hence, Joseph Goebbels's Propaganda Ministry tried to make it appear as if the British had sunk the *Athenia* to entice the United States to join them in war. Germany's spin machine failed. The Allies were furious and accused Germany of flouting international laws of the sea and engaging in unrestricted submarine warfare, as it had during the First World War.

The *Athenia* became the first of many merchant and civilian boats on the receiving end of German attacks during the Battle of the Atlantic, between 1939 and 1945. Germany's U-boats pursued and attacked British surface ships, destroying supplies. The United States officially declared war on December 8, 1941. In the early years of the war, German U-boats had to operate on the surface of the water for maneuvers under cover of darkness. They would dive to attack. But, in the summer of 1943, the Germans began to pull their subs out of the Atlantic—the Allies had better radar and better and more powerful depth charges. This led Admiral Karl Dönitz to push the idea of a super U-boat with Adolf Hitler.

The U-boat began as Nazi Germany's agent of terror during the Second World War.[7] Indeed, from the outset of hostilities, German U-boats menaced the Baltic Sea. After World War One, the German navy had faced restrictions on the number and size of boats German shipyards could build. According to the 1935 London Treaty, the German navy could not exceed 35 percent of the number of British surface warships. Yet the German navy was allowed to have an equal number of submarines as the British had. So, when Great Britain started rearming in 1936, Nazi Germany ramped up the construction of its U-boats.[8]

As supreme commander of the German navy, Admiral Erich Raeder supervised the build-up. Raeder served as the navy's number one man until December 1942. Following an argument with Hitler about the Battle of the Barents Sea, Raeder suggested that either Admiral Rolf Carls or Admiral Karl Dönitz replace him.[9] The Führer chose the 51-year-old Dönitz.

The new navy commander could focus on the Soviet navy since the US and British fleets were occupied elsewhere. Even so, the Russian submarine fleet presented no more than a pesky intrusion in the Germans' side, at least during the early years.

At the start of the war Nazi Germany felt confident about its naval superiority.[10] "No German officer who had fought the Russians in 1914–1917 had any real respect for their fleet. It is true that the ship's crews knew well enough how to fire their guns, and in a tight corner they would fight bravely to the end," wrote a vice admiral of the German Imperial Navy who sailed in the Baltic during World War One. From this admiral's perspective, the Russians didn't think quickly and didn't exploit tactical and operational opportunities that were fluid during wartime. The German navy was confident to the point of arrogance, but it wouldn't retain superiority for long.[11] In fact, when Captain Alexander Marinesko attacked and sank the *Wilhelm Gustloff,* the Soviet Union and Germany had already been engaged in unrestricted warfare in the Baltic Sea since 1942.

eanwhile, the Russian navy pursued its own build-up. After Vladimir Lenin died in 1924, Josef Stalin took a direct role in decision-making concerning weapons development and production.[12] During the prewar years the Soviet regime stressed submarine development and construction, moving to increase the size of the entire Soviet fleet.[13]

During the uneasy days of the Molotov-Ribbentrop Pact, the German navy had used Soviet port facilities at Teriberka, just east of Murmansk. The navy welcomed these harbors as they offered safe haven for German blockade-runners trying to escape the British navy.[14] In September 1940, the Russian navy built three battleships, one of which was about 45,000 tons. The Russians also started building several 2,800-ton submarines.[15]

Because whoever controlled the Baltic controlled vital supply lines, the German naval command grew somewhat obsessed about conditions in the Baltic Sea. On February 23, 1940, for example, General Wilhelm Keitel, General Alfred Jodl, and Commander Karl von Puttkamer fretted about how the "ice situation" froze German naval activity: "The Naval Staff considers the present time—after the conclusion of the economic pact with Russia—suitable for reviewing the agreements with Russia regarding the boundary line for warfare against merchant shipping. We cannot forgo control of the merchant traffic in the eastern Baltic."[16]

The Russians wanted access to the sea, and occupation of the Baltic States guaranteed that by giving its navy a trio of virtually year-round ice-free bases at Revel, now Tallinn; Libau, now Liepaya; and Baltiski Port, now Paldiski. Ice plagued both the Reich and Russia. The winter of 1941–1942 was quite severe, causing Germany to postpone the training of new U-boat crews.[17]

In the spring of 1942, the German navy concentrated on stopping Anglo-American aid shipments to Russia; Russian convoys became target number one for the Third Reich. The German navy also launched various Black and Baltic Sea offensives to help the Wehrmacht push through Russia.[18] To avoid U-boats, Allied convoys transporting war material for Russia no longer traveled the waters of the Arctic to Murmansk; instead, they passed through the Mediterranean to the Persian Gulf.[19]

The German U-boats had at best another year of impunity before the Allies started to dominate the seas. In the spring of 1941 code breakers at Bletchley Park in England cracked the Enigma code. While breaking the code helped Americans and the British protect their vessels from the German navy, it initially didn't do much to improve the strength and force of the Soviet fleet. For one, the Allies didn't want the Germans to know they had broken the code.

In Germany, Adolf Hitler pushed Admiral Karl Dönitz to devise a plan for the eventuality of Russian boats breaking through the Gulf of Finland into the Baltic Sea. In turn, Dönitz assured the Führer that "control of the Baltic is important to us."[20]

Retaining naval supremacy in the Baltic Sea allowed German surface ships and U-boats access to the Atlantic and the North Sea, and of course kept the Soviets at bay. Admiral Karl Dönitz considered the possibility of beginning submarine operations in the Arctic Ocean. Although this might have seemed an obvious alternative to the Baltic Sea for the Soviet Navy, harsh conditions and frigid temperatures severely limited operations.

"The arctic night is unfavorable for submarines as it renders it difficult to locate the targets. Winter weather, with blizzards, storms, and fog, has an adverse effect," Dönitz told the naval command gathered at a meeting with Adolf Hitler.[21] Ice can cover up to 45 percent of the sea in winter. The Arctic Sea rarely freezes over, but water temperatures average 4 degrees Celsius (39 degrees Fahrenheit). In addition to manmade obstacles, mines laid by the Germans filled the Arctic Sea.

Moreover, Admiral Dönitz and his immediate subordinates decided not enough air reconnaissance existed to make it worthwhile. Submarines in World War Two relied on air reconnaissance to help guide them and locate targets, as well as for protection. Since the submarines still had no radar, they used the radio to communicate with aircraft. Those communications could be intercepted.[22] The Arctic also posed a problem because the currents in the sea were simply too strong.

At least ten Russian submarines operated in the Baltic Sea region. However, not one submarine had so far successfully attacked a German vessel. As winter set in, Dönitz said, the possibility that any of those Soviet ships still able to operate might break through diminished. During Germany's invasion of Russia, German U-boats had made quick sport of the Soviet submarines: the Soviet Baltic Fleet lost 12 subs between June 23 and June 26. To protect against further losses, the Russian navy moved the remaining units of the Baltic Fleet to the North Black Sea before the inland waterways froze.[23]

"When war against Russia broke out, eight boats were dispatched to operate in the Baltic. There they found practically no targets and accomplished nothing worth mentioning. They were accordingly returned to me at the end of September," Dönitz wrote in his memoirs about early summer 1941.[24]

Throughout the war, the United States closely watched and reported on the ever-increasing Russian and German military presence on the Baltic Sea. In 1939 Ambassador Laurence Steinhardt wrote to Secretary of State Cordell Hull to alert Hull not to trust the Molotov-Ribbentrop pact. The Soviet government's agreement with Nazi Germany about the Baltic States—namely the expulsion of millions of Baltic Germans according to Molotov-Ribbentrop pact—appeared to have been part of the Soviet's long-time strategic aim to gain access to the sea, he said. In addition, the Russian navy wanted to secure Soviet naval and air bases on the Finnish islands in the vicinity of Kronstadt and possibly a base at Hanko as well.[25] Controlling these locations would help them launch and repel attacks against Germany.

At the time, many Russian warships found themselves effectively hostages of Sweden. In the early fall of 1944 Sweden closed all its territorial waters in the Baltic to foreign shipping because of Allied pressure. This had the effect of hurting German communications, and also that of the Soviets.[26]

The closure of Sweden's territorial waters wasn't the only thing hindering the Soviet navy. Earlier in the war the Germans had heavily mined the Gulf of Finland. Yet, in spite of an estimated 13,000 mines, Russian submarines based in Kronstadt broke through and made it to the open waters of the Baltic Sea.[27] This was of little concern to the Germans. Most in the German naval high command regarded this as a bit of a fluke, still believing that generally mines would heavily damage Russian forces.[28] This fit in with Germany's plan to prevent Russian naval forces from leaving the Gulf of Finland.[29]

Also in 1944, the German and Finnish navies met in Kiel, Germany, to discuss completely blocking the Gulf of Finland.[30] They had finished laying steel nets, which reached to the bottom of the sea by the spring of 1943. These double antisubmarine nets, called *walross,* or walrus, were successful; Russian submarine attacks on German shipping ceased until about autumn 1944.[31] Attacking German ships posed a peculiar challenge because the Luftwaffe was a constant deterrent—until June 1944, when the

Soviet Union achieved air supremacy in the east and the Americans and British attained it in the west.

Consequently, in August 1944, the Nazi leadership decided to only use small vessels in the Baltic to fight growing Russian naval power. Mines became the region's most effective weapon. Only two or three Russian submarines broke through the minefields into the Baltic compared with at least 20 others that were destroyed in trying to reach it.[32] The Germans also used floating mines to blow up the many bridges that spanned the region's rivers. To defend against these German floating mines, Soviet ships tasked artillery watches with identifying and destroying suspicious objects floating on rivers and sea. The Russian ships attached old wooden barges at their bows as rudimentary bumpers that would take the force of an explosion before the mine could damage or sink a ship.[33]

In 1944 the Soviet Union opened its counteroffensive against Nazi Germany. Not only did the Red Army push back the Wehrmacht on land, the Russian navy began to exert control along the Baltic coast. The Soviet navy took advantage of the winter of 1944 and 1945 to establish submarine bases all along the Finnish coast.[34] Finland allowed the use of its harbors and anchorages under the shaky armistice between the two nations for as long as the war with Germany lasted. By the end of October 1944, Helsingfors and Nadendal, and even Hanko, operated as Soviet naval bases.

Submarine patrols in the Baltic Sea stopped when the Germans withdrew from eastern portions of the Baltic coast. About 2 million soldiers, Gestapo troops, military dependents, and other Prussian and Pomeranian civilians needed to be relocated after German defensive positions along the coast collapsed.

In 1944 the Russians reclaimed the Black Sea port of Odessa, Captain Alexander Marinesko's childhood home. This Soviet victory didn't end in Odessa; rather, it helped push the Soviets forward. It was part of a powerful Red Army offensive designed to push the Wehrmacht out of the Crimea. If successful, the Soviet fleets would have the run of the entire Russian Black Sea coast.[35] During the offensive, the Soviet navy captured many German sailors. Descriptions of these captures reached American shores: "Captured German submarine crews were described by the Americans and Allies as no longer 'spitting in our eyes like they did when they were cocky.' There is now an appreciable loss of spirit in the crews of the U-boat which our men have recently captured. . . . Now they seem to realize the cause is lost."[36]

Yet, in spite of the Soviet victories, and in spite of the fact that the Soviet navy failed to sink or damage any of the major German vessels employed at the time in the Baltic Sea, the German forces were able to retreat from the area's coast.[37]

Even while the Soviets regained some control of the Baltic Sea, the Germans still dared to use its waters as a training ground for their new U-boats. The Baltic training area, known as Baltic Station, was one of Germany's three key naval bases. As late as January 1945, a new generation of German U-boats had test runs in the Baltic and training was going on at full speed.[38]

Before World War Two started, Soviet submarines often worked in pairs and often gave away their positions in frequent radio communications with command headquarters located on shore.[39] One Soviet submarine captain described the Soviet navy as facing some of the most "inconceivably difficult conditions," during the war. Between net barriers, minefields, and constant attacks from the Luftwaffe, the Soviet navy simply had to contend with incredibly difficult challenges.

The Soviet navy sought to reduce these difficult circumstances and to mitigate losses, and so Soviet submarines initially hunted individually in contrast to the German "wolf packs." The Soviet submarines kept a distance of up to 5 miles from each other so they wouldn't endanger one another, and for the most part, they relied on aerial reconnaissance to locate targets. Each submarine patrolled its own territory, known as a box, along German shipping routes. At first most attacks happened in the daylight since Soviet submarines didn't have radar. However, later in the war the Russian Navy increased its nighttime attacks.[40]

During the war's early years, Soviet subs waited passively in preset locations until a target appeared. Unsurprisingly, this strategy didn't yield many hits.[41] The strategy changed when those below the sea started communicating with reconnaissance planes above the water. However, because the planes needed visual sighting, daylight attacks outnumbered nighttime attacks. Of course, once submarines began using radar, nighttime attacks increased.

During the latter part of the war, the Soviet military pushed back their German enemies on land too, as the Russian armies choked off many possible escape routes. That left the Baltic Sea as the most viable refugee option. As the United States Office of Strategic Services reported from its Stockholm station during the period January 24 to 30, "nine ships totaling 18,500 tons passed through the Great Belt northward bound and during the same period seven ships totaling 14,500 together with a ten thousand ton hospital ship." The *Wilhelm Gustloff* was among these boats. But the United States didn't yet know the size of the Soviet's prize.

Meanwhile, German military strategists understood they needed to protect the coastline along the Baltic Sea to help thwart Russian incursions onto their land. They also needed to secure the Baltic training areas and U-boat building harbors, such as Gotenhafen and Danzig.[42] They employed coastal artillery and defensive mine barrages, and they mined the waters to close all entrances to the Baltic Sea. This, they hoped, would hamper merchant shipping and vessels used to supply Russian civilians and troops.[43]

The lone wolf strategy of the Soviet navy suited Alexander Marinesko, who now moved his boat silently along the Baltic Coast, hunting for a suitable target. It is the end of January and he has received word that the Germans will be stepping up naval operations in the Baltic. Back in Gotenhafen the *Wilhelm Gustloff* prepared to leave. The *Hansa,* also anchored in Gotenhafen, was supposed to escort the former KdF cruise liner to safety in Kiel. Hundreds of naval personnel and thousands of refugees waited—anxious and desperate.

This bell is one of the few artifacts that was recovered from the Wilhelm Gustloff. Author's collection.

Seaman Walter Salk, 19, of Essen, Germany, perished on the Wilhelm Gustloff. It took his parents more than a year to learn his fate. Walter's older brother, who served on a U-boat, was killed a year before. Courtesy of Rita Rowand.

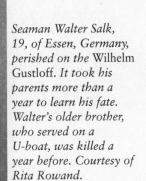

Inge Reuter, sister of Helga Reuter Knickerbocker. The last image Helga had of Inge was her floating away in the dark night. Courtesy of Helga Reuter Knickerbocker.

The Tschinkur family; sisters and cousins with father Herbert Christoph and Serafima, in Gotenhafen. Courtesy of Irene Tschinkur East.

Left to Right: Irene Tschinkur, Serafima Tschinkur, and Ellen Tschinkur. The girls and their mother survived the sinking. Courtesy of Irene Tschinkur East.

Lighting Christmas Advent candles during a blackout in Gotenhafen. Left to Right: Ellen, Evi, and Irene Tschinkur. Evi would not survive the sinking. Every few years Irene takes out an advertisement with her picture in her hometown paper as a way to remember and memorialize her cousin. Courtesy of Irene Tschinkur East.

The Wilhelm Gustloff. *Author's collection.*

Helga Reuter Knickerbocker. Courtesy of Helga Knickerbocker.

Poſtkarte
mit Antwortkarte

Sammler-Gemeinſchaft der NSG "Kdf" / Abgabepreis: 10 Pf.

REICHSTAGUNG 1938
DER N·S·G
KRAFT DURCH FREUDE
HAMBURG

"Strength Through Joy" postcard celebrating Wilhelm Gustloff. *The Nazi's Strength Through Joy program was designed to bring leisure to the German middle and lower classes who weren't able to afford a vacation on their own. Cruise liners such as the* Wilhelm Gustloff *were part of this program. Author's collection.*

The Reuter furniture factory and showroom in Königsberg. Next door a store had been named "Enemy." The Nazis commandeered the factory and turned it into a uniform factory. Russian prisoners of war worked in the factory. Courtesy of Helga Knickerbocker.

Geſchäftshäuſer ——— Steindamm 137/38 und 139

Staff working at Baltic Home, a place for newly repatriated ethnic Germans when they first arrived to East Prussia from Baltic States such as Estonia, Latvia, and Lithuania. Under the Molotov-Ribbentrop Pact hundreds of thousands of Baltic Germans were moved to East Prussia. Courtesy of Irene Tschinkur East.

In 1945 Serafima Tschinkur, mother of Irene and Ellen and aunt of Evi, wrote to family friends about the sinking. The letter was recently recovered in a suitcase in Paris, France. Courtesy of Irene Tschinkur East.

Nienburg 28/IV. 45.

Meine lieben, lieben Otti und Felix! Wie waren wir froh, wenn wir von euch Brief erhalten! Wie oft haben wir an euch gedacht! Gott sei Dank Ihr seid alle gesund und zusammen. Das ist ja nun jetzt hauptsache. Schließlich alles verloren und kahl sind ja nun alle egal, aber bei diesem drunter und drüber das ist ja kleinste verlust. Uns freut es dass euch gut geht.

Wir sind ja auch alle vier zusammen, aber leider wir mussten sehr vieles erleben. Ganz zuerst liebe Otti die traurige Nachricht für dich persönlich: Rudy ist schon im Juli Monat gestorben in Marz und Oskar ist bei Schiffskatastrophe umgekommen. Von Heinz wissen wir nichts, aber von Billy haben wir eine Nachricht (nicht direkt von Ihm, durch einen Kriegsgefangenen), dass Billy ist in Gefangenschaft in Russland (Ural). Ob er bald zurück kommt und ob überhaupt kommt, dass kann keiner wissen. Arme Junge er ahnt auch nicht dass die Mutter und Oskar nicht mehr leben. Das schicksal war zu hart für ganze

Nearly 70 years after the sinking of the Wilhelm Gustloff, Horst Woit stands in front of his lakefront home in Ontario. A day doesn't pass that Horst doesn't think about the night his knife saved him, his mother, Meta, and the people inside his lifeboat. Courtesy of Cathryn J. Prince.

Meta Woit, Horst Woit's mother. Meta moved to Canada with her son after the war. Courtesy of Horst Woit.

Milda Bendrich and baby Inge Bendrich Roedecker, Gotenhafen. Just two years old at the time of the sinking, Inge remains the youngest known survivor of *the* Wilhelm Gustloff. According to a letter from Milda, Inge didn't cry once during the entire ordeal. Courtesy of Inge Roedecker.

Inge Bendrich Roedecker after the war on King Island, Australia, with pet wallaby Skippy. Inge's father spent nearly three years in a Soviet prison camp after the war. After he was released the family moved to Australia. Courtesy of Inge Roedecker.

Eva Dorn Rothschild in Ascona, Switzerland. A music student at the University of Leipzig when the war broke out, Eve joined the Women's Naval Auxiliary. She was helping in the ship's hospital when the torpedos hit. Courtesy Cathryn J. Prince.

Evelyn "Evi" Krachmanow, cousin of Irene and Ellen Tschinkur. The three cousins were very close, and Evi's death left an impossible hole to fill in Irene and Ellen's hearts. Courtesy of Irene Tschinkur East.

Alexander I. Marinesko, commander of the S-13. The sailor from Odessa knew he needed a significant "kill" in order to redeem himself in the eyes of his superiors. Courtesy of Edward Petroskevich.

Statue honoring Alexander I. Marinesko in Kaliningrad, Russia (formerly Königsberg, East Prussia). Today the Russians consider Marinesko a hero for sinking the Wilhelm Gustloff.

Seven

CHAOS ON DECK

Before the war, Gotenhafen had been an orderly seaport on the Baltic Sea. Eva Dorn, who served with the Women's Naval Auxiliary, recalled that German sailors were stationed on and near the ships, but they rarely interacted with civilians. Now, as Operation Hannibal got underway, the population had tripled, and members of the military—some of whom had deserted, while others had been assigned to transport ships—mixed with the refugees.

Five years into the war, the seaport was unrecognizable. People scavenged for food and scoured the streets for shelter. Throngs of refugees pushed and shoved while waiting to get a place aboard the *Wilhelm Gustloff* or other ships. Etiquette and civility broke down.

Refugees who had arrived in the port one or two days before the ship left boarded in a more orderly fashion than those who boarded in the last hours. For the recent arrivals it was chaos. Accounts from survivors tell of mothers throwing their children into the water in a vain effort to protect them from crushing crowds. With discipline unraveled, people looted homes in and near the large port. Coal barges, submarines, minesweepers, and former

cruise liners waited at the docks. Some soldiers deserted by don-
ning civilian clothing and trying to board the waiting ships.

Admiral Karl Dönitz urgently needed to transfer the German
submariners to Flensburg, the naval base near Kiel. He hoped
they could refresh depleted units. Among these sailors were those
who had been training in the new, more powerful type of U-boat,
the XXI. In addition to civilian refugees, some of the *Gustloff*'s
passengers included these trainees.

People waited in the harbor for days before the *Gustloff* departed. They saw other boats taking part in Operation Hannibal, including the *Löwe,* which, until Germany's 1938 invasion
of Norway, had been a destroyer originally commissioned in the
Royal Norwegian Navy with the name HNoMS *Gyller.* Many of
these waiting refugees had tried to leave East Prussia at the beginning of the month but were denied passage. For example, Peter
Siegel, a doctor from Homburg-Saar, who had been stationed near
the Baltic Coast for most of the war, had brought his wife to Pillau
the week of January 20 when it was clear the Soviet army couldn't
be repelled. In Pillau he saw the *Robert Ley,* another former KdF
cruise liner, dock and take on refugees. The officer in charge told
Siegel that East Prussian gauleiter Erich Koch had "ordered that
no one was to go on a ship, not even women and children."[1] Five
days later Siegel received orders to transport injured soldiers to
the port of Pillau. This time the local authorities permitted him
to bring his wife. The couple arrived in Pillau on January 31 and
boarded the *Togo.* The ship "was so stuffed with refugees it had
to leave," Siegel wrote. About 9 P.M. the ship raised its gangplank.
Panicked refugees stormed the gangway and 20 people fell into
the water. The first officer dove into the water to save the people
from getting crushed between the pier and the hull. Finally the
Togo left the pier and set off toward Kiel.

As a member of the German Navy's Women Auxiliary, Eva
Dorn, 18, boarded the *Wilhelm Gustloff* one week before it left

port. The former music student from Halle (Saale) was assigned to the *Gustloff* with other naval personnel who would be transferred to Flensburg. Upon boarding she was issued a mattress and a pillow and was assigned to sleep in the drained swimming pool. Eva took one look at the area, already crowded with hundreds of other Naval Auxiliary officers, and decided it too closely resembled a cage. Deciding to find sleeping accommodations later, Eva climbed a few steep flights of stairs to the ship's infirmary. She made herself useful there for a few days, helping dress wounds and preparing for arriving refugees. Starting on January 28, Eva began helping to register refugees as they arrived in Gotenhafen.

"The children came on, frozen. Their frostbitten cheeks had holes in them. Every child that came on got a dab of salve on each cheek. Mothers came on, some with dead babies in their arms," Eva remembered. "People were pushing, but they were elated to be on the boat, they were relieved."[2]

The *Gustloff*'s crew showed people to cabins, assigning two and three to a bed. Many of the refugees promptly collapsed from mental and physical exhaustion. After helping refugees register, Eva returned to the infirmary. When Eva did leave the infirmary for fresh air, she noticed the ice on the deck was getting thicker and there was no sand to spread across the ice to prevent people from slipping and sliding. The lifeboat davits and ropes were frozen and the inflatable boats were frozen together.

After nearly 70 years, it remains unclear exactly what passengers were told to do in case of a crisis. According to Eva there were no preparatory exercises. At no point prior to sailing did the crew tell passengers what to do or where to assemble in case of an emergency.

However, according to Captain Paul Vollrath, who also served on the ship, the ship's officers did give the refugees a crash course in basic boat safety.[3] This was important considering most of the refugees had never before set foot on a ship. After instructing them how to properly put on their lifejackets, the crew also instructed the passengers not to smoke, not to use a flashlight, not to turn on radios. The crew told passengers to keep portholes firmly closed and to keep the steel blinds lowered so as not to let light leak out during the night. Lights would attract not only enemy ships operating in the region but also Allied aircraft. By this time in 1945 the Allies airplanes were making nearly round-the-clock sorties over the Baltic Sea. Earlier in the war the Allied planes had protected shipping against U-boat attacks. Now much of their activity involved firing on cities and laying mines.

Word spread rapidly of the vast operation underway to move civilians from the path of the Soviet army. Therefore, many passengers boarded the *Wilhelm Gustloff* a few days before the lines that bound her to the pier were cast off. These passengers settled in, their thoughts drifting between the horrors they'd seen and the unknown into which they headed. Just three days before the *Gustloff* sailed, passengers were roused from what Helga Reuter remembered as a state of limbo. An order blared over the ship's public address system: "Everybody Off!" The screech of an air-raid siren filled the air.[4] Every man, woman, and child shuffled off the boat. Crewmembers carried those who couldn't walk, the wounded rode on stretchers, the newborns in their mothers' arms. Once again the passengers stood bunched in the frigid air trying to stay warm. Air raids were frequent in January 1945. In this late stage of the war, Germans spent many hours in bomb shelters and basements as sirens seemed to sound 24 hours a day. For those who didn't take refuge in the shelters, bags of sand and buckets of water stood ready to douse flames.

Not every person who came off the *Gustloff* during the air raid found shelter in cellars or other underground locations. Some simply tried to hunker down as best they could. Finally, the all-clear whistle sounded and the thousands of people returned to their hard-won nooks and assigned cabins aboard the vessel.

Fortunately, no bombs had fallen on Gotenhafen that night. When bombs did fall, it was difficult for the authorities to establish order. Rubble and bodies intertwined, making identification of the dead nearly impossible. Proper burial was also a luxury; at this point in the war many bombing casualties were buried in mass graves.[5]

On January 25, five days before the *Wilhelm Gustloff* started her engines, Rose Rezas and her father trudged roughly seven miles under gunmetal-gray skies to reach the harbor in Gotenhafen, suitcases and purse in hand. Rose Rezas was most definitely not inured to the devastation she saw on the way. Rose and her father set their sights on safety. The 25,000-ton *Gustloff* gave her a glimmer of hope.[6]

Once in Gotenhafen, Rose stared openly at the refugees. Not everyone had come from a city like hers where, before the war, shop windows beckoned and sidewalks were swept. There were tens of thousands of refugees holding their few belongings in rucksacks or valises. Some people camped in abandoned trolley cars. And yet, Rose and the others—Horst, Helga, Irene, and Ellen—had more in common with these people than she could ever have thought possible, because they all shared a common purpose: escape and survival.

The time finally came for Rose and her companions to board the nearly 700-foot long ship. A sailor, one of hundreds on board, handed the group life jackets, and along with 18 other girls they were assigned to a space in the once-grand ballroom. The ballroom was on the same level as the promenade deck. Refusing to feel claustrophobic, Rose tried to sleep on the granite-like floor. Her feet throbbed.[7]

Knowing that passengers now outnumbered available life jackets, Friedrich Petersen, the ship's military captain, ordered all men with life vests to pass them out to women and children. There was not enough safety equipment onboard. The ship had only 22 lifeboats and, even with extra safety equipment brought aboard, there were still only enough flotation vests and life-rings for less than half of the ship's passengers and crew.[8]

"Don't take your clothes off. Everybody put on your life jackets," commanded a disembodied voice over the ship's loudspeaker. The air was so hot in Rose's small corner of the ship; she ignored the voice and shed her life preserver and her shoes. Indeed, few passengers complied with the order to keep their life jackets on; the air was simply too thick with sweat and fear. Dirty people crowded the space and babies' cloth diapers needed changing. No matter how uncomfortable, the thought that soon she would be relatively safe bolstered Rose's spirits. She tried to rest, to close her eyes.

On the evening of January 29 the harbormaster instructed Captain Friedrich Petersen, who was officially in command, to prepare to weigh anchor. There were actually four captains on the bridge. Captain Wilhelm Zahn, who had been in charge of the U-boat training division aboard the *Gustloff*, was also aboard. Zahn stayed on with the submariners under his command being transferred to the naval base of Flensberg. There were also two captains from the German merchant marine, Karl-Heinz Köhler and Heinz Weller.

During these final hours, the German military police boarded the *Wilhelm Gustloff*. The police hunted for deserters in the corridors and rooms. The police had the power of summary court martial and although they didn't wield this power against anyone on board the *Gustloff*, they had used it often on the front lines. This time it seemed an intimidation tactic, nothing more, Paul Vollrath wrote.[9] The crew raised the gangways under cover of darkness. They had been ordered to sail on January 30.

A coat of gray paint and antiwar craft weapons mounted on the ship's upper decks made it hard to discern the true face of the one-time cruise liner. However, the *Wilhelm Gustloff's* dull color did nothing to mask the near elation Horst Woit felt as he marched up the gangplank with his mother, Meta, his mother's friend Hildegard, and her daughter Christa. From the posture of the two women, the young boy sensed they were incredibly lucky to have escaped Elbing.

"The temperature was 20 below Celsius. Oh, the four of us were very happy to be on board and thinking we were safe from those Russkies," Horst said, smoothing his crown of white hair.[10]

The Woits felt blessed for another reason. Proper boarding passes were becoming scarcer by the hour; indeed there were virtually none to be had at this late date. Previously, the ship's printing press had printed boarding passes in German Gothic type. Some passes bore the stamp of the U-boat training division's headquarters.[11]

One bit of gossip making the rounds on the pier was that Erich Koch, the East Prussian gauleiter, had decreed that only Nazi party members could board the ship. The struggle for boarding passes intensified as word spread through the swarming harbor that the *Wilhelm Gustloff* was prepared to leave. Those who got boarding passes had to supply authorities with their name, address, and city of origin. Those with money and influence boarded the former KdF luxury liner first. For example, Wilhelmina Reitsch, sister-in-law of Hitler's favorite test pilot, squeezed and searched for spare room among the thousands now on board, all vying for space.

The 373 female naval auxiliaries of Eva Dorn's group, aged 17 to 25, sheltered in the empty swimming pool in their blue-gray uniforms with winter overcoats. The sunlight above the pool let in the barest of light. An enormous Roman-style fresco of fit and fertile bodies, fierce horses, and shining chariots adorned the wall at one end of the pool. The female auxiliaries rested and slept on mattresses in the pool and on the surrounding deck. At the last minute, officials and high-ranking Nazi Party leaders scurried to board, some of whom were shown to the Führer Suite located on B deck. The 13 members of the Danzig *burgermeister*'s (mayor) group took over the suite; the entourage included the county's Nazi Party leader, and his wife and five children, a maid, and a parlor maid.[12]

Along with the Woits, Helga and Inge Reuter and their aunt Ruth Walloch, Rose Rezas, Irene, Ellen, and Serafima Tschinkur and their cousin pushed against the dense crowd forming around the ship. After helping Nazi Party officials and German military board, the ship's crew turned their attention to those traveling with children. In dire straits, adults passed children and babies to and fro between strangers; this helped hundreds more secure passage on a boat whose hull already seemed to sag from the extra weight. Sometimes the children fell into the water or onto the pier or were caught by strangers. There were stories of soldiers taking children and disguising themselves as women, or carrying rolled blankets made to look like babies. If they were caught, they could be hung for desertion.[13] Women smuggled husbands and sons in their trunks, rolling and pushing them on board so the males could avoid being pressed into the Volkssturm (Home Guard).

Serafima Tschinkur knew her group had escaped from Gotenhafen just in time. They reached the ship on January 28 and sat in it for two days before it set sail. Like most passengers, they didn't know that January 30 had been set as the departure date.

Never before had the *Wilhelm Gustloff* carried so many people. Later, Heinz Schön, a purser in training, would devote much of his life to tallying the number of people who had been aboard the doomed vessel in order to calculate the loss of life. By his count the ship's official manifest would show the number of passengers and crew stopped somewhere just above 6,000.[14] Schön, who had been just 19 at the time of the sinking, spent many hours over the years to corresponding with surviving crewmembers and civilian passengers to piece together the story. Through his work, he learned that in fact thousands of people smuggled themselves aboard disguised or inside crates. The crew worked hard to situate everyone. Refugees who didn't have passes waited forlornly on the pier for other ships to come. Some said 60,000 or more refugees waited on the quays hoping for a chance. One soldier reported the most pathetic sight was of children who had lost their parents in the mad race to escape: "Even their tears froze." These children were among those given priority and assigned places aboard.

Flocks of small boats packed with refugees followed the *Wilhelm Gustloff,* their passengers screaming: "Take us! Take us!" In the last hours in the harbor and as it left shore taking on those from smaller boats, the *Wilhelm Gustloff* added an estimated 2,000 additional undocumented passengers.[15]

The Hamburg-based shipbuilding firm Bloss & Vohm had designed the *Wilhelm Gustloff* to accommodate fewer than 2,000 passengers. However, given this emergency, the crew knew that with a little ingenuity they could pack scores more on board. They emptied the dining rooms and removed the seats from the onboard movie theater, a luxury from another time. The crew transformed the sun deck into a maternity unit and another deck served as an extra infirmary in which nearly 162 military casualties, many of whom were amputees, lay on stretchers. Nurses and medical orderlies from East Prussia attended these soldiers. Aside from the sundeck, the infirm recuperated in larger lounges and halls. The *Gustloff* crew tried to make these soldiers and sailors as comfortable as possible on whatever mattresses, chairs, settees, and lounges they could find.[16] In addition to helping situate the sick and wounded, the crew needed to feed the soldiers and refugees, and the catering staff was asked to find food.[17]

"The catering staff had been instructed to get as much food ready as possible with emphasis on much, for many people had to be fed and there could not be a question of choice selection. After all the ship had originally been designed to carry approximately 1,500 passengers and a crew of approximately 500. We now had already over 5,000 people on board and more were coming all the time. The main thing was therefore to have something hot, never mind Cordon Bleu standards," Vollrath wrote.[18]

"They let the ramp down for us to go on board," Helga Reuter said. "We got registered. The soldiers that ran the ship had to give us their life vests. Then we were told to go to the dining room—to get our ration of bread and find ourselves a place to rest." Upon boarding the ship, the three young women felt secure.[19]

Helga and Inge Reuter and their aunt, Ruth Walloch, three months pregnant, found a place to camp. The stately dining room, now devoid of any furniture save for a grand piano, once had a lustrous parquet floor. The white columns, which once separated long tables and supported the paneled ceiling, stood like silent waiters. The last fine meal had been served long ago.

"There were no tables, no stools, and we were lying like sardines," Helga said. "They gave us a half a loaf of bread. Finally we found a toilet so we could wash our faces and hands. So we were happy to get to lie on a clean floor. It was next to the staircase. We were in the middle of the top deck. One staircase up to the lifeboat."

Sapped of strength, the three young women fashioned bedrolls using their life vests as mattresses. The girls spread their fur coats atop the vests. Then the trio curled up, closed their eyes, and searched for sleep.

The Reuter sisters and their aunt had now been aboard the ship for two days.

On January 29, the ship's crew directed Horst, his mother, and her friend Hildegard and daughter Christa to a place in a large empty hall. Horst doesn't remember if it was the ship's ballroom or dining room. Even before they had a moment to put their belongings down, a sailor told them to relocate to a cabin on the upper decks on the port side at the stern. "The four of us slept in one cabin together," Horst said.[20] They were fortunate that they didn't have to share the space with anyone else.

While his mother and her friend settled in, Horst decided it was time to explore the vast ship. To the 10-year-old boy, the *Wilhelm Gustloff* was fascinating and, as Horst remembers it, the ship seemed, however briefly, to promise adventure. Before Meta could tell Horst to stay put, the boy scampered out of the cabin—he was certain he'd seen a dog padding about nearby. Hassan, the German shepherd, belonged to Lieutenant Commander Wilhelm Zahn. The 35-year-old officer had a strong, chiseled face; a goatee and mustache framed his set jaw. Horst laughed and chased the dog up and down stairs and back and forth in the upper corridors, weaving in and out of streams of people. He glanced over the ship's rail and saw other KdF liners-turned-refugee-ships tethered to Gotenhafen's piers. They were the *Deutschland* and the *Hansa*. He spied the two lighthouses at the mouth of the harbor.

Irene and Ellen Tschinkur, their mother Serafima, and cousin Evi settled down in the upper-deck dining room. Using their lumpy lifejackets as pillows, the four lay alongside one of the room's four walls.

Only six years old, Ellen Tschinkur not only didn't fully understand the gravity of the situation, she decided to make her complete displeasure and discomfort about the situation known to everyone, especially to her mother.

"I was very naughty. I complained the whole time," Ellen Tschinkur said, her eyes lighting mischievously at the memory. "My poor mother. I just kept whining that it was hot, that I didn't want to be on the boat. I asked when we could go home."[21]

Finally the rocking of the boat lulled the three girls and Serafima to sleep.

Nellie Minkevics and her father squeezed on board with everyone. They were assigned a space on the highest deck above the women's auxiliary.[22] They were in an unfortunate location, below decks and far from the lifeboats. Yet, the pair was grateful to be aboard. Like so many on board, they had a moment to savor the idea that peace and safety was upon them.

Clutching baby Inge to her breast, Milda Bendrich allowed herself the quickest sighs of relief. She paused before gladly handing the last of their possessions to the crew of the *Wilhelm Gustloff*. Milda and her parents received life vests in exchange.

"We were directed to our places. My parents and the old ladies were to sleep on mattresses in the theater, you and I in a cabin with several berths, which, as time went on, were insufficient for the increasing numbers of mothers and children. On the second night there was an air-raid warning, and many, including us, left the ship to seek refuge in an air-raid shelter," Milda wrote to her daughter Inge long after the war. "I cannot remember in detail any of my companions in fate except a 50-year-old East Prussian lady who had already made the arduous journey from Königsberg. I had noticed her because she was terribly nervous, as if she had an inner feeling of the impending disaster. Shortly before the W.G. received the order to leave, this woman left the ship. I don't know if she returned. I never saw her again."

Four captains occupied the bridge of the *Wilhelm Gustloff*, each with his jurisdiction, and they all vied for control. No one agreed on the best route to safely cross the Baltic Sea. Of the four, two were the dominant force: Lt. Commander Wilhelm Zahn and Captain Freidrich Petersen. Zahn, the military commander and former submariner, thought the *Gustloff* should follow the shoreline and maintain total blackout conditions. Zahn,

33, had been commander of the department of the 2nd U-boat Training Division and had recently been appointed Military Transport Leader. Petersen, the 63-year-old civilian captain, vehemently disagreed. Petersen wanted to maintain a speed of less than 12 knots, about 10 miles per hour. The broad-faced captain, who also sported a trim goatee and mustache, was anxious about taxing the ship too much, thinking its years in dry dock had robbed its engines of the ability to handle any stress. Nonsense, thought Lt. Commander Zahn. He argued for the *Gustloff* to travel at least 15 knots, or about 17 miles per hour, to better avoid an enemy attack. A naval dispatch had reported enemy submarine activity off Pomeranian coast. They bickered. They fought. Zahn tried hard to assert his position.

Captains Zahn and Petersen also quarreled about whether the *Wilhelm Gustloff* should follow the coastal route though the waters there were shallow and mined.[23] Theoretically, this route in an outward shipping lane offered more protection to the vessel from a Soviet submarine attack. The other option required heading for deeper water, miles off the coast. German minesweepers would have already cleared floating mines dropped by aircraft, but this route put the *Wilhelm Gustloff* in a more vulnerable position regarding a possible submarine attack. In the end, they settled on following a zigzag route, relying on decades of military practice. In World War One and World War Two, surface ships often steered a zigzag course to impede torpedo attacks.

However, the zigzag carried its own risks, in fact it could be quite dangerous. There was always the danger of collision—if a ship poorly executed a turn, it could venture into the path of an oncoming vessel. Or, sometimes, as in the case of the British liner *Arabic,* a U-boat found its mark and sank the boat in spite of it having zigzagged.[24]

After the *Gustloff* sank, a naval board of inquiry called Zahn to testify. He told the board that a contributing factor to the extreme loss of life was that Croatians had replaced many of the ship's German crew members. He blamed them for neither following nor understanding orders. In addition, Zahn said that he hadn't received orders about whether or not to zigzag. "Before we left I got three phone calls and was told to leave," Zahn said. "I was confirmed to take the deep water route. I had gotten neither verbal nor written orders to zigzag. As it related to submarines, I knew from discussions with other colleagues that there were no submarines in the area. I had also assumed the sea area in question had been reconnaissanced and had a submarine been sighted, I would have been notified."[25]

As the gray cruise liner sailed past the harbor mouth, Friedrich Petersen and Wilhelm Zahn agreed to take it through a channel that was "officially" mine swept. Even so, Petersen made another fatal mistake when he switched on the ship's red and green navigation lights to avoid colliding with the German minesweeper colony operating in the area.[26] The *Wilhelm Gustloff* twinkled like a Christmas tree.

In the meantime, the crew struggled against stubborn winds and sea spray to chip ice from the *Gustloff*'s antiaircraft guns, rigging, and davits. The upper deck gleamed like an ice skating rink. It was windy, but so far the visibility remained fair. Lookouts with night glasses were stationed on the upper decks. They searched the infinite darkness for signs of enemy ships. The wind howled, whistling in the antiaircraft turrets. Night fell; the cold intensified, and many refugees became violently seasick. Some of the queasy moved to the center of the boat, amidships, where they wouldn't feel the pitch and roll from choppy seas. It took a long time for the rolling and rocking ship to reach deeper waters of the Baltic Sea.[27]

The pier in Gotenhafen did not easily relinquish the *Wilhelm Gustloff*. When the liner finally pulled away around 1 P.M. a heavy coating of mud encased its hull.[28] Engines churned the water into a murky brew. Four tugboats helped the ship to the harbor, and as it reached the open sea, the tugs dropped back one by one. Captain Paul Vollrath noticed the *Gustloff* was almost all alone as it sailed toward the Hela peninsula. Rather than a convoy of protection, a single minesweeper served as escort. Normally several ships served as escort to help protect against submarines. These support ships traveled at high speeds to search for submarines and lay depth charges as precautions against the U-boats. The *Löwe*, a torpedo boat, joined the minesweeper just after the *Gustloff* passed the harbor's mouth. Also, a smaller torpedo-retriever ship, the *TF-1*, which was about 100 tons, announced it too would serve as escort. There were supposed to be two other escorts, but to wait for them would have been to risk air strikes or artillery barrages.

"This was our spectacular escort force, two small units of the German navy without any practical experience of escort duties, no submarine chasers, and that in spite of a submarine warning having been circularized and being imminent in the very area we were to pass through," Vollrath recounted in a memoir penned some 35 years after the sinking. "For the first time during the whole war, Russian submarines had been able to clear the very extensive minefields and nets laid at the mouth of the Gulf of Finland and had broken out."[29]

After Captains Petersen and Zahn received their orders to embark, the *Gustloff* proceeded to a mine-swept channel called route No. 58. It ran about 20 miles north of the Pomeranian coast. This was to avoid the coastal lane, which was reportedly infested with mines. Although a minesweeper had preceded the *Gustloff*, there were always stories of ships that blew up after a completed sweep. The intricate devices incorporated into the last magnetic and acoustic mines defied many normal mine detecting devices, no matter how modern they were.[30]

After the *Gustloff* left, the *Hansa* remained tied to the pier. It continued taking refugees on board, some of whom came alongside the ship on tenders. The *Admiral Hipper*, which was also supposed to help, was evacuating 1,500 wounded soldiers.[31] These ships sailed after the *Gustloff* had ventured further out to sea. However, engine problems soon forced the *Hansa* and the *TF-1* back to shore. Only the *Löwe* remained. Well aware that scores of mines lurked beneath the churning sea, the German navy had dispatched minesweepers ahead.

"Already we felt safe," Milda said. "It was not long before the first victims of seasickness clung to the washbasins. An attempt to reach the toilets in time would have been useless because the corridors and stairs were crowded with people, mostly women and children. Of course, I was sick, too, as the heavy swell together with the foul smell in the cabin would have turned anybody's stomach. I can still remember that I fed you porridge for dinner and that I had a little of this myself to settle my stomach. We were told not to undress but we took off fur coats and boots. You were partly undressed. We were all so exhausted that it quickly became quiet and dark in the cabin."

The ship left in a heavy snowfall, the four captains confident the blizzard would shield the ship from aerial attacks. The captains, the crew, and the passengers could not know that a certain Soviet submarine captain, Alexander Marinesko, had entered the Gulf of Danzig in his *S-13*. Marinesko didn't relay his position to command.[32]

It was no secret that the *Wilhelm Gustloff* had left Gotenhafen; it would have been impossible to conceal the ship's movement from the Soviets.[33] On the pier, a dejected and envious crowd stood. Hundreds watched what they thought was their last best hope for survival sail away. This time, unlike the days when the *Gustloff* sailed the Mediterranean as a KdF pleasure boat, no music played and no flags waved. In the distance, the night sky flashed red.

Eight

PLUMMETING TO THE SEA FLOOR

During the *Wilhelm Gustloff*'s days as a KdF liner, passengers would gather in the common areas to play cards, listen to music, or read. Now, the round tables and upholstered chairs had been removed to make room for refugees. Sailors and officers assigned people arbitrarily to cabins, which they might share with strangers, or to one of several community rooms. When the larger common spaces and smaller cabins were filled, people bunked down in whatever space remained, whether stairwells, holds, closets, the spaces under stairs, and hallways.

The refugees understood that sailing across the Baltic Sea aboard the *Wilhelm Gustloff* presented the easiest and fastest way to escape the Soviets. Some were cautiously optimistic as they tried to ignore the sea's own dangers, such as mines and submarines. The upper decks were safer since one could get stuck below deck in an emergency. However, space in the dining room and ballroom quickly filled. The more crowded the ship became, the more it stank. People were hot and body odor pervaded the cabins and halls. Toilets clogged. Some people, sick from nerves, vomited over the sides of the ship.

The crew divided up the hundreds of wounded on board and billeted them into large lounges and halls. Pregnant women were shown to one of the makeshift hospital rooms, and though the ship wasn't fully equipped for labor and delivery, an unknown number of babies were delivered on board. The Naval Auxiliary women helped and held the hands of many mothers-to-be.

Officially the crew forbade anyone from coming on board after the night of the January 29. However, some survivors recall people coming on hours later.

"Perhaps since Dad belonged to the Baltic Sailing Club—on the other side of the quay where the *Gustloff* anchored—Dad had made friends with sailors on that ship and they got us into that dining room in the last hours—but, it's all speculation on my part. I do have some old black-and-white pictures where sailors are in uniform partying with members of the Baltic Sailing Club," said Irene Tschinkur, thinking back on that time.[1]

The night between January 29 and 30 was "hell" as more and more refuges, wounded soldiers, and sailors boarded the ship, Vollrath wrote. All the while the *Gustloff*'s officers tried to go about their duties. They pushed through crowds and climbed over personal belongings. The ship's purser and his staff tried to get a head count and keep up with the ship's manifest. Much of the crew hurried about gathering equipment. They brought additional life rafts on board but didn't properly secure them. These new rafts, similar to pontoons, had floors made of net. They were put on the ship's upper decks. The crew told passengers that in an emergency the rafts would float up from the water.

Around 8 P.M. on January 30, 1945, Adolf Hitler delivered a speech commemorating the twelfth anniversary of his rise to power under the banner of the National Socialist German Workers Party. The *Wilhelm Gustloff* broadcast the speech over the ship-wide public address system. Passengers couldn't blot out his words. His lengthy monologue obligingly addressed the situation on the eastern front:

"The horrid fate that is now taking shape in the east and that exterminates hundreds of thousands in the villages and market places, in the country and in the cities will be warded off in the end and mastered by us, with the utmost exertion and despite all setbacks and hard trials. . . . In this fateful battle there is therefore for us but one command: He who fights honorably can thus save his own life and the lives of his loved ones. But he who, because of cowardice or lack of character, turns his back on the nation shall inexorably die an ignominious death."[2] As he spoke, each word seemed to punch the air. Nearly 70 years later, Helga Reuter from Königsberg remembers trying to ignore the long speech and rest.[3]

The *Wilhelm Gustloff* approached the gravel-rich bed known as Stolpe Bank, located off the coast of modern-day Poland. Captains Friedrich Petersen and Wilhelm Zahn breathed a little easier. They shared a cognac toast, believing the worst had passed.[4] Their détente was brief. At this point Zahn and Petersen couldn't agree on whether the *Gustloff* should increase its speed. Zahn later told a naval board of inquiry that he wanted the boat to go faster but that Petersen and others told him the ship couldn't maintain a high speed for long. "While we were debating this at 21:20 there were three detonations within two second intervals," Zahn said.[5]

Just after 9 P.M., almost immediately following Hitler's fevered address, Alexander Ivanovich Marinesko, the captain from Odessa, commanded the *S-13* to fire all four of her torpedoes at the *Wilhelm Gustloff*. Packed with 660 pounds of explosives, the torpedoes streaked toward the ship. One of the four torpedoes got stuck in its launching tube, with its primer fully armed. Torpedoes of this period traveled a few thousand meters under water to their target. Batteries or electric motors propelled the torpedoes forward until they detonated either when close to or upon contact with the target. The slightest jolt would blow up the *S-13*. The crew disarmed the failed torpedo; it was the one labeled "For Stalin." Generally, a submarine had to be between 2,000 and 3,000 yards away to hit its mark. The *S-13* was less than 1,000 yards away. Captain Marinesko made a brief note in his log.

"Immediately the ship had a 5 degree port listing," Zahn testified before the naval board of inquiry five days after the sinking. "All of the officers met on the bridge and the refugees were told to go to the upper deck and not to panic."[6] Zahn said the frozen davits weren't the only reason lifeboats weren't lowered. Again, he pointed to the replacement crew for the reason. "Only four to six boats were lowered with the help of soldiers, under difficult circumstances. The davits were iced and the Croats were absent." The captains tried to maintain calm, and Zahn remembered that for the first 20 minutes after the strike the boat didn't list much. Then it did, and there was panic. "We calmed them [the refugees] down by calling to them that we had run aground." Zahn ordered his subordinates to destroy the radio room. The boat listed more, the people panicked more. Zahn said they announced that the ship could float for several hours. As the listing increased to between 25 and 30 degrees, Zahn realized the ship was doomed.

At this point Zahn saved himself. He knew the crew had stored much of the safety equipment aft and so he went there. He climbed into a lifeboat and waited for rescue.[7]

Clad in a too-large life vest, Horst Woit was asleep when the first torpedo punched through the bow. The boy heard nothing. It was 9:10 P.M.; the ship was 25 nautical miles off shore. The second and third hits thundered through the vessel. The ship shuddered and Horst awoke to see his mother's face fixed in terror. Horst and his mother stumbled inside the dark cabin to open the door. Outside, mother and son saw a crush of people, as the hallway had been filled with passengers once the cabins and the larger halls had run out of space. The two rushed for the stairs. Again the ship quaked. Fire extinguishers exploded, coating the stairs with a toxic mousse. Meta slipped.

"Mama get up! Mama get up!" Horst screamed from the top of the stairs, his cries mixing with the howls and shrieks from other passengers. Hurt, Meta hoisted herself up and slowly, but deliberately, she climbed the stairs to her young son. As they edged toward the lifeboats across the slick deck, Horst saw flares shoot into the onyx sky.

The evacuation quickly devolved into an exercise in panic. Passengers groped the walls along dark passageways that started tilting upward. Some found luggage and were able to dig out coats, hats, and boots if they weren't already wearing them.

The second torpedo struck the swimming pool where the 373 members of the Women's Naval Auxiliary were billeted. Most of the young women died instantly.

Irene Tschinkur East, now 78, remembers being slammed against a wall in ballroom when the first torpedo hit. The force jolted the grand piano from its position in the room. It rolled like a boulder toward Irene and her younger sister, Ellen. Their cousin Evi and mother Serafima were also in its path. Torrents of water rushed into the room. Hysteria washed over many of the women, children, and men inside the room.

"We all just hung onto each other," Irene said. "The lights were flickering. All of us quickly ran upstairs; people were coming from all directions."

"However, our journey was brief. We were torpedoed three times at 10 P.M. and hell was upon us. How I was able to find my three children in the dark and was able to get out I do not know. The ship was halfway in the water and we kept climbing higher and higher," Serafima wrote after the war.

Milda Bendrich scooped up her 2-year-old daughter, Inge, and made for the stairs, desperate to find a way off the ship. She hadn't had time to dress her baby girl. A heap of bodies, crushed under the stampeding feet of escaping passengers, blocked her way like corks in a bottle. Somehow Milda reached an open deck.

"We would not have been asleep more than half an hour when I was suddenly flung from my berth," Milda wrote to her daughter Inge after the war. "You were asleep against the wall and stayed there quietly but that first hit had sent me flying. The second and third hit came in quick succession. In the meantime I had picked you [Inge] up quickly and headed toward the door to turn on the light. Nothing happened. Soon a pale red light glowed in the corridor, scantily lighting the path."[8]

"Suddenly there was a 'bam.' And then two more: 'Bam. Bam,'" recalled Rose Rezas. "People were yelling and screaming."[9]

Seconds after the blow from the first torpedo, Rose and her sister, Ursula, locked hands so as not to lose each other in the mad rush. Running, they jumped over bodies and found they had to sidestep trampled children if they wanted to get out.

Then an announcement from the ship's loudspeakers cut through the racket: "Everyone quiet. We will save the ship!" Rose remembers another very different announcement barely one minute later: "The ship is sinking. Women with children go now to the lifeboats." Hundreds of passengers wouldn't survive the frenzied stampede to the uppermost of seven decks. Captain Wilhelm Petersen ordered sailors to secure the lifeboats and guard the exits from the sundeck and promenade deck. They could not effectively carry out orders.

One of the captains spoke over the ship's public address system. He pleaded with passengers to remain calm and keep order. The voice was ignored, lost in a roar of panic and the ship's bleating alarm sirens. The traditional "Women and children first" order was overtly ignored as terrified people pushed their way to the decks and lifeboats. People slid, rolled, and skidded; piles of people were crushed when they careened against a wall. Many refugees got stuck in the hallway and stairwells. Some of them simply sat down, succumbing to their fate. Others were lifted to the upper decks on a wave of people desperate to survive.

In the moments after the attack, Rose Rezas became disoriented; the ship sloped like a crazy fun-house mirror. But somehow she and Ursula clawed their way to the glassed-in promenade deck. Behind the glass, it looked as if humans were trapped like fish in an aquarium. Together with other passengers, they tried to smash an opening in the glass. Rose and her sister pushed through a stairwell jammed with people to escape the rushing water that was sure to reach them. If they were to fall, they would die.

"Then all the lights went out and we couldn't see a thing," Rose said. "My sister and I were holding hands so we wouldn't lose each other. I can't describe the screaming that was going on. A woman next to us said, 'Kids, now it is time to die.'"[10]

The third torpedo struck the *Wilhelm Gustloff* amidships, near the engine room where sailors stood at their posts. Freezing water rushed into the lower decks. It's quite possible Walter Salk, the young sailor from Essen, was here below decks when the impact came. This blast disabled the engines and cut the ship's power. It also extinguished the lights and silenced the ship's communications system. With the radio dead, the ship would not be able to send out a mayday. The radio room operator used an emergency transmitter to hammer out an SOS in the scant hope of a rescue ship.[11] Unfortunately, the transmitter only had a range of 2,000 meters, so the torpedo boat *Löwe* was the only vessel to receive the distress call. Under the command of Lieutenant Commander Paul Prüfe, the *Löwe* saw the red flares fanning out in the night sky. He headed the *Löwe* toward the damaged ship, all the while retransmitting the *Gustloff*'s SOS, hoping other boats would hear it and respond to the scene.

From the bridge Captain Friedrich Petersen ordered any able-bodied crew members below decks to shut the watertight doors. This effectively sealed off the forward part of the ship, trapping many of the off-duty crew in their quarters. While a few sailors escaped to the sundeck by climbing emergency ladders located in the ventilation ducts, most were trapped in the engine room that soon became their coffin. They clawed and scratched at the locked steel doors. Petersen's decision robbed the ship of many of the sailors who were schooled in emergency procedures. There were few sailors left who knew how to lower the lifeboats.

The ship listed to the port side. This made escape from lower decks impossible. Staircases tilted at crazy angles and stairs were hard to climb, especially for those with young children and babies. Indeed, between 1,000 and 2,000 people died in the first few minutes after the attack. Suddenly the emergency lights blinked to life. It seemed an unknown crewmember had started the emergency diesel engines.[12]

At 9 P.M., Captain Heinz Weller stood in the chart room. In his memoir, Weller recalled how, just when the *Wilhelm Gustloff* passed the mouth of Gotenhafen's harbor, off to port side the lighthouse at Stilo seemed to blaze a little more brightly. During war, lighthouses on the German coast shone only at certain preset times that each sailor knew. The navigation officer noted the ship's bearing and recorded it on chart. Weller returned to the bridge. As he passed through the doorframe of the chart room, a shockwave blasted through ship. The force threw Weller in the air and he smashed his head on the top beam of the doorframe.[13] At first he thought the ship was in the middle of a minefield. After the second and third explosion he realized the ship had been torpedoed.

At the same time, bulkheads began to collapse and burst. Steel braces throughout the ship tore apart as rivets popped, and the *Wilhelm Gustloff* listed to port side. Weller lost his balance. He felt the bow dip deeper into the water and the ship tremble. The boat started rolling toward one side.

Weller skidded to the port-side bridge deck, pulled up, and climbed to the bearing deck. He ordered the signalmen to fire off every flare they could. Red blooms rose upward into the night.

Initially, Zahn, Petersen, and a few other officers remained on the bridge trying to maintain order. They felt the stern rising higher and higher as the bow tipped further beneath the sea. They knew the ship was lost. Although many of the crew died instantly or were sealed off from the rest of the ship and were thereby prevented from aiding the civilian refugees, many stories of crew members behaving badly surfaced years later.

Some of the survivors recall naval personnel firing their weapons in the air to quell the creeping hysteria. Yet, it seemed panic seized some of the crew, not all of whom went down with the ship. Some sailors didn't wait—they put on life vests and jumped. Some of them were squished and smashed by other lifeboats. Each lifeboat could hold 50, yet one lowered lifeboat held a captain and 12 sailors. There weren't enough lifeboats, and even for those who reached them, there was no guarantee of salvation. Water from swells splashed over the sides of the vessels, soaking everyone inside. Some of the lifeboats capsized; others were adrift on the water.

Horst Woit and his mother had been fortunate enough to acquire a cabin on the top deck, so they were spared the lower decks' pandemonium with children slipping from their mothers' arms and people being crushed under panicking feet. After climbing over bodies and pushing through the crowd, the Woits reached the ship's railing. Shouting people beseeched the sailors to help them, to save them. Two crew members pointed to the Woits and assigned them to a lifeboat fairly quickly. As he, his mother, and family friends climbed aboard one of the few lifeboats filled to near capacity, Horst recalls seeing flares burst over his head.

The Woits' boat cranked lower and lower, the inky sea tantalizingly close. It was slow going because, as with the other lifeboats, ice seemed to have turned the lines on this vessel into steel. The small boat began to swing slowly at first and then more violently with every turn of the crank. Horst pushed his face against his mother. He doesn't remember if they spoke or if she tried to calm him. Instead, he remembers how one man howled against the wind for something with which to cut the line. Suddenly, Woit remembered his uncle's jackknife. He passed the black knife to his mother. Each passenger carefully passed it forward, each afraid it would slip from between cold fingers. The man opened the blade and sawed through the thick, ice-covered rope, a difficult job since the lifeboat rocked with force. Finally, the boat broke free. The knife saved 70 lives.

"Otherwise we would have been pulled under," Horst Woit said. Even now, nearly 70 years after that night, when Horst tells the story, it's as if he is telling it for the first time, as if he is surprised the knife wasn't lost, that it worked. It's as if he's unsure the knife will still save him, save his mother, and all those people.

The boat landed on the water. All the while the din of human voices dying filled the air. As more lifeboats hit the sea, crammed lifeboats ignored outstretched hands lest they sink from the weight of one more body. Children's faces were plastered in terror, their parents' faces etched in agony at their helplessness of the situation. The atmosphere in many a lifeboat had turned feral.

"People tried to pull themselves onto the boat, and people hit them on the heads and hands saying 'Get 'em off, they're going to top us over!'" said Woit.

In the water around their lifeboat, Horst noticed legs stuck straight up into the air. Later Woit realized that they were the legs of children whose too-large life vests had pulled them underwater headfirst. Blood-red flares fired by desperate sailors danced across the sky.

Nellie Minkevics had just shut the door to the putrid bathroom when, boom! She flew out of the lavatory, trying to stay balanced on the ship that now rolled and pitched terribly. She looked around for her father and her friend. She felt strangely alone in the mob. Then Nellie saw her father go one way, running away from her. He didn't see her. She couldn't reach him. The last glimpse she had of her father was his back disappearing into the rush. A tap on her shoulder summoned her from a trance. Her friend had returned to fetch her mother's suitcase. That single irrational act saved the pair because they had headed off in one direction searching for the suitcase while everyone else ran the other way. Eventually Nellie and her friend reached the deck with the lifeboats and sailors helped them into one.[14]

Rather than endure death in the frozen sea, one father shot his family before turning his pistol on himself, remembered Vollrath. Pistols weren't used exclusively for suicide. Many armed officers used them to try and control the panicked passengers. Sometimes an officer shot into the air to get people's attention.[15] However, suicide in the face of near certain drowning was a rational choice for some. Some stripped off their clothes before jumping into the sea, knowing the cold would grant them a faster death. Some survivors told stories about passengers who slit their wrists. At that time of year the Baltic Sea hovers around 4 degrees Celsius (39 degrees Fahrenheit). A body doesn't have long in that frigid water.

Carrying baby Inge, Milda Bendrich stood in the midst of a mountain of people blocking the stairs from C-deck to B-deck. They had to trample over the dead to save themselves.

She couldn't understand why so many people didn't make any effort to mount the stairs, especially when they could clearly see the sea of passengers from the cabins trying to climb them, Milda wrote to Inge. "Anyone hesitating to climb across the people below them or losing their strength would end up under stampeding feet. The panic had started. At this stage we did not even know why we were fleeing. Nobody had experienced a torpedo hit before. We were women and children, not experienced seamen. It was much later that we understood why the people sitting on the stairs could do nothing to escape from the stampeding masses. I just hope that they were beyond feeling anything."

Milda stared at the two flights between C-deck and B-deck, and started her ascent, pausing for breath on a small square landing.

"I climbed [them] countless times in my mind in the coming years. You in my arms, fighting against the wave behind me and the women in front of me who, like me, lacked the strength to fight on," Milda Bendrich wrote.

Those who surrendered to the mob simply became one more obstacle for Milda to cross. She, too, almost succumbed to the calamity when she reached the second half of the stairs. But then a woman behind her pushed her up one step, and then another step, saying, "For God's sake, don't fall." Suddenly a wider passageway opened ahead of them. Milda wanted to rest, just for a moment. Looking down at the deck floor, she thought that she was too tired to go on and was tempted to stop trying. Then she saw the tiniest clump of snow. She guessed someone had tracked it in on their shoes. She picked up the snow and put it in her mouth.

"I could not have cared less about hygiene as I devoured this snow," Bendrich wrote. "Now I was able to continue. I did not have to fight for every centimeter now. There were no bodies barricading my way. The torpedo hit had its harvest further below, not here."

Revived, Milda Bendrich searched for her parents. She found the mattresses they had rested on, but they were empty. Indeed, the entire hall was empty except for a few old people who told her the others had left a long time ago. It seemed as if quite some time had elapsed since the first torpedo. For a while she searched aimlessly for her parents, a task doomed to fail because of the sparse emergency lighting and increasingly impassable corridors. Later, Milda would learn that her parents, Rosalie and Karl Felsch, never escaped the glassed-in promenade deck.[16]

The ship now tilted at an angle of 30 degrees. In the search for her parents, Milda hardly realized she was actually walking up-hill. Then, clutching her baby girl, she stepped out onto a mirror-smooth sheet of ice, which turned out to be the boat deck.

"I stood, pressed against the wall of the ship, but again, as if by instinct, I worked my way across to the railing, as I could see men working on a boat by the light of the moon. Now, imagine me climbing this icy hill, without being able to gain a foothold and carrying a small child. I kept on ending back against the wall where I started," Bendrich wrote. As the ship leaned, people slid over the side rails straight into the water. She was standing at the rail when she saw a lifeboat filled with people fall and dump everyone inside into the water.[17]

About a meter away from Milda stood a marine officer. He made no attempt to get to the railing. He appeared to be listening to noises, which sounded like whipping. Later she realized it might have been some officers shooting their families and children rather than gamble on making it into a lifeboat. Something seemed to pull the officer out of his trance, and he barked at a soldier to help Milda and Inge into a lifeboat. The soldier held onto the parapet with one hand. He took Milda's hand in his while the other officer pushed the mother up as far as he could. "So by pushing and pulling, we arrived at the railing and were lifted into the lifeboat. While our boat was being freed, another which was already being lowered into the water capsized and lost everybody."

While Milda Bendrich struggled to survive, the Rezas girls, Rose and Ursula, remained riveted to a railing to stop themselves from tumbling into the glacial waters. They saw bodies flailing in the water below, and they heard the howling of those desperately cleaving to life. They tried to smash open a porthole. They failed. A German officer shot the glass. It shattered. Ursula and Rose crawled through the hole and were swept into the sea. The cold salt water stung their bloodied hands; it felt as if it was cutting through their skin and bones.

Fortunately Rose could swim. But so many didn't know how to stay afloat, so many drowned. "An old man came floating toward me and grabbed me. I began to go down and kicked him away from me," Rose recalled. "I can't forget his face."[18]

Rose swam to a dinghy filled with refugees. The passengers smacked at her hands, trying to shoo her away. She climbed onto the rustic sea vessel. Chest-high water sloshed inside the small craft. The cold water felt prickly lapping at her feet, legs, and chest. Her hair froze like strands of spun glass. She prayed she would lose consciousness.

Just before 9 P.M. Eva Dorn was passing cotton balls to a doctor in one of the makeshift delivery rooms. He told the 18-year-old not to worry, that the ship was pretty much out of submarine territory. In the next room a woman was in labor. Then, just as a nurse opened the door to tell the doctor that the baby was crowning, the first torpedo struck.

A skeleton in a glass case fell in front of the infirmary's door and shattered. Another boom. The second torpedo hit. The door was blocked. Then, on the third strike the door sprang open. Eva stepped over the glass and over the skeleton. "I thought to myself 'You have stepped over death. Nothing will happen to you,'" Eva said, her left arm starting to tremble as she recounted this part of her story.[19]

Eva hurried out of the room and turned left down a small stairway to the lifeboats. A pile of life vests lay on the floor. She took one. She reached the railing and a crowd of people. There were soldiers in front of the boats, and Eva helped put women and children into the lifeboats. Suddenly a lifeboat filled with people tipped and fell. As Eva tells this part of the story her fingers tighten around her cigarette. Her left arm shakes and she tries to hold it down.

The soldier looked at Eva. "'Girl, now you go in,' he told me," Eva said. "I was on automatic pilot. I got into the boat. It was silent." Two men, dressed in civilian clothes accompanied the women, children, and Eva, who wore only her uniform. They rowed. Eva Dorn sat in the crowded lifeboat, a girl and a boy under each arm. One of the children cried, the other vomited over her shoulder. She clamped the lifeboat's rudder under her arm. The *Wilhelm Gustloff* was to her back.

All around Eva, people in the water thrashed and flailed. They tried to hang on to the boat. The two men in Eva's boat and some of the women hit their hands to knock them off.

"A man in the water, he looked at me. He wanted to come in. I could sketch him now. His eyes looked at me. As he was slowly letting go, going under, his eyes were fixed at me. I couldn't leave the rudder," Eva said. It was dark, but it didn't seem dark. The water shone like silver, she said.

Eva now faced the *Wilhelm Gustloff*. She saw it sink. She heard the screams: "I have that always in my ears."

Serafima Tschinkur grabbed her daughters, Irene and Ellen, and their cousin Evi by their arms. They ran upstairs to the next floor, by now a veritable ice rink. They gripped the railing. Irene felt Evi's hand slip from her grasp. By then the *Wilhelm Gustloff* slanted so much, the four slid into the sea with so many others. An avalanche of suitcases, bags, and even a baby carriage tumbled over their heads. Water pulled them down and pushed them up. Irene thought her lungs would burst. Masses of people roiled in the water. Irene screamed for her mother in the watery darkness. In the water Serafima lost her last rings off her fingers—her wedding ring and one with a large light blue stone in it, which Irene had always admired.

"It was stormy, cold, and there were high waves. I gave ourselves up in God's hands when we reached the highest deck. I held all the three children as long as I could until there was a loud bang and we were torn from each other and fell into the water. I personally was under water and hoped, may God grant me a quick death (I assume there was an ice floe above me)," Serafima wrote.

Somehow mother and daughter found each other and managed to swim to a boat. Evi vanished into the deep. "I remember it was snowing," Irene said. "The moon hid behind the clouds and then it would come out again."

"It was not long as the first detonation exploded," Helga Reuter recalled. "The air got dusty. We knew what happened. I grabbed my fur coat and put it on, then the life vest. My sister and aunt left their fur coats on the floor and took their [life] swim vests. I had to crawl like a dog, my knees buckled; they gave way for panic. People tumbled over me and I hurt my back."

At the door of the promenade deck, Helga breathed in a lungful of fresh air and stood. She, her aunt Ruth, and her sister Inge moved as quickly as possible in the darkness. On deck, the combination of ice and lack of trained crew members exacerbated the frantic situation. The ship canted more and more with each passing minute. Lifeboats remained frozen to their davits. People clawed and smashed at the lifeboats with bare hands trying to free them. Reportedly, only one lifeboat was lowered correctly during the sinking. Other lifeboats made it down, but just barely. The cables on many lifeboats snapped, fell, and capsized, tossing their occupants into the icy water or crushing those who were in the water beneath. Some useless antiaircraft guns broke free and plummeted overboard, landing on a fully occupied lifeboat.

Some survivors reported seeing a high-ranking officer with his wife lowering a motorboat only half-filled with people. The craft passed right by the plate glass of the enclosed promenade deck, jammed with desperate women and children. Helga could only imagine what those on both sides of the glass were thinking. It seems selfish acts weren't reserved strictly for the passengers.

When Helga and her companions reached the lifeboats, they were told the vessels were reserved for mothers with children. They watched, helpless as crewmen hammered the boats loose from the mother ship. The *Wilhelm Gustloff* started rolling violently to the other side. Shots suddenly fired into the night; SOS flares lit the sky. All the while Helga, Inge, and their Aunt Ruth gripped the railing and watched, stunned, as people slid to their deaths in the frigid waters of the Baltic Sea.

Helga saw rafts being lowered into the water. Unlike the lifeboats, the rafts, with their net flooring, had much less stability. She inhaled sharply and without hesitation she decided they should slide down a rope into the water after the rafts. Inge didn't want to follow. Helga persuaded her older sister to shimmy down the rope after her. Her aunt refused.

The girls wore layers of clothing and boots so heavy that they soaked up the water and threatened to pull them beneath the waves. Inge wore a yellow and brown sweater underneath a green-and-white striped sweater she had knitted herself.

When Helga's turn came to descend the thick rough rope, she noticed her sister's raft had already drifted away, without her sister on it. Once on her raft, she pushed herself up and searched everywhere for her sister. Helga looked up at the ship, squinting her eyes against the snow and cold. She saw her Aunt Ruth still standing at the railing in her black dress with pockets trimmed in white fur. Helga neither yelled nor waved; the screaming people made it impossible to hear.

Then Helga saw her sister Inge.

"With the white stripes it gave a light through the night. She was petite. Her skirt was flowing around her like a circle, very nicely, very neatly. She just drifted away," Helga said, whispering the memory. "I thought about her riding boots she had on, and then, the water must be icy."

Inside Helga's raft she and the other refugees worked furiously to balance the craft against the heaving sea. The high waves made this hard work. They tried to move their legs in the small space. After a while they saw empty rafts float past. Their occupants had succumbed to cold and exhaustion, and had fallen into the sea like trees felled from a lumberjack's axe.

Helga's raft was not immune to the enemies of cold and sea swells. "We had been 18 sitting or hanging on the raft. Now I counted four seamen. Their uniforms were as hard as a board. Our 'icicle hair' started to dry," Helga said. One of the young men in the boat had fallen forward inside the net. He stared at her, saliva foaming at the corner of his blue-tinged mouth. She tried to lift him to a sitting position but couldn't. Across from her sat a young seaman. He begged his comrades for one cigarette. Another delirious man kept talking about his wife and baby girl who had been born on Christmas Day. He'd never seen the infant. Another soundlessly fell backward yet again. He had no more strength to balance. After the third or fourth time, the other two men just tipped him back and he was gone. They were afraid he would pull them into the water with them.

Helga's two remaining companions soon vacillated between despondency and complaints. They feared their feet would be amputated. Then they grumbled about her feet. She wanted to move them to keep blood circulating through her toes. They wanted her to hold still. She couldn't help bumping her feet against theirs. Then one of the men started snapping. He said he had been torpedoed before but that it had never taken so long to be rescued. The lifeboats lacked rudders and there was no gasoline to power them, they simply bobbed on the waves. Helga looked up at the starless night; snow fell on her blonde lashes.

"Then I saw the lights from the ship flare up. People screamed. The tail went up and the ship was gone," said Helga.

Captain Paul Vollrath ate his supper in his cabin with other officers. The cabin was the only place left to eat since refugees and naval personnel occupied the entire ship. They were in every hall, every room, and every closet. Vollrath and his shipmates talked a bit of shop after they ate, and then, just before 9 P.M., two officers of his watch left for their own quarters. Moments later, as Vollrath was about to swing himself into his bunk fully dressed, the first torpedo slammed into the *Gustloff*'s hull.

"We stepped on a mine!" was his immediate thought, but shortly after that a second and third explosion almost tore the ship apart. He no longer doubted—these were torpedoes. Vollrath jumped into his shoes, which he had taken off against his better judgment, and tied the strings on his life vest.[20]

His hands trembled, his body shivered with fear. For some reason he grabbed two small parcels, cigarettes, a bottle, flashlight, and tucked his revolver under his life vest. He made his way to the chart room; the doors to it were now blocked. Vollrath passed onto the bridge deck through a side door on the starboard side.

"What I had to face here already so soon after the explosions made me forget altogether to get to the bridge. Immediately after we had been hit by the torpedoes, the ship stopped and listed to port side. Emergency lights had been switched on in the meanwhile and at least one could see better. I lit a cigar, perhaps just to cool my nerves, and a lady came up to me, begging to be saved. 'Well,' I said, 'there is nothing to worry about, don't you see I am enjoying a cigar?'" Vollrath wrote.

On the starboard side of the boat, people waited to get on the lifeboats that hung from davits. But the heavy list of the ship had shifted the center of gravity. Many lifeboats dipped too much to the port side and couldn't be moved. In addition, the rope falls and rollers of the lifeboats were iced up and acted as stoppers. Try as they might, the crew couldn't budge the boats.

"How were we to save all the thousands of people in so short a time, because the ship was listing fast and I knew that she would not last much longer. I knew too that not by far enough life-saving equipment and lifeboats were available. Regretfully I have to admit that. We survivors may always remember that thousands of people drowned or froze to death for us in the biggest of all sea disasters," wrote Vollrath.

Vollrath said rumors were already circulating among the panicked passengers: murmurs that Captain Friedrich Petersen and Captain Wilhelm Zahn, as well as other officers on the bridge had committed suicide. That story started after many people mistook the firing of the flares for pistol shots. There were rumors that the captains had escaped with a case of champagne in tow.[21] Vollrath scrambled to the other side of the boat.

Vollrath made his way to the lifeboat he'd been assigned to, No. 6, which hung on the port side. He tried to convince a group of people to follow him, but most preferred to stay rooted in place. They feared crossing to the other side, where the ship dipped precariously close to the water. They feared they would fall into the water and be sucked under the boat. On his way to the lifeboat, Vollrath passed through the main hall and saw a casual female acquaintance of his, whom he'd once given some advice on what to do in case of a torpedo attack. "I asked her, in an act of bravado, to give me a kiss, which I got without hesitation, though kisses were not so easily exchanged then as they are now," Vollrath wrote.

When Vollrath reached the port side, empty davits seemed to mock him. The chief officer, an old man of 68 years of age, was lying in the scuppers with a leg injury, visibly shaken and unable to move. Vollrath helped him into the boat. He returned to the starboard side to get more people. It was an uphill struggle since the list was so heavy. Vollrath got into a lifeboat and descended about 15 feet "into the dark uncertainty." By now the *Wilhelm Gustloff* nearly lay on her side. He had difficulty steering the lifeboat away from the ship because of the floating debris and the people in the water.

This was the only time that Captain Vollrath took his revolver in hand and threatened to shoot people if they were not instantly silent and if they didn't follow his command. "Perhaps my shouting did more to restore order than the gun, which could not be seen anyway. In any case very quickly I had the boat under control and away we went," he wrote. "One of the captains stood in the bridge wing, about 20 feet above us and shouted who was in charge of the boat and I replied to that. To this his reply was 'Mach's gut!'—'Good luck!' Around us, all around us were humans floating and shouting for help, debris, floats, wooden planks, rafts, everything that could float."[22] The *S-13* lurked off port side of the boat—wanting, waiting to fire a fourth torpedo into the cruise liner, or sink any ship coming to rescue.

Inside the lifeboat, Horst snuggled against his mother and stared at the sinking ship. A mere 15 feet lay between Horst's boat and the *Wilhelm Gustloff*. It was about 10:30 P.M.; about 90 minutes had passed since the first torpedo strike. Inexplicably, the ship's lights suddenly blazed, only to be snuffed out in the next second. The ten-year-old watched as the liner gave one final lurch before spearing the water and plunging 150 feet to the seabed. The moon shone and the snow fell.

Nine

THE LITTLE RED SWEATER

The *Wilhelm Gustloff* sank about 12 nautical miles off Stolpe Bank, an underwater shoal near present-day Poland. Any ship within 10 nautical miles of the *Wilhelm Gustloff* when the *S-13* fired its torpedoes that night would have heard the explosions, Captain Paul Vollrath said.[1] The news of the sinking reached the German signals staff in Gotenhafen via the SOS relay that had gone out a few minutes after the attack. In turn, the headquarters relayed the message.

Refugees aboard other transport ships heard the news. For example, aboard the *Togo,* Dr. Peter Siegel from Homburg-Saar remembered, "During the trip it was noticed that the crew, who was initially in good spirits and talkative, all of a sudden turned stern. I heard that they had just received the news of the sinking of the *Gustloff.*"[2] All available ships from the Hela peninsula, Pillau, and Gotenhafen left their courses to find survivors.

Helga Reuter estimated that perhaps four and a half hours had passed since the *Wilhelm Gustloff* sank before she spied searchlights on the horizon from inside the lifeboat. Her feet were swollen stiff from the cold and she could no longer feel them in her leather boots. Her face was numb and the saliva in her mouth felt like a thin layer of ice. Her blonde hair lay plastered to her scalp.

Then lights came closer. They belonged to the *T-36*, a torpedo boat. Upon hearing the distress call, Captain Robert Hering headed straight for the scene of the attack. The *T-36* belonged to the Elbing class of small, fast torpedo boats, and throughout the war she had served in the Baltic Sea.

Captain Robert Hering had heard the transmission from the *Gustloff* around 10 P.M., just about an hour after Marinesko attacked. The boat neared the site at the same time as a barge. The large swells pushed the barge and it kept colliding with the *T-36*. The *Gustloff* had not yet gone under, and some passengers on the cruise liner's upper decks took a chance and jumped into the water. Some made it onto the bucking barge; others were crushed between the barge and the *T-36*.

Hering couldn't steer close enough to the *Wilhelm Gustloff* without risking his boat and crew. He resigned himself to picking up survivors. Each time the torpedo boat found a lifeboat, the crew threw over the side rope ladders, lines, or hawser netting. The stronger survivors climbed aboard. The weaker ones were pushed and sometimes pulled up in a sling. It quickly became apparent which lifeboats and rafts had able-bodied, experienced seamen inside. Those craft had little trouble maneuvering alongside the *T-36*, making for an easier rescue. The other boats drifted about. Captain Hering worried that the submarine that had attacked and sank the *Wilhelm Gustloff* still prowled the waters. He and his crew pushed that thought aside and worked diligently for hours.

The German navy didn't coordinate the rescue effort; rather those ships that heard the distress call headed toward the scene.

"We yelled and waved our arms," Helga Reuter said of trying to flag down the *T-36*. "Finally they came near us and called with a bullhorn. They had to turn around to get us from the right angle to the raft."[3]

Reuter's two exhausted companions mustered enough energy to align their little raft with the rescue boat. The rescuers shouted through the bullhorn to them. Their voices barely carried over the cold air. The rescuers told the three survivors in the raft to get ready to catch a rope. They needed to secure their life raft to the rescue boat, otherwise, it wouldn't be steady enough for the *T-36* crew to pull the three survivors up and over the gunwale, one at a time. The rope flew through the air, but the hands of Helga's two companions were frozen. Time and again they tried to catch it, and time and again their fingers couldn't close around the rope. Helga, however, had kept her hands tucked underneath her armpits, beneath her giant fur coat. Every so often she remembered to wiggle her fingers and rotate her wrists. She was able to catch and fasten the rope.

"I was the first to be lifted on this torpedo search boat. I could not stand up," Helga said, pointing to her feet, which today plague her, nearly 70 years later, with arthritis and cold sensitivity. "They had to carry me inside where all the refugees and rescued sat on the floor or were standing. They got a stool from somewhere for me."

By now it was nearly 2:30 in the morning on January 31. With nearly 500 survivors aboard, the *T-36* quickly ran out of room. Inside the engine room, two sailors helped Helga shed her ice-encrusted clothing and don warm, dry apparel, all of it donated from the crew's own clothing. A third sailor wrapped her in a woolen blanket. A fourth sailor handed her a double vodka. She looked down and realized she had only one shoe. It was missing a heel. Slowly the icebox chill left her body and the heat, painful at first, flooded her body. Helga opened and closed her fingers to encourage blood flow. Then, the awful truth about Inge and Ruth came as her body warmed.

"As for my sister and aunt," Helga said. "I never heard from them again."

Since the *T-36* had escorted the *Wilhelm Gustloff* out of Gotenhafen, it was the first rescue vessel to arrive on the scene. It had been working the area some time before it found Helga and her companions in their life raft.

The young captain and his *T-36* crew also rescued Captains Wilhelm Zahn, Friedrich Petersen, and Heinz Weller, in addition to pulling several hundred people out of the Baltic Sea. Not all of them were alive and some were dying. Rescuers kept coming upon an all too familiar sight; aimlessly drifting lifeboats filled with the frozen dead. Some of the people had died from exposure, others from the sheer exhaustion of trying to balance on rickety life rafts. People were sucked under the propellers of rescue ships. From inside the rafts and lifeboats, a maddening chorus of screaming women, children, and men filled the air. Dead bodies floated past.

Most rescue boats took hours to locate survivors from the *Wilhelm Gustloff,* searching for bodies to match the pleading voices calling over the black waters. Many lifeboats and bodies had drifted far from the site of the attack. When rescue boats did arrive, their captains and crews found a floating debris field filled with dangerous pieces of metal, splintered wood, rucksacks and bodies.[4]

"On January 31, 1945, at about 1 A.M., we passed the sinking spot of the *Gustloff.* Despite submarine alerts we were able to save a woman and a petty officer amongst the drifting bodies," wrote one officer who had been on a rescue vessel.[5]

Two decades after the sinking, Maj. Erich Schirmack wrote to Dönitz's subordinate Vice Admiral Conrad Englehardt about the rescue effort. While returning from a mission with five other boats, Schirmack heard the *Gustloff*'s distress call. His boat was heading back to Pillau to pick up refugees. Schirmack's vessel arrived on the scene an hour after hearing about the sinking. It sailed as fast as possible, but "could only recover corpses."[6]

The *Admiral Hipper*, a heavy cruiser that *T-36* had escorted from Gotenhafen, arrived on the scene soon after hearing the distress signal. It had left Gotenhafen with 1,377 refugees and 152 crewmembers already on board. The *Hipper* had seen quite a lot of combat during the war, from operating against Allied merchant shipping in the Atlantic to participating in operations against Allied convoys trying to supply the Soviet Union. The ship and its crew had been drafted into doing construction work in Gotenhafen. The boat was actually on its way to Kiel for refitting when it heard the distress call. The *Hipper*'s crew tried to pluck survivors from the black waters of the Baltic Sea. Her captain, fearing another submarine attack, didn't stay long. The ship sailed away.

His fear was understandable, but Alexander Marinesko never saw the *Hipper*. In fact, he'd dived far beneath the midnight-dark sea to escape the punishing shock waves of depth charges.[7] Three more minesweepers eventually arrived and saved nearly 200 more people from drowning or exposure.

Dramatic scenes played out throughout the night, aboard the rescue ships and in lifeboats such as Captain Paul Vollrath's. The lifeboats were built to safely hold between 60 and 70 people. After a quick head count Vollrath realized close to 90 people sat on board. The boat was heavy, the bodies and sodden clothing pushed the gunwales nearly flush with the water.

For the rest of his life, Vollrath's decision to refuse more people remained one of the hardest and yet the most necessary choices he ever had to make. Inside the boat meant life, or at least a chance at life. Outside the boat death was certain. "Even today I often ask myself, 'Why did you not at least attempt to get some more into the boat?' But still my answer is that should I have done so, the boat would have capsized, there were too many people swimming in the water," said Vollrath.[8]

Finally the wind no longer whipped about, the sea calmed, and the swells came less frequently. Just after 10 P.M., an hour after the three torpedoes hit, Vollrath decided to stop rowing away from the ship so he could conserve his energy. He also didn't want to take the craft too far from the site of the attack. About 50 yards separated his boat from the *Wilhelm Gustloff*. Vollrath saw the emergency lights glimmering against the ship's upper decks; they cast a spectral glow. He thought he saw a person standing on the side of the ship, which now rested at sea level. He wondered if his mind was simply playing tricks on him. When he looked again, there was nobody there and quite suddenly the *Wilhelm Gustloff* was gone, pulled into the watery abyss.

Among the 90 people inside the lifeboat was a doctor, and for that Vollrath was thankful. He asked the physician to look after people as best he could. Meanwhile, Vollrath passed around his cigarettes and bottle, which, if nothing else, helped shore up morale. "There was not much else one could do," Vollrath said. Every now and then one of the survivors saw what appeared to be the shadow of a ship moving on the water's surface and then stopping to pick up survivors. The people in lifeboat No. 6 waited, and waited, for their turn.

Shortly before midnight, nearly two hours after the *S-13* fired its torpedoes at the *Gustloff*, the *Löwe* moved alongside Vollrath's lifeboat. Vollrath told the captain of the torpedo boat that he and his passengers were stable and in fair shape, and he suggested that the crew continue searching for those hapless souls still in the water or those people floating on the more exposed rafts. Before the *Löwe* left Vollrath's location to do so, one of its crew announced through a megaphone that they were preparing to drop depth charges. The British had developed depth charges in World War One to use against German submarines. It was unlikely that *Löwe's* action would sink the *S-13* or any other submarine still prowling about. However, its shock waves could loosen the submarine's joints or perhaps damage its instruments, which would force the sub to surface, allowing guns from the *Löwe* to finish it off.

Explosions rumbled beneath the water and Vollrath's lifeboat creaked. The severe shockwaves threatened to split the lifeboat open. The depth charges, however, yielded no results: Captain Marinesko's submarine was no longer in the vicinity.

At this point silence filled the lifeboat. Passengers sat alone with their thoughts. To Vollrath, it felt as if only a short time had ticked by since thousands of lives were literally swept away, frozen to death. When he rowed away from the *Wilhelm Gustloff*, Vollrath glimpsed a gigantic hole in the *Gustloff*'s foredeck, the size of which had nearly eviscerated the boat. The hole was just below where the drained swimming pool had sheltered the Women's Naval Auxiliary. "In one hour this inferno had lasted and dragged love, hopes, and wishes down to the bottom of the sea. What is one hour, 60 minutes, 3,600 seconds? Sometimes it may appear to be [an] eternity and I am sure no one will ever forget this," Vollrath wrote in his postwar memoir.

He remembered the ship's siren screaming as the *Gustloff* went down. "Landlubbers always say that ships do not have a soul. Technically this behavior is easily explained by stress, but I thought that it so very much reminded me of the last outcry of a dying animal," Vollrath said.[9]

In his memoir, Vollrath recounted how the *Löwe* worked for several hours more, picking up survivors here and there, until its captain realized nothing more could be done. It was time for the *Löwe* to return to lifeboat No. 6. The beacon from Vollrath's flashlight helped guide the torpedo boat back into position.

That night the *Löwe* saved more than 400 people. Vollrath wondered how many others might have lived had their lifejackets been supplied with flashlights. The survivors in lifeboat No. 6 scrambled over the side of the lifeboat and onto the torpedo boat, which was fairly low in the water. Only then did Vollrath notice a crippled old man, unable to move, lying in the boat. Vollrath reached for him and helped carry him aboard the *Löwe*.

Once the survivors were safely on board the *Löwe*, the crew worked furiously to warm them. They cut away nearly frozen clothing from men and women and hosed their frigid bodies with warm water. Then they tucked the survivors into bunks in twos and threes. Hot drinks were served and blankets handed out. Members of the ship's crew gave their clothes to the survivors.

After he had boarded the *Löwe* and changed into warm, dry clothing, a woman approached Vollrath. She told him that she and the others from the lifeboat had been angry that he had repeatedly turned away the *Löwe* to rescue others. Now she wanted Vollrath to know she understood his decision, and that he had been right after all.

The *Löwe* also plucked Horst Woit from his lifeboat. He doesn't remember his mother pushing him up and over the side, or her telling him it would be okay, that they were now safe. He doesn't remember any motherly words of consolation or assurances. One minute he sat next to her and 68 other people, and the next minute strong arms lifted him through the air. Being carried up from a lifeboat to a rescue boat didn't guarantee safety. Some people slipped through rescuers' arms into the sea and drowned; others died minutes after being pulled from the water. Horst Woit was lucky.

On board, an officer guided the young boy to the engine room. The room radiated heat. The officer helped Horst out of his frozen ski pants, jacket, and socks and into dry, if slightly large, clothes. He gave Horst something hot to drink. The officer asked Horst if he would like a marmalade sandwich.

"Yes, of course," Horst remembered answering, "with butter too please."[10]

Though alone, Horst said he didn't feel frightened but he was anxious to find his mother. So much had happened so quickly, he hadn't much time to think, but now he began to wonder where the crew had taken his mother. Meta Woit had been pulled aboard the *Löwe* a little after Horst; it took time to transfer all 70 people inside the lifeboat. When Meta boarded the *Löwe,* sailors offered her a change of clothing and something hot to eat and drink. Then she searched for Horst. It was a story she often told Horst in the years after the sinking.

"Have you seen my son?" she asked every crewmember, every passenger. No one answered the wild-eyed mother because no one knew the answer. There were so many people, so many families split apart in the confusion of the sinking and rescue operation. An officer pointed Meta toward a scratchy-looking woolen blanket piled at the bow. Meta forced herself to peer beneath the mound. Small bodies lay tucked together in lifeless slumber. Though her little yellow-haired boy was not among them, she nearly retched at the sight. At dawn, Meta found Horst asleep in a bunk, wedged between the wall and an elderly man.

Others weren't so fortunate. Children, mothers, fathers were stacked like cordwood on the boat's decks. There weren't enough rough wool blankets to drape all the corpses.

Around 5:30 A.M. on January 31, a small patrol boat, the VP–1703, spotted a dark shape bobbing on the waves. At first the sailors couldn't figure out whether it was debris or bodies. It was a lifeboat, but its passengers appeared dead, all of them twisted and frozen, floating inside the water-filled craft. Nonetheless, Petty Officer Werner Fick jumped in to inspect. To his astonishment he found an infant wrapped in a woolen blanket snug between frozen corpses. He was the last official survivor of the *Wilhelm Gustloff.* Fick and his wife adopted the baby.[11]

Rose Rezas thinks she was rescued around 4 A.M., but since she had no watch she couldn't be certain.[12] Inside her lifeboat, which was only half full, one little boy kept yelling over and over for everyone to stay strong, to not give up hope. Finally, after what seemed an interminably long time, a ship appeared. The crew threw over a rope and the refugees ascended to safety one at a time. Rose promptly passed out upon hitting the deck. She woke to find herself wearing men's clothes. A sailor handed her a whiskey to drink. With each sip her anguish grew. Where was her sister Ursula? Feeling quite worried, Rose almost didn't notice the officer standing before her.

"There's a girl who looks like you in the next cabin," the sober-looking officer said. Rose timidly got to her feet and followed him, cautiously hopeful. She passed through the door, her eyes searching. Leaning against a wall, Ursula sat eating.

Nearly 70 years later, Irene Tschinkur, who was 11 at the time, doesn't remember the moment her body hit the sea. She doesn't remember feeling a slap as the waves rushed to meet her. She does remember feeling afraid she would drown. While submerged beneath the icy surf, she felt her lungs might pop. She doesn't remember seeing bodies or debris. But those memories pale in comparison to the moment she and her mother, Serafima, found each other in the dark water and swam together toward a lifeboat packed with people. They tried to hang on to the outside of the little vessel. Their exertion was in vain; the people inside boat smacked at their hands with oars. Irene and Serafima treaded water. When Irene remembers it today, it seems that they waited for hours in the water. Naturally, there was no way to tell how long they were in the water until the *T-36* picked them up.

"The German navy men were so helpful, stripped our wet clothes from us, and put us in hammocks with warm blankets," Irene said, remembering how she studied the beads of condensation on the ceiling as she lay in the hammock. Getting out of her wet, frozen clothes was relief and torture, the sudden warmth painful. After more than six decades, certain sights and sounds can still pull Irene back in time.

"We watched somebody operate on a woman's leg which showed a big hole, and most of the night we kept throwing up seawater," Irene said.

Irene and her mother still had no inkling if little Ellen had survived. The thought that she too had died twisted the mother's gut since she was fairly certain that Evi, or Evchen as she was also called, had drowned. So mother and daughter thawed and sipped hot liquids, and if they talked, Irene doesn't remember what they said.[13] They simply waited in limbo together with the hundreds of other refugees aboard the boat. So many were waiting for news of loved ones.

The pair spent the night on the *T-36*, and the next morning the ship arrived at Sassnitz, a seaside port on the Isle of Ruegen, just off the coast of present day Stralsund, Germany. The Red Cross had set up a makeshift camp with the German authorities to help sort out the survivors. The sailors had given them their clothes but had no shoes to provide. They tramped barefoot through the snow to the camp.

Hitler had envisioned using the 30-mile-long island of Ruegen with its deep bays and narrow straits to build a British-style beach resort. He wanted the Baltic Sea island to be the largest resort ever to have existed, with room for up to 20,000 people at a time in a 2.5-mile-long complex. The hotel Prora, situated between Sassnitz and Binz, was built between 1936 and 1939. Like the KdF cruise liners with which the *Wilhelm Gustloff* had once sailed, the hotel too would offer affordable vacations for the average German worker. It was called a "Seaside Resort for the Common Man." Each room boasted two beds, a wardrobe, and sink; guests would have used communal toilets, showers, and ballrooms located on each floor. In spite of Hitler's ambitious plans, no guests ever checked into the hotel, for when Germany invaded Poland, the idea and the buildings were abandoned. Today the island is a popular tourist destination and can be reached by ferry or car over a causeway.

German authorities processed the refugees, recording their names and where they wanted to go. Like many survivors, Serafima and Irene Tschinkur were assigned to a Red Cross ship. Once on board they found a place to sit. They still didn't know Ellen's fate. No one on the island remembered seeing the child, but then again many children and parents had become separated. The mother was heartsick. If her little daughter hadn't made it into a lifeboat, she was dead. She told Irene to wait while she looked for their clothes, which supposedly had been transferred from the *T-36* to this Red Cross ship. Suddenly, a cry of joy pealed through the boat. Serafima had found Ellen's little red wool cable-knit sweater in the survivors' clothing pile. After survivors had been pulled from the sea and given dry garments, rescuers had gathered up the sodden clothes. The Red Cross had taken the clothing, hoping to match the garments with their owners. Surely, she thought, this little hand-knit sweater was proof of life. She scooped it into her arms and tore through the ship, going from room to room until she came upon a room full of crying children who had lost their mothers. There sat Ellen, quiet and bewildered. She did not speak one word.

A lifeboat had rescued the six-year-old. When the *T-36* came on the scene and began transferring people from the lifeboat, it was clear the blond-haired girl was too small to climb the rope ladder on her own. Instead, she was transferred aboard in a sling seat. Just before Ellen's turn came to ride the sling, she watched a lady in a rescue chair. The lady was pulled up, but her frozen hands were unable to firmly grasp the ropes. She slipped and fell, hitting her head on the lifeboat. She sank.

The terror of falling into the water and being submerged remains with Ellen Tschinkur to this day. She has trouble talking about her rescue. She still cannot wash her hair under the shower since standing under the faucet reminds her too much of being submerged under the sea. So few children Ellen's age were rescued. Her white fur coat helped save her life; it shone like a beacon in the dark.

Milda Bendrich couldn't believe her 2-year-old Inge made nary a peep the entire time, from the moment the first torpedo slammed into the *Wilhelm Gustloff* until they were rescued aboard the *T-36*. Like survivors in the other lifeboats, Milda too climbed a ladder from her lifeboat to the safety of the *T-36* deck. Her hands were frozen but she maintained her white-knuckled grip on her baby girl. Once on board, Milda tried to warm Inge. "A woman with a fur coat put me inside and kept me warm," Inge Bendrich Roedecker said.[14] Together, the lady and Milda made sure Inge was warm, safe, and unscathed. Medical personnel took Inge in another cabin for further examination. Only then did Milda tend to her own basic needs. She changed into dry clothing before sitting down on a hard chair.

"I spent this night sitting on a chair. Around me were women, each one engrossed with her own fate. As if in a fog, I heard a woman in another room screaming hysterically. Somebody explained that this woman had to leave her three children on the W.G.," Bendrich wrote in her letter. "I must have suffered from shock as from the first moment I had felt no fear and instinctively knew that I would not give up."

Milda and Inge were reunited the next morning. A doctor assured the young mother that he had examined the baby girl and that she was well. The baby slept peacefully through the night.

Wilhelmina Reitsch, who supervised the evacuation of the Women's Naval Auxiliary, had remained in Gotenhafen until the end of March when the port was under fire and she left on a fishing boat.[15] She had decided to put the auxiliary women on the ships because the few trains available were deemed unsafe and there were no other options. Even when she heard about the *Gustloff*'s fate, she continued putting her officers and sailors on board ships. However, just about a day after the sinking, she faced a grim task. The recovered dead auxiliaries found in lifeboats or floating in the waters around the *Gustloff* were taken to Gotenhafen. There she and other auxiliary leaders identified them whenever possible. Reitsch received the Iron Cross in recognition of her service. Because the catastrophe happened on January 30 in very cold temperatures and because they knew them, Reitsch and her staff were able to identify the young women on sight. Most casualties of the army, Luftwaffe, and other refugees were not identified. Unidentified bodies were buried in the seaside city of Gotenhafen. Irene and Ellen Tschinkur believe their cousin Evi was buried in a mass grave with the other dead.

Once Helga Reuter reached Sassnitz, she tried to find Inge. "I went to the Red Cross to look for my sister. Maybe find information from the camp. The last I saw of her she was in the water," Helga said. Although Helga asked and searched, she held out little hope that Inge lived. The water had been too cold, the wait for help too long. Besides, she couldn't deny that last vision of Inge floating away like a frozen lily pad.

Helga realized it was time to plan. She wouldn't return to Königsberg. That left her with only one option, to continue her journey to Berlin. The Soviets were still coming on one side, the Americans and British on the other. Other survivors in similar situations joined together. Helga decided it would be safer to travel with someone else. So Helga paired off with a lady who had sat and rested next to her on the rescue boat. The lady hoped to reach

Dresden. Helga can't remember the woman's name, but her face lights up when she speaks of her these many years later.

"She had lost her oldest son in Königsberg and her youngest slipped out of her arms on the *Gustloff*. Now she had to write to her husband who was in army and tell him. She asked me to come with her. I said 'I have no shoes.' The lady said 'I have no coat.' We left together after a nurse scrounged up a coat for the lady and shoes for me," Helga said.

Together the mother without a child and the sister without a sibling walked to an airfield. It took them nearly two hours. Helga's legs felt numb. Finally, they arrived in Dresden. Almost two weeks later, Helga decided to continue on the road to Berlin. She was so appreciative of the woman's graciousness but now it was time to leave.

What should have been a two- or three-hour trip took eight hours. At one point the train stopped in its track in the middle of the forest. Helga peered out the window. She saw a phantasmagoric outline of trees and little else. The train shook up, down, and from side to side. The Allies were firebombing the baroque city of Dresden, best known for its delicate porcelain dolls. In four raids in mid-February 1945, British and American planes participated in the firebombing of Dresden in support of the Red Army's drive on that city.[16]

Eva Dorn isn't sure how long she floated in the lifeboat before the *T-36* under the command of Captain Hering came alongside. Sailors from the torpedo boat started pulling *Gustloff* survivors up from the lifeboat. Eva was the last one in the lifeboat when the *T-36* crew received a warning that enemy submarines were in the area. It was going to leave, even though Eva remained. "Throw me something," Eva yelled. Down came a seaman's chair. Shaped like a triangle, it's what sailors sat on while cleaning or painting the side of a ship. She had to jump over the water to catch the chair and she worried she'd miss. A dead woman floated in the water. With every wave her head banged against the side of the *T-36*, her hair undulated like seaweed. Eva held her breath and jumped. She caught the chair and was pulled up. Eva Dorn became the last of the 564 survivors pulled aboard the *T-36*.

The sailors ushered her down iron steps to the engine room, the warmest part on the ship. She undressed and put her clothes on a machine to dry. The room was crowded with survivors and smelled of wet clothes.

Hours later the *T-36* reached Sassnitz where the Red Cross was busy helping sort out the survivors; because Eva was a member of the Women's Naval Auxiliary, she was directed to a military barracks on the island. She spent the night there in a room with 14 other young women. In the morning Eva went to the laundry and washed her seawater and vomit-encrusted uniform. She received a four-week leave of absence and decided to go home to Halle (Saale). Her mother, Aliza, opened the door. She thought Eva had returned because she'd received the cable about her sister-in-law dying in childbirth. No, Eva told her mother, she hadn't heard. Rather, she was on leave. She sat next to her mother on the sofa. She told her the story of the *Wilhelm Gustloff.* "My mother looked at me and said, 'How terrible, but couldn't you have saved at least one suitcase?' She just didn't get it," Eva said.[17]

Finally, Serafima Tschinkur understood that her niece, 13-year-old Evi, had not survived the torpedo attack and had drowned in the icy sea. Neither Ellen nor Irene remembers talking about their despair at the time. After a day or so at the Sassnitz camp, the three Tschinkurs were taken to the mainland where they received train passes from the German authorities. They were lodged in a home for a couple of days and were given clothes to wear. "For many years we kept a handmade lavender-and-white triangle shawl until it fell apart in Canada. That's all we had to remember from the Isle of Ruegen," Irene said.

Serafima decided to travel to Poznan, a risk since the Russians were headed there; however, she needed to find Evi's mother, her sister. Their train passes allowed them to sit in a compartment normally reserved for officers. So the three sat, not talking very much, when two officers entered the cabin. Ellen still remembers the high sheen of their boots and just how clean they looked. The pair sat facing the Tschinkurs. Ever so meticulously the two peeled opened wax paper bags. Inside were neatly cut sandwiches.

"We just looked at those sandwiches. We couldn't turn our eyes away from them," Ellen said.

Before taking their first bites, the officers motioned for the conductor. Clearly agitated, the two demanded to know, "What are these persons doing in our car?" The conductor explained the family had just survived a torpedo attack. That quieted the officers but didn't make them generous. They ate slowly, methodically chewing every morsel.

Once in Poznan the three Tschinkurs went directly to their Aunt Irene's house.

"The worst part of all of this was not the shipwreck. It was when they got to my Aunt Irene's house," Irene said. "When she opened the door, she held my face in her hands. 'Evi?' My mother gently pushed me aside. She had to tell her Evi died." Their Aunt Irene quaked with grief.

Nearly seven decades later, Irene and Ellen sit together in Irene's home. An advent candle, much like the one they lit when they were children, sits on the table covered with a cream-colored hand-crocheted cloth. Irene tells how she publishes Evi's picture in the local newspaper every five years. It's just a reminder, she said, a simple, but important way to memorialize her.

Irene pushes back her chair and takes a framed picture off the wall. Under the glass is the two-page letter their mother wrote to a friend after the war. The yellow lined paper is an unexpected gift; they only recently discovered its existence. Irene and her sister Ellen now know how their mother remembered those first moments after they literally fell off the *Wilhelm Gustloff.*

"After a long search I found Ellen two days after the catastrophe in Sassnitz, nobody could give me any news about Evchen. We were not allowed to stay in Sassnitz and had to move on. Without clothes (even the clothes we wore disappeared while "drying"), in torn clothes, without food, no food stamps and without . . . bread I went with my 2 children to Harz where Oma and Reny [Aunt Irene] were. That is how I got to Gandersheim. Now, dear Otti, you can imagine my situation, how could I tell Reny that I did not know where Evchen was. At this moment I wondered, why Evchen? It would have been better if one of my children had gone missing," Serafima wrote.

Ellen speaks. She looks around, her eyes settling on one of the many black and white photographs covering the table. She looks at the photo of Evi, in which her light hair is pulled back in a braid, her face tilted away—a happy, serene look on Evi's face.

"How do you tell parents you lost their child? I just felt so guilty," Ellen said, adding that their Aunt Irene died of tuberculosis soon afterward. "Truthfully? We never talked about it. We never talked about. Why did the three of us survive? It's not fair. But then I ask, how could three members of a family survive it at all? It boggles my mind."

Ten

THE FORGOTTEN STORY

For nearly 70 years the survivors of the *Wilhelm Gustloff* have lived in a world where most people are ignorant of the tragedy they endured. Upward of 9,000 people died in this event, making it the worst maritime disaster in history. By contrast 1,517 died when the RMS *Titanic* sank on its maiden voyage in April 1912, and 1,198 people died when the *Lusitania* sank in World War One.

In his report on the sinking, Admiral Karl Dönitz highlighted the situation in the Baltic Sea as the main reason for the disaster. He said the lack of German aerial reconnaissance and the need for the German navy to concentrate on securing refugee convoys rather than hunt for enemy submarines enabled the Russian submarines to "go about undisturbed in the Baltic Sea."[1] Even so, Dönitz stressed that Operation Hannibal saved the lives of nearly 2 million people. Yet, the operation and the sinking remain one of the lesser-known events of World War Two.

The reasons why this story has remained unfamiliar are varied and complicated. There were no celebrities or tycoons aboard the *Wilhelm Gustloff,* and the German media controlled everything about the ship's departure and sinking. These two factors helped the catastrophe become a non-event from that perspective. Furthermore, that a Soviet submarine operating in present-day Polish territorial waters sank a German ship was not something the West was especially concerned about in the war's immediate aftermath. Cold War politics took precedence.

While it is now estimated that fewer than 1,000 people survived Captain Alexander Marinesko's swift torpedo strike, there can never be a precise count of either the survivors or the dead since no exact record of passengers exists.[2] This is often the case with World War Two events in which figures might be expected but the tragedies are so often measured in estimated numbers.

The survivors had lost not only their belongings but their documents too. Very few survivors had papers and precious objects, such as the photos Helga Reuter had in her trousers or the pocketknife Horst Woit had hidden in his ski pants. The priority for the survivors was to connect with family and figure out where to go. Meanwhile, German authorities handled the sinking with their customary clinical precision; they recorded the names of survivors, processed surviving sailors and Women's Naval Auxiliary, and buried the dead in communal graves in Gotenhafen. They also made sure not to allow news of the sinking to spread.

On February 21, 1945, 22 days after the S-13 attacked and sank the *Wilhelm Gustloff,* the Swedish newspaper *Afton Bladet* published an article about the tragedy. The event received scant attention in the American press. The *New York Times* published a brief mention: "The Finnish radio reported tonight the sinking of the 25,000-ton German liner *Wilhelm Gustloff.* . . . The *Wilhelm Gustloff,* a passenger liner before the war, had been converted into a troop transport."[3] The event wouldn't be mentioned again until 1955, when a news brief in the *New York Times* marked the tenth anniversary of the sinking, calling it "the greatest single toll on the European seas during World War Two."[4]

Likewise, Soviet newspapers didn't mention the attack. Of course, not one word of the sinking appeared in German newspapers since the Third Reich buried the news. In its final death throes, Nazi Germany would not permit such clear evidence of its defeat to be publicized. The *Gustloff* had shone as the crown jewel of the KdF fleet. The *S-13*'s sinking of the ship delivered an irreparable blow to the Third Reich. It was a death knell for Hitler's grand scheme. A strategic success for the Soviet Union, Alexander Marinesko's attack had destroyed a Nazi symbol.

An Allied propaganda newspaper in German, dropped over German territory by Allied planes, did publish a full-page article headlined "*Wilhelm Gustloff*, Catastrophe," on February 19, 1945.[5] The article related how the former KdF liner turned refugee ship was attacked:

Eastern fugitives and armed forces members were onboard when the ship ran out of Gotenhafen. . . . The *Wilhelm Gustloff* left nevertheless on the evening of January 30th with the perfectly insufficient security of an outpost boat and two R boats. All decks of the *Wilhelm Gustloff* so were stuffed that no person was able to move. . . . Many passengers who were hurled into the sea in the capsizing of the ship hardened in the icy water before aid could be brought them. Survivors report of the frightening scenes that happened after the explosion on board the ship. . . . Women and children were involved in the embittered battle that ensued around the few lifeboats; women and children were knocked ruthlessly overboard.[6]

Still, after these early and brief accounts, the postwar literature veered away from anything having to do with East Prussia, the eastern front, and the fate of German civilians. Few knew, for example, that Royal Air Force bombs and Soviet ground troops nearly destroyed historic Königsberg. In the aftermath of the war, few knew about KZ Stutthof, the first German extermination camp in East Prussia, where more than 85,000 Jewish and non-Jewish inmates perished. Few knew of the *Steuben,* another KdF boat that sank with more than 4,000 people on board after Marinesko's sub attacked it too. The *Steuben* was a hospital ship but its markings were not visible in the dark night with foul weather. Indeed, few knew of the many other boats, large and small, that were sunk. Marinesko and the *S-13* were ultimately responsible for about 14,000 deaths at sea.

Nearly 70 years ago, on January 31, 1945, Admiral Karl Dönitz conferred with Adolf Hitler during a meeting with naval leadership. The sinking of the *Wilhelm Gustloff* merited an ever-so-brief mention. Rear Admiral Conrad Englehardt had heard the news first and immediately informed his superior, Dönitz.

Thus, when Admiral Karl Dönitz heard of the sinking, he reacted pragmatically. Operation Hannibal was in its first phase. Hundreds of thousands of more refugees needed to cross the Baltic Sea. Dwelling on the catastrophe would serve no one.

"In connection with the sinking of the passenger steamer *Wilhelm Gustloff* by submarine torpedoes on the outer route north of Stolpe Bank, the Commander-in-Chief, Navy, declares that with the extensive transports in the Baltic Sea, it was realized from the start that there would be losses. Painful though these losses were, they represented only 1 percent of the total brought out by sea; 99 percent succeeded in arriving safely at ports on the western Baltic," Dönitz said in a meeting with key aides. "On the other hand, the percentage of refugees lost on the overland route was very much higher."[7]

Dönitz stressed that Soviet submarines continued to operate undisturbed throughout the Baltic Sea only because there were no German aircraft overhead ready to strike. Moreover, Dönitz said, the only practical defense against submarines is the radar-equipped aircraft, "the same weapon which enabled the enemy to paralyze our own submarine warfare."[8]

Admiral Dönitz remarked that even had a U-boat escorted the *Wilhelm Gustloff* on her bold dash across the sea, it's not likely that would have prevented the *S-13*'s assault. Still, they decided to make sure more escorts attended future transports across the sea. If nothing else, a more pronounced presence would give an appearance of safety and reassure the hundreds of thousands of people still awaiting evacuation under Operation Hannibal.

Earlier in the war, U-boats had escorted Germany auxiliary cruisers, blockade-runners, and supply ships as they left and entered harbors. But U-boats stood very little "chance of being able to protect its charge if it were attacked and would be quite powerless to help if it were sunk by the enemy. Such enemy attacks would, of course, be delivered either from the air or by long-range gunfire from an enemy warship, and it would take good care to keep well beyond the range of the U-boats, which it would [be presumed were] escorting the surface vessel; accordingly having sunk the ship, it would still keep its distance and then disappear."[9]

In spite of the small attention paid to the sinking during Admiral Karl Dönitz's meeting with Hitler, Captain Wilhelm Zahn was called before a board of inquiry five days after the sinking. He told the board that his orders included supervising the rescue equipment and signaling, as well as counseling the ship's leadership in all military matters. However, Zahn said, he never received an order to take command over the civilian leadership, namely Captain Friedrich Petersen. "It is naturally difficult without a higher order to give a 63-year-old captain with 50 years of experience an order without the authority to do so," Zahn said.[10] "In this particular case all of my suggestions were deemed unfeasible." Zahn told the board that he was given no orders to zigzag, no indication that such a defensive maneuver was even necessary.

Although his superiors didn't discipline Zahn, his naval career essentially ended when the boat went down.

In the first decade or so after the war, those directly involved in Operation Hannibal and the *Gustloff* rescue efforts exchanged correspondence. Admiral Robert Hering of the *T-36* exchanged some letters with Admiral Conrad Englehardt, who had served under Admiral Dönitz.

"All in all we can say there were many mistakes in the leadership of the *Gustloff*. However, whether the submarine would have been successful without those mistakes no one can say," wrote Admiral Conrad Englehardt. "At least one has to ask why the ship's leadership did not go high speed or zigzag. It's easy to talk about that today. This much is for sure, dear Mr. Hering—that you and your boat did all that was humanly possible to save as many people as you could given the bad weather."[11]

Heinz Schön, who was a 19-year-old assistant purser aboard the *Wilhelm Gustloff,* spent decades trying to piece together what happened on January 30, 1945. The German archives in Bayreuth, Germany, hold his correspondence with Englehardt, Hering, and others. Credit is due to Schön who worked to gather the names of those who perished and those who survived. The event troubled him always, and he made it his mission to try and confirm details and figure out who was responsible for the catastrophe. Schön repeatedly wrote to Englehardt, explaining that his memory of the incident compelled him to pursue the story. In a November 17, 1965, letter to Captain Robert Hering, who had commanded the *Admiral Hipper,* Englehardt said Schön was so far the only surviving crewmember of the *Gustloff* who had agreed to help piece together the events of January 30. Englehardt also said that understanding needed to be extended to Schön since he had suffered as a result of the tragedy.[12]

These early efforts to construct a narrative were important, particularly because much of the papers and documentation regarding Operation Hannibal and the *Wilhelm Gustloff* were lost when the Russians advanced and subsequently occupied former East Prussia. The Soviet navy sank 206 of 790 ships used to evacuate refugees during those last weeks of the war.[13]

World War Two not only wiped away whole villages and populations. It also wiped away pieces of history. The German Red Cross records were lost. Their headquarters, which used to be in Babelsberg near Potsdam, were largely destroyed in the Soviet advance on Berlin; later, the Russians collected and destroyed most of the remaining records.[14] In addition, the German Red Cross never had a central archive for its records; instead, the Red Cross societies operated independently in Germany, including in Prussia, Wurtemberg, Bavaria, and Baden.

The *Wilhelm Gustloff* now lies on the sandy bottom of the Baltic Sea. Almost six times as many men, women, and children perished in this attack than in the April 15, 1912 sinking of the *Titanic*. Yet, until recently the enormity of the *Gustloff*'s story was too awful to deal with for many of the survivors. For many, the tragedy lasted beyond the sinking. They had difficulty trying to create a life afterward. For many, coming to terms with January 30, 1945 required coming to terms with what it meant to come of age in Nazi Germany.

In the first decades after the sinking, cold war politics, debates about German war guilt, victimhood, and justifiable military targets all conspired to push the story to the sidelines. Initially, when Nazi Germany invaded Poland on September 1, 1939, the idea of collectively blaming all Germans wasn't considered. It wasn't until years later, after the full scale of the war's atrocities were revealed, that this attitude emerged and the distinction between Nazis and non-Nazis in Germany blurred.[15] Ignored was the idea that Germany, the nation responsible for unleashing an inferno of violence across the European continent, had also been the recipient of considerable violence: Allied strategic bombing campaigns, evacuations from cities, towns and villages, the westward flight of East Prussians and others trying to escape the Soviets, and the postwar expulsion of millions of Germans.

A few divers have visited the *Wilhelm Gustloff*'s final resting place off the Polish coast. Between the late 1960s and 1970s, the Soviet Union worked over the shipwreck site and, according to the divers, they seemed to have paid particular attention to the ship's midsection, which would have housed much of the ship's inner machinery and cargo.

In 2004 Mike Boring, a diver with decades of experience on various shipwrecks, obtained a permit from the Polish government to dive the *Gustloff*. A mass of twisted and broken metal waited on the sea floor; there was evidence of explosions and cutting saws. Boring described his dive as incredibly emotional and interesting. The low oxygen and cold waters of the Baltic Sea have preserved hundreds of shipwrecks resting on the bottom, the oldest dating back to the 1300s.[16] This environment left the *Gustloff*'s stern and the bow very much intact, Boring said. The teak of the deck and the wooden cap of the handrail were also well preserved. However, the midsection looked as if it had suffered from damage unrelated to the 1945 torpedo attack. Normally when a wreck sinks intact, as the *Gustloff* more or less did, it collapses from the pressure of the sea. The ship's bow, which absorbed the first two torpedo hits, showed a significant amount of damage. Yet, several signs one would expect to see on a wreck weren't there, he said. For one, there is a dearth of personal effects. The nature of the Baltic Sea, its temperatures and oxygen, make it ideal for preserving evidence of the dead, but there was no evidence of the thousands of passengers. There were no bones. For some reason the wreck was stripped of all association with humanity.[17] As far as cargo, the *Wilhelm Gustloff* was primarily carrying people, not possessions. For the most part, whatever belongings were on board had little monetary value; refugees mostly brought aboard clothes and other necessities such as identification papers, easily disintegrated over 50 years in the water. Certainly, aside from salvaging metal in the engine and mechanical rooms, the ship didn't carry the types of cargo that invited the kind of salvage operation that appears to have occurred.[18]

The absence of objects has invited speculation that the *Wilhelm Gustloff* carried more than desperate refugees and soldiers and sailors. There are theories that the Amber Room, which was a chamber in the Catherine Palace in Russia paneled in amber, or pieces of special rockets were secured in the ship's hold. King Friedrich Wilhelm I of Prussia had given the Amber Room, a study in Baroque excess, to Tsar Peter the Great in 1716. The lavish gesture honored the friendship between the two nations. Germans moved the room from the Winter Palace in St. Petersburg to Catherine the Great's summer palace on the outskirts of the city. When Germany invaded the Soviet Union in 1941, soldiers from the Wehrmacht took down the amber paneling and sent it to Königsberg. Soldiers packed the panels into more than 70 wooden crates and drove them to a mysterious location. Erich Koch, the gauleiter of East Prussia, maintained that the Germans had stored the amber paneling in a castle to avoid damage from Allied air raids.

Koch escaped East Prussia in April 23, 1945, aboard an icebreaker from Pillau. His flight was interrupted when the British caught him on the Island of Ruegen. The Soviets wanted to try him; instead, the British handed him over to Polish authorities. Koch stood trial in 1958 in Poland for killing 400,000 Polish citizens. He was sentenced to death for planning, preparing, and organizing the mass murder of civilians. The authorities commuted his sentence to life imprisonment due to ill health, however, some insisted the commutation was because the Soviets thought Erich Koch knew where looted art, in particular the Amber Room that once graced the Catherine Palace in St. Petersburg, was stashed.

The original panels remain missing; however, reproductions are now on view in St. Petersburg.

After the war ended, the Russians believed the *Wilhelm Gustloff* carried some of the priceless objets d'art and the panels of the wondrous room aboard.[19] They sent multiple dive teams to search the former KdF liner as well as other refugee ships that were sunk during the war. Historians say the panels, intricately inlaid amber with gold leaf and mirrors, were likely buried in Austrian or Czech mine shafts, which may very well have been dynamited and destroyed during the German retreat from the Soviet army. Until the 1950s, Russia banned Poland from diving to the wreck except under strict Soviet supervision.

Another reason for the repeated postwar dives was that some in Soviet military circles believed the *Wilhelm Gustloff* carried secret, improved military weapons and equipment in addition to the refugees. Rumors persisted that the ship was carrying parts of newly developed U-boats with batteries that enabled them to remain below the sea longer and move undetected by radar. These boats had completely isolated motor housings and were electricity-driven; they could travel up to 15 knots (17.3 miles) per hour under water and up to 23 knots (27 miles) per hour on the surface.[20] Indeed, the German navy had developed and manufactured more than 100 new U-boats in the second part of the war. The US Office of Strategic Services noted in January 1945 that the "new-type of German U-boats have their training stations in the Baltic and training is going on at full speed. The U-boats will shortly be removed to Bergen via Storebaelt and Oersund."[21] It was also rumored that the Germans had developed rockets capable of shooting shells from German territory across the English Channel that could reach all the way to London. The submariners being transported aboard the *Gustloff* were supposed to sail these new U-boats.

A July 1958 article headlined "6000 Victims" in the American magazine *Battle Cry* argued that Adolf Hitler ordered his own navy to purposely sink the *Wilhelm Gustloff*. The article, which was loose with facts, claims Hitler wanted to halt Operation Hannibal to show East Prussian refugees that the Baltic Sea evacuation route was too dangerous.[22] If his dastardly ruse succeeded, the article said, Hitler would then have used the refugees, men and women alike, to stand their ground in Gotenhafen and fight the Red Army. This article's unsubstantiated thesis ran counter to the evidence that Admiral Karl Dönitz and Rear Admiral Konrad Englehardt wanted to and did orchestrate the evacuation of 2 million refugees.

The silence that enveloped the world's greatest maritime disaster lasted well after the war ended. In the case of the *Wilhelm Gustloff,* some survivors kept silent because they felt complicit; they were German, or had German ancestry. This group felt culpable for Nazi Germany's crimes against the Polish and Russian peoples, the Jews and the Gypsies, and every other group targeted throughout Adolf Hitler's regime.[23] They were afraid to talk, cowed by the idea that though they had suffered, they hadn't suffered the same way as others. Some felt guilty about their decision to bring their family on board or their inability to save those they were responsible for. All these survivors experienced survivor's guilt. The German leadership also imposed silence on the survivors in the months and years following the sinking. Hitler Youth warned survivors not to speak of the *Wilhelm Gustloff*. Inge Bendrich said her mother was threatened with dire consequences if they uttered one word about the sinking. To the Allies, Nazi Germany was the enemy. In the war's aftermath, there was no room to consider that German civilians suffered.[24] A conspiracy of silence attached itself to the events of January 30, 1945, like barnacles to the sunken ship.

The Soviet Union had its own motives for suppressing the story. During the cold war, as the Soviet Union supplanted the Third Reich in its control of civilian populations, it shuttered access to free information. Those East Prussian and Baltic German refugees who faced another brutal regime quickly discovered they weren't able to talk about the war without reservation. To question the events surrounding the *Gustloff* and its sinking could have sparked questions of why those civilians felt a visceral need to flee the oncoming Red Army, an army that liberated people from Adolf Hitler and his Nazi Party. It could also have the unintended, but dangerous, consequence of spotlighting Soviet brutality and Josef Stalin's policies of mass deportations and suppression. Clearly this was intolerable to the repressive regime. Along this line, there was no mention of the Holocaust in the Soviet Union, in spite of the fact that the Soviet forces liberated camps such as Majdanke, Auschwitz-Birkenau, and Stutthof. Again, talk of this might invite talk of the Soviets' own atrocities, such as the Katyn Forest massacre near Smolensk, where an estimated 22,000 Polish officers, customs officials, and intelligentsia were taken into the woods and shot in the back of the head.[25] The NKVD, the Soviet secret police, dumped the bodies into mass graves and blamed the atrocity on the Germans in order to garner sympathy from the west. The truth did not surface until after the war.

In time, German war guilt accomplished what government censorship could not. In the same way that survivors of the Dresden firebombing had difficulty finding an audience receptive to listening to and learning about their ordeal, so too did survivors of the *Wilhelm Gustloff*. According to Gertrud Baer, the postwar political climate in Germany dissuaded overt expression of mourning for the nation's "4 million fallen soldiers, the 12 million civilians expelled or fleeing from Eastern Europe . . . or the 600,000 others killed by Allied air raids."[26] Mourning was seen as tantamount to clinging to an immoral and evil past.

Some survivors thought discussing the sinking would be self-pitying and laid claim to an innocence that they felt they didn't own. Few spoke about the Russian invasion and horrors associated with those times. Others worried that talking about their ordeal would put them in the same category as the German far right, which wanted compensation and revenge. And some felt the destruction of the ship was payment for hubris, for their country's quest to dominate the world.[27]

"The reason of man, like man himself, is timid and cautious, when left alone; and acquires firmness and confidence, in proportion to the number of which it is associated," President John Adams once said.[28] Adams's quote applies to those who survived the *Wilhelm Gustloff*. It has only been possible for many to begin speaking out in recent years because their social circles and the process of reaching out to one another have allowed it. There were simply more Germans and more Soviets who kept those who had been on board the *Gustloff* from speaking out. As the great ideological wall bifurcated Europe and the cold war froze into place, the fate of a boatload of German civilians and military refugees had little importance.

In the minds of many people after World War Two, Germany and the Nazis were one and the same. In the United States, knowledge of what happened was boiled down to one narrative starting with the Japanese attack on Pearl Harbor on December 7, 1941, followed by D-Day on June 6, 1944, V-E Day on May 8, 1945, and V-J Day on August 8, 1945. In between were the stories of the Holocaust, the Bataan Death March, hard-fought naval battles and island-to-island combat in the Pacific, and dropping the first atom bomb on Hiroshima. It wasn't fashionable to talk about humanity as it related to German civilians. Until recent times. Today in Germany many more know about the *Wilhelm Gustloff* tragedy. With that increased attention and focus comes the realization that the story of World War Two is full of difficult truths.

Eleven

"WE HAD TO GET OVER IT"

Some *Wilhelm Gustloff* survivors, like Ellen Tschinkur, kept closemouthed about the incident for decades because they worried that telling their story would isolate them from their peers and coworkers.

The shipwreck survivors were trying to assimilate in their newly adopted nations; they simply didn't want to do anything that might further set them apart. Also, their experiences were so singular, they felt those around them couldn't sympathize, whether they were survivors of other World War Two tragedies or were born after the war. The scope and scale of suffering meant there were literally millions of such stories.

"It was hard during and after the war until I came to the USA," Rose Rezas Petrus said. "You're right, most people don't understand it all and don't know that the *Wilhelm Gustloff* was the biggest maritime disaster in history."[1]

Some survivors secured visas to go west. Others wanted to return home but couldn't under the terms negotiated by the victorious powers. Albert Schweitzer, the 1954 Nobel Peace Prize laureate, spoke about how the war continued to disrupt lives long after the armies stopped fighting. "The most grievous violation of the right based on historical evolution and of any human right in general is to deprive populations of their right to occupy the country where they live by compelling them to settle elsewhere," Schweitzer said in his Oslo acceptance speech. "The fact that the victorious powers decided at the end of World War II to impose this fate on hundreds of thousands of human beings and, what is more, in a most cruel manner, shows how little they were aware of the challenge facing them, namely, to reestablish prosperity and, as far as possible, the rule of law."[2]

After the *Wilhelm Gustloff*'s sinking, those with family in the west or those who made it to the British or American zones of occupation fared better than those stuck in the Soviet zone of occupation. Perhaps as many as 16 million German civilians were forcibly relocated from lands that were returned to Poland, and from those countries overtaken by the Soviet Union between the years 1945 and 1948.[3] The dislocations were agreed upon in the summer of 1945 during the Potsdam Conference, when Britain's prime minister Winston Churchill, US president Harry S. Truman, and Russian premier Josef Stalin authorized the transfer of East Germans to the remaining territory of the Reich. Both Hitler's and Stalin's massive population swaps opened the way to the decisions of Yalta, Tehran, and then Potsdam to move East Germans.

Yet, even if they wanted to, the Tschinkurs couldn't return to their spacious apartment above the bakery. The Soviets had usurped their home and business in Riga, Latvia. In 1948 the family, then living in Nienberg, Germany, received visas to immigrate to Regina, Ontario. The Tschinkurs spent their first years after the war living in what the sisters still refer to as "DP housing." The poorly insulated, white clapboard units had outhouses in the backyard. In spite of the Spartan accommodations, the Tschinkurs were immensely grateful; they had shelter, they were living in a free nation, and they had survived. In 1950 the family of four moved from Regina to Windsor, Ontario, where there were many jobs. Ellen and Irene stayed in Windsor and the nearby town of Tecumseh, married, had children and grandchildren. The sisters' philosophy has been to move forward: "One could go bonkers if you let the past live within you," Irene said.

It was another story for Irene's and Ellen's uncle, Heiner, and cousin Bill, Evi's father and brother. In the last months of the war, the German military had conscripted Heiner and Bill into the Volkssturm. After the Germans surrendered, the Soviets arrested the father and son and put them on a cattle car bound for a Siberian prison camp. The two survived three years of forced labor in a Siberian gulag. Once released from the gulag, Heiner moved to Bavaria to live with his second wife, a woman he'd known previously. Irene and Ellen's dad, Herbert Christoph Tschinkur, had saved enough money to sponsor Bill to emigrate to Canada. The two pounded the streets of Windsor, Ontario, looking for work.

Irene and Ellen recently discovered a letter from their mother containing new information. In November 1948, Serafima had written to family friends, Otti and Felix von Lieven, to inform them of the tragedies that engulfed the family the year before. The von Lievens lived in West Germany after the war and later settled in Toronto. The sisters didn't get a hold of the letter until just a few years ago. It had turned up in an old suitcase in Paris. Irene said it was a mystery how it got there, because as far as she knows the von Lievens never lived in Paris. She believes after the von Lievens died the valise containing the letter was sent on to relatives.

My dear Otti and Felix. How happy we were to receive your letter! We have thought about you often. Thank god you're in good health and together. That is the most important thing. Finally we have lost everything. . . . We are happy to hear that you are doing well. The 4 of us are together but we have lived through a lot. First, dear Otti a sad news for you personally:

Reny died in July in the Harz and Evchen died during a "ship catastrophe." We have no news of Heiner, but we have news from Billy (not directly from him, but through a POW) that he is a POW in Russia (in the Urals). Whether he will return soon or not at all, no one knows. Poor kid, he has no idea that his mother and Evchen are no longer alive. Fate was too bitter for all of the family Krachmauer. One asks often: why? You know, Otti, that Evchen was with us in Gotenhafen.

This letter was Serafima's only allusion to the sinking. She never spoke directly about it after the war, Irene said.

In Ontario, life regained a rhythm of normalcy. Irene and Ellen went to school, their mother sewed them new dolls to help replace their massive collection left behind in Latvia. The girls fondly recall one in particular that had a bright red skirt. The girls learned English, and slowly life resumed. The death of Evi left a great hole in their hearts. The family never talked about the *Wilhelm Gustloff* outside their home. Yet once, about 15 years ago, Ellen had a brief moment where she considered sharing her story with her coworkers. She started to tell them about what happened to her family. One of her colleagues interrupted her. "'Oh the war. That was hard, we had to use margarine,'" Ellen remembered the woman saying. Ellen's mouth clamped shut, never to speak of it again with her colleagues.

Ellen's story helps explain why survivors of the *Gustloff* remained reluctant to talk with outsiders for so many years. Instead, they reached out to each other. In the past few years they've formed a community of sorts where they can and do talk amongst themselves. They call each other on January 30; they call each other on birthdays and anniversaries. Today Helga Reuter Knickerbocker, 82, who lives in Las Vegas, counts among her friends Rose Rezas Petrus, 86, in Littleton, Colorado. Though the two have never met face-to-face, circumstance threw them together—with Horst

Woit, Eva Dorn Rothchild, and other survivors. In their lifeboat of shared memory, they became a small community with a shared history, able to talk freely without worrying about the judgment of others.

"You think about it all the time. Fortunately or unfortunately," Horst Woit said. "You dream about it. It's not easy, particularly that lifeboat. I will never, ever forget the face of my mother when I pulled that knife out of my ski pants. It's even hard to describe. It's very emotional."

After Alexander Ivanovich Marinesko torpedoed the *Gustloff* and the following month torpedoed the *Steuben,* he returned to the Russian naval base Turku near Finland. He was certain he would receive his nation's respect. What he got was food: Marinesko's comrades feted him by arranging a feast at which the banquet table held two enormous glistening roasted pigs symbolizing the *Wilhelm Gustloff* and the *Steuben.*[4]

However, other than that sumptuous meal, recognition eluded Captain Alexander Marinesko. He received the Combat Order of the Red Banner at the end of World War Two, and his crew received the Order of the Red Star.

Unfortunately for Marinesko, his commanders failed to consider his actions brilliant. In fact, they doubted the magnitude of the hit. The NKVD gave credit for the *Gustloff*'s sinking to a Soviet air force attack. Still irate over the disorderly conduct Marinesko had displayed in January 1945, the NKVD ultimately pulled strings to get him ousted from the navy. Before that could happen, Marinesko's superiors demoted him two grades and wanted to station him on a minesweeper. His insubordination had irritated too many of his superiors. Marinesko declined the offer and found he no longer had a place in Russia's navy.

After the war, a blood transfusion institute hired the former submarine commander as a deputy manager.[5] Ever the concerned commander for his crew, Marinesko now worried about his employees. He got in trouble for letting employees take home peat bricks to heat their homes. The peat was considered state property and so Marinesko received a three-year sentence in a prison camp near Vladivostok.[6] After serving, he was released and lived in relative obscurity. He married and had a daughter, Tatania, who lives in Krondstadt, traditionally the home port of the Russian Baltic Fleet on a small island near St. Petersburg, Russia.[7]

Ultimately Alexander Marinesko received the redemption he craved. In 1990s, just before the Soviet Union collapsed, Premier Mikhail Gorbachev posthumously awarded the submariner the nation's highest military honor: Hero of the Soviet Union. Marinesko had died in October 1963 at the age of 50. Grim-faced Soviet naval officers attended Marinesko's funeral, bearing his casket that had his captain's hat atop it. Russians consider Marinesko a hero and often visit his tomb in St. Petersburg, a dark granite stone etched in gold letters and topped with his likeness. A large statue of the submarine captain stands in Kalingrad, Russia.

Today, the question nags. Did the Wilhelm Gustloff present a legitimate target since it was transporting military personnel across the Baltic with the intention of using them to boost troop strength? Or did the fact of the overwhelming number of civilians negate the fact that there were service members aboard? Was the sinking merely one man's attempt to win a medal and national recognition, or was it a necessary step to stop the war? For every person who argues that Captain Alexander Marinesko sank an innocent refugee ship, there are those who point out the thousands of soldiers and sailors on board, many of whom were destined to replenish German troops.

Some see Marinesko's decision to fire on the Wilhelm Gustloff as a brilliant military operation. It showed Soviet submarine commanders possessed a prowess that enabled them to seize the initiative and utterly and completely dominate the Baltic Sea battleground. "Acting as they did, the submarine 'S-13' crew advanced the end of the war. It can be rightly considered the huge strategic success of the Soviet Navy while for Germany it was the most disastrous sea catastrophe. The greatness of Marinesko's deed lies in the fact that he destroyed the symbol of Nazism itself, which seemed unsinkable, the dream-ship emphasizing and promoting the might of the Third Reich. The civilians, who happened to be on the ship, became the hostages of the German warmachine. That is why it is Hitler's Germany, not Marinesko, that must be blamed for the 'Gustloff's tragic death."[8]

All of Horst and Meta Woit's belongings sank to the sea floor with the ship. Every photo Horst has today came from generous relatives and friends. After the Woits arrived at Sassnitz on the Isle of Ruegen, the Red Cross sent them on to Kolberg, Pomerania, where the German authorities issued the family new identification cards affirming they had been on the *Wilhelm Gustloff*.[9] The Woits were one of the few survivors to have such cards. From Kolberg, Horst and Meta Woit traveled to Schwerin, East Germany, then in the Soviet occupation zone. Ironically, the two now resided in the town where the *Wilhelm Gustloff*'s namesake had been born and buried, and they would spend a year behind the iron curtain, living under the very forces they had just fled.

Refugees from the *Wilhelm Gustloff* and those transported during Operation Hannibal were sent to one of the four occupation zones. The large German populations in territories returned to Poland and the Soviet Union meant large population transfers. In the Russian zone, refugees like Horst and Meta were supposed to view the Russians as their saviors and ignore the atrocities they had seen or heard about. "I cannot recall being asked to keep quiet about the sinking on the *Wilhelm Gustloff*, but perhaps my mother was," said Woit. She never spoke about the sinking outside their home because keeping quiet became necessary for their survival. They now depended on the good will of the Soviet occupiers. To talk about the sinking to anyone outside the home was dangerous. Going to school each day frightened Horst to the core. Yet, he also used to follow the Russian soldiers to try and get something to eat from them and he still remembers some Russian phrases.

Horst can't forget the grim faces and menacing body language of Russian officers in the area. Their fears were realized when one afternoon a Soviet soldier grabbed Meta. What happened next was never clear to Horst, yet this memory chills him to this day.

During the postwar period, the Russian population had been portrayed as a lewd, rapacious horde. No one knows how many rapes went unreported or how many rape victims never received medical attention, but rape was a very real threat for the wandering refugee population as well as for those living in temporary shelters.[10] The situation was grave enough to warrant a telegraph from the American ambassador in France, Jefferson Caffery, to Secretary of State Cordell Hull: "We may however expect some vigorous complaint from the Russians and possibly other Allies over present treatment of their displaced nationals. Incidentally, Russians are by far the most difficult to handle in view of their greater tendencies towards looting of and violence towards Germans. For this and other practical administrative reasons I believe our military authorities have taken the only course in, wherever possible, concentrating and temporarily virtually confining displaced persons."[11]

Horst and his mother stayed in East Germany until 1946 when they moved to Frankfurt, West Germany. Horst's father rejoined the family in West Germany about 20 months after the sinking of the *Gustloff*.[12] Horst's uncle, from whose possessions he had lifted that important knife, arrived in Frankfurt in 1948, a fortunate survivor of three years in a Siberian gulag. By the war's end, the Soviet Union had taken nearly 2.4 million German soldiers and slightly more than 1 million combatants from other European nations as prisoners. More than a million of the German POWs died.[13]

Although life in Frankfurt improved each day, the Woits yearned to cross the Atlantic Ocean to start anew, far from Germany where they had seen so much violence and destruction. They wanted to immigrate to either Canada or the United States. The quota in the United States for European refugees was filled, and in the summer of 1948 they received their visas to Canada. A few years later, Horst found a job with the Canadian railroad. He lived in Toronto and commuted to Montreal.[14]

Today, Horst's home in Kimberly, Ontario stands as a shrine to the *Wilhelm Gustloff*. Paintings, models, books, and magazine articles about the *Gustloff* line the shelves of his study and adorn many of the home's walls. Horst married and has two children; his mother, Meta, died several years ago. He has helped keep the band of survivors together through emails and by phone, calling many on their birthdays and always on January 30.

Horst remembered many things about his young boyhood before boarding the *Gustloff*, and occasionally he felt a twinge of homesickness for Elbing, but he and his mother realized quickly they would never return. "Once we found out after the war that East Prussia would become part of Russia, we knew we would never make it back. I went back to Elbing in 2000 by myself for the first time. I flew to Berlin and drove to Elbing. It was hard on the nerves, but I found the house."

"We're alive."

Those words played often in Irene and Ellen Tschinkur's heads in the days, weeks, and decades following the sinking.

Because they lived in the British zone of occupation, they were not officially silenced. But nothing was said about the sinking and rescue; the family had more pressing matters to consider such as where and how to get food, or whether to enroll the girls in school. Above all, they were preoccupied with securing visas for the West. "I didn't talk about it with mom or my sister," Irene said. "We had a life to live. Then we were busy with school, fitting in, learning the language, work."[15]

All that Herbert Christoph Tschinkur carried when he left Gotenhafen were the clothes on his back, his baker's cookbook, and some money. The sisters cherish the book, with its cracked binding and lovingly handled pages. When the Tschinkurs lived in Nienberg, Germany, all in one room under a mansard roof, they often paged through the book, looking at the luscious photographs of cakes, creams, and cookies. An evening spent fantasizing about the sugar delights helped sate their appetites. "Food was rationed, but [our parents] were good to us. Just nothing left, no food, no coffee," Irene said.

They were, of course, hungry all the time, but safe. Finally the lines of communication with America opened. They started hearing from two aunts who lived on Long Island. One day a package arrived from C.A.R.E., an organization that allowed Americans to send relief packages to friends and family in Europe. Aside from honey, sugar, beef broth, and other staples were packets of coffee. Real coffee.

"The whiff of that coffee was just heaven," Irene remembers.

Helga Reuter Knickerbocker didn't receive strict orders to remain silent, but she too never spoke of the incident until decades passed. "We had to get over it," Helga said.[16]

When Helga arrived in Berlin after the sinking, she stayed with her younger sister and brother-in-law. They took her in and fed her, in spite of the scarcity of food in the city. She soon learned that her parents were stuck in Königsberg; they could not get out from under the Soviet occupation. Her father, Kurt, who had fed prisoners and had defied orders to try and ensure his daughters' survival, died of starvation 18 months after the war in a Soviet prison camp. The Soviets had also captured Helga's mother, Marta, who spent three years in a forced labor camp. By the time she returned to Königsberg, it had been renamed Kaliningrad. Their home had been virtually destroyed, and her mother went to work as a street cleaner. The town was starving and life under the Russian occupation was difficult. "My mother was walking through the town one afternoon and a lady said to her, 'Come, I have to show you something. Look in through the window, look into the basement.' She looked in and saw a mother and child who had been eaten alive by rats."

In 1952 Helga Reuter left Berlin and made her way to Zurich, Switzerland. She found a job working as a seamstress in a high-fashion enterprise. After a year Helga decided she'd had enough of Europe and decided to emigrate to the United States. Congress had just passed the 1952 Immigration and Naturalization Act that maintained a quota system for various ethnic groups. Labor qualifications were a big factor. Helga got a visa to work as a nanny in Dayton, Ohio. After that, she found a job with an older couple who lived in California.

Helga will never forget the moment she saw the Pacific Ocean. "When I saw the Pacific, that was it. I was a water girl set on dry land. I was a water rat. I had no trouble after that [the *Gustloff* sinking] with water," she said.

At first Helga had little love for the United States. She found it difficult, particularly because she spoke halting English, having studied it for only six years as a child in Königsberg. She remembers her teacher who came from Great Britain. She favored wearing black shoes in winter and showed a penchant for brown shoes in summer. Tired of living in a country where she couldn't converse, Helga said she finally just "opened my mouth and learned English."

In 1966 Helga met her husband, Roy Knickerbocker; they married in 1968. "My husband always wanted to know how I felt when they said the *Titanic* was the greatest shipwreck. He couldn't stand hearing about that," Helga said.

Milda Bendrich remembered, too, the painful years after this traumatic event and how she came to shroud her story in silence.

Milda recalled arriving with her daughter Inge in Sassnitz on the Isle of Ruegen on January 31, 1945. "Here I have a gap in my memory, which I simply cannot fill. When I left my cabin on the *W.G.*, I could not possibly have put on my boots, as if I had done so, then I would still have had these boots when I arrived in Ochtersum. And I know exactly that I had no boots after the flight until, with the help of a few bartering items, I managed to have a pair of boots made by a bootmaker who was a friend of my in-laws. So I arrived on the *TZ-36* (and so did you) without any shoes. After we berthed, we walked with other shipwrecked people to a camp on a path made of trampled snow. A part of this path I can still remember clearly, but I cannot judge if it was much more than a kilometer. Could someone from the *TZ-36* have provided me with shoes?"

Bendrich remembered the Red Cross camp had shelters with long rows of double-decker bunks. On two of these bunks lay two of the Marinehelferinnen, Women's Naval Auxiliary, who were rescued from the water. Both were naked under their blankets. Their soaked uniforms had been cut from their bodies. One of the girls had a high fever and was somnambulant. Milda spoke with the other girl, trying to comfort her.

While in Sassnitz, the Red Cross gave Milda the most necessary basic items of clothing so she and her baby could continue their journey. Milda wanted to get to Ochtersum, where she had once lived for a month with Fernande (Nanni) Pape. Nanni and Milda had lived together for quite some time in Gotenhafen and the two became good friends. Naturally, Nanni told her friends and acquaintances about the sinking of the *Wilhelm Gustloff* and how Milda and Inge had survived.

"A few days after our arrival, the doorbell rang and at the door were two boys from the Hitler Youth. They threatened us with dire consequences should we insist on spreading rumors about the *W.G.* As things were at that time, we decided on the path of caution," Milda wrote. "The only document to prove that this was not just a bad dream is the enclosed certificate of the local group leader in Sassnitz."

The Russians didn't release Inge's father, Franz Bendrich, from the Siberian prison camp until 1951. Her mother gave up on ever seeing him again sometime between 1949 and 1950. "She talked about him as if he wasn't coming home," Inge Roedecker said. "Then we got a telegram saying he was coming home." She remembered him as a naturally stout man, "but he came home totally emaciated."[17]

Inge remembers lying awake in bed at night and hearing her parents talk. In the morning she'd ask them what they'd been talking about. Her father told his only child stories about what they used to eat—very little, and sometimes the occasional cat. He told Inge about how the guards in the Siberian prison camp subjected them to a type of torture in which they were put in a room for hours and could only stand. The guards shone bright lights into the eyes of the men, and when they got out of the room, they couldn't see. Inge remembers her father telling her "it was very white, like snow had fallen."

Finally, their visas arrived. Milda, Franz, and Inge left Germany aboard the *Skaubryn* from Bremerhaven in the last week of June 1954. The family arrived in Melbourne, Australia in the first week of August. From Melbourne the Bendrichs took a train to

Bonegilla in northern Victoria. They lived in a former Australian army barracks with other newly arrived immigrants.

Recently Inge and her partner, Ian Fieggen, visited Bonegilla, which has been turned into a museum. They met other visitors who had also stayed there as immigrants. "It was quite emotional. Being an eleven-year-old child then, I loved Bonegilla, as everything was so different from Germany. The birdlife, wallabies, and kangaroos were fascinating. I remember having a lot of friends, some that I had already met on the *Skaubryn*," Inge said. She recalls that some adults who had been there for six months to a year said that they hated the place. Her father was offered a position as mechanic on King Island, an island in Bass Strait, where they moved with two other families about five weeks after they had arrived in Bonegilla. The people in King Island were lovely, Inge recalled.

"What hurt me about it the most was everybody would talk about the *Titanic*," Inge Bendrich Roedecker said, remembering her mother's experience. "My mother said, 'I was on a boat that sank.' And people snickered. I feel the ridicule in the room to this day."

Captain Paul Vollrath fled Germany in 1948 aboard a yacht and ended up in Waterford, Ireland.[18] "Fleeing from the frightful conditions prevailing in Germany, and the fear of another world war, nine German refugees, seeking permanent homes in a quiet land far away from war-ravaged Europe, arrived by accident at the little village of Checkpoint, seven miles from Waterford City, on Friday night or early on Saturday morning. Natives of Hamburg, the intrepid adventurers have figured in one of the greatest dramas of the turbulent Atlantic Ocean when their 32-foot yacht was tossed about on the angry waves in one of the fiercest gales they have ever known," read an article in the *Waterford News*.

According to the story, after Vollrath and the rest of his party left Germany, they spent 25 days floundering about in the North Sea.[19] Apparently engine trouble plagued the yacht. That was followed by a broken diesel engine. The groups had no tools to fix either engine. In desperation they hoisted the one small sail on board, which carried the craft over 900 miles of sea around the English coast and to Checkpoint. Moreover, the boat's cooking stove broke and the party was "forced to eat cold tinned food, which had run out by the time they reached the Irish coast."[20]

In Ireland Captain Vollrath met 18-year-old Vera. She was volunteering in a seaman's center. The two feel in love with the force of a thunderclap and had three children, Gerard, Anna, and Paul. Vollrath died in 1996. Vera had a stroke in December 2011 and suffered from Alzheimer's. Her son, Gerard, was charged with the unlawful killing of his 83-year-old mother at Killure Bridge Nursing Home in Waterford in January 2012.[21]

In Essen, now a city of rubble and wreckage, Walter Salk's mother Hedwig "clung to a thread of hope" that perhaps the Red Army had captured her second son and middle child. She prayed he lived, be it in a Russian prison camp or in hiding. To lose another son would be more than she could bear.

It took the family more than a year to unravel the story of the young seaman's fate.

Two days after the sinking, on February 1, 1945, his mother and father sent a letter to their son from Essen-Altenessen: "My dear Walter! I want to send my greetings to you. A lot has changed in the East recently. I am writing to let you know that Aunt Martha left on January 16th. We didn't hear from her until January 25th. She was in East Prussia and may not be able to get out. She was going to try and visit you. Maybe we'll hear more from her soon. Your father is feeling a little better, and Inge will be having her 17th birthday on the 9th of February. Send me your new address as soon as you know it. You are my good boy. Heartfelt greetings and kisses from your Mother and Father."

Hedwig and Willi Salk wrote the poignant letter after Walter had already died.

On March 8, 1945, Walter's parents did receive a letter, but not from their beloved son. This letter, written on thin graph paper, from Flensburg, was from a young woman named Christa Hausen:

> Dear Mrs. Salk! You will be surprised to get a letter from someone you have never met. My dear Mrs. Salk, I would be very grateful if you could give me some news. I know your son very well; I was Canteen Helper on the *T.S. Murwik*. Walter and I became good friends. Now, I have not received any mail from Walter since the 21st of January. Since he was living on the *Wilhelm Gustloff,* and it was torpedoed, I am dreading that Walter was on board. Perhaps, Mrs. Salk, you can tell me if Walter still lives? Walter told me shortly before he was repositioned from Flensburg, "If you don't hear from me, you will know I am dead." One of his friends gave me your address, and so I beg you dear Mrs. Salk, give me some information if you have gotten any news of him, and I would be eternally grateful. With kind regards, Christa Hausen.[22]

It wasn't until December 18, 1945 that an official missing-in-action notice arrived, informing Hedwig and Willi that their 22-year-old son, Mech. Maat Walter Salk, had indeed been on the *Wilhelm Gustloff* when it sank near Stolpe Bank in the Baltic Sea.

Hedwig and Willi clung to hope, as did Inge, Walter's younger sister. Finally, news came on September 28, 1946, from the Naval Documentation Center, British Naval Headquarters. The letter mentioned Rudolph Dommash, Walter's uncle, who had been making frequent inquiries regarding the fate of his nephew, the last being on March 7, 1946. It confirmed that Walter had been stationed on the *Gustloff* and that it had been sunk: "Your son was not one of the survivors to be rescued, so you must reconcile yourself that he is no longer among the living. The possibility that he could be in a Russian prison camp is extremely unlikely. Russian ships were not in the area at the time of the rescue operation. Should you not have heard from your son by now, we officiate that he is legally declared dead and recorded as such in Hamburg. . . . German Controller Naval Document Center." Hedwig and Willi Salk received official notice from the German authorities on September 28, 1946. The brief missive concluded that Walter had indeed died in the torpedo attack; it said it was virtually impossible that Salk could have been captured since no Russian ships were in the area around the time of the sinking to pick up survivors. Salk was thus pronounced dead one year after being listed as missing for over one year.[23]

The Salks' letter exchange with German authorities is just one of thousands of such letters from families searching for their relatives. Millions of men were now dead, millions of men were listed as missing, and millions were languishing in prison-of-war camps near the Arctic Circle. Letters like the Salks' show the painstaking search of survivors to find their relatives.

For years, Nellie Minkevics imagined her father had survived the shipwreck as an amnesiac. She imagined he lived somewhere in Sweden or Norway, unaware of his previous life. Daily she asked the Red Cross if they had any information on Voldemars Minkevics. She never heard a word, and slowly she came to terms with the fact that her father had perished on the *Wilhelm Gustloff*. Her mother remained in Latvia, now firmly under Soviet rule. Nellie ended up moving to England, where she met Peter Zobs in Scotland. She came to Nebraska in 1958 and became a nurse. Minkevics didn't communicate with her mother until the 1980s, when Mikhail Gorbachev came into office with a new policy of perestroika.[24] Minkevics and her mother suffered separation because of the postwar redrawing of maps. Leonilla Minkevics Zobs died on March 16, 2011, at the age of 89 in Lincoln, Nebraska.[25]

After spending several uneasy days with her mother in Halle (Saale) after the *Gustloff* sank, Eva Dorn decided to travel to Hamburg. More than 40,000 of the city's residents had died from Allied bombings alone. Countless more had died in concentration camps and on the front lines. The city was destroyed.

Six decades later, sitting on her terrace in Switzerland, Eva remembered sitting on a pile of rubble, the ruins of a restaurant. She wondered what she would do now. Then she remembered that she once knew someone in Hamburg and searched him out. He gave her an address of a small bed and breakfast. Bombs had considerably damaged the building. Where there should have been a staircase, a ladder leaned. Eva climbed to the second floor. There was a room and a sofa, and the woman told her she could stay. In exchange for helping repair the inn, Eva could have shelter, sleep, and food. Eva worked for the woman for a few months; she later fell ill with tuberculosis and spent six months in the hospital.

Eva married soon after the war; it lasted less than a week. She married again and had two daughters; that marriage lasted just over four years. Then she found true love. She married a Jewish man—Rothschild. Their marriage lasted 44 years; he died a few years ago. They lived in Chile and then in New York City. About twelve years ago Eva traveled to the Isle of Ruegen with her daughter, Constantine. Though the pier is no longer there, Eva and Constantine found the place where the *T-36* docked on January 31.

Today a model of the *T-36*, which the Soviets later sank in May 1945, occupies the mantel above Eva's fireplace. The long gray boat, built to scale, was a gift from its captain, Robert Hering. It shows a sailor pulling Eva up on the seaman's seat. Every day Eva walks by this model to see herself rescued.

In 1995 Irene Tschinkur East rested on a hammock in Tecumseh, Ontario. She was admiring the sun-dappled leaves when she seemed suddenly jerked back in time 50 years, when she also lay on a hammock watching condensation on the ceiling of her rescue ship. It was the first time she'd really thought about what happened to her all those years ago.

There is a certain agony in surviving. These are memories one can't forget. Irene can't get over what has happened, but she has had to live with it so she could have a life for herself and for her children. She succeeded; she emerged in one piece from the nightmare. In the end, Irene, Horst, and all the survivors learned to cope with their lives. They learned to survive, because they just had to.

APPENDIX

According to Heinz Schön, who had served aboard the *Wilhelm Gustloff,* the survivor tally was as follows:

Torpedo boat *T 36,* Kapitänleutnant Robert Hering, picked up 564 survivors; the *T Löwe,* Kapitänleutnant Paul Prüfe, picked up 472; minesweeper *M 375/TS 8,* Oberleutnant d.R. Karl Brinkmann, picked up 98; minesweeper *M 375/TS 8,* Oberleutnant d.R. Walter Weichel picked up 43; the steamer *Göttingnen,* Handelsschiffskapit Friedrich Segelken, picked up 28; the steamer *Gotenland,* Handelsschiffskapit Heinz Vollmers, picked up 2; torpedofangboot *TF 19,* Oberleutnant Walter Schick, picked up 7; and the Vorpostenboot *Vp* 1703, Kapitänleutnant Helmut Hanefeld picked up 1 person.

Throughout the book German place names have been used instead of their Polish or Russian counterparts. Their names today are:

Gumbinnen—Gusev
Gotenhafen—Gdynia
Elbing—Elblag
Danzig—Gdansk
Königsberg—Kaliningrad
Insterburg—Chernyakhovsk
Thorn—Turin
Breslau—Wroclaw
Stutthof—Sztutowo

NOTES

CHAPTER ONE: "YOU HAVE TO GO ON THIS SHIP"

1. Alfred-Maurice de Zayas, *Nemesis at Potsdam: The Anglo-Americans and the Expulsion of the Germans* (London, Boston: Routledge & Kegan Paul, 1977), 61.

2. Edward A. Westermann, *Hitler's Police Battalions: Enforcing War in the East* (Lawrence: University Press of Kansas), 191.

3. Michael H. Kater, *Hitler Youth* (Cambridge, Mass.: Harvard University Press, 2004), 191.

4. "Nazis Fight for Time and Political Miracle," *New York Times,* February 11, 1945, final ed.

5. Victor Shiff, "'Last Fortress' of the Nazis—in the Alps East of Switzerland Hitler's Henchmen Are Expected to Make a Final Stand." *New York Times,* February 11, 1945, final ed.

6. "Red Army Wins Elbing Port, Threatens Danzig Rail Line" *New York Times,* February 11, 1945, final ed.

7. Author email with Horst Woit, Kimberly, Ontario, July 25, 2007.

8. National Archives and Records Administration, http://www.archives.gov/central-plains/kansas-city/finding-aids/lincoln-naturalization.html, last accessed May 16, 2012.

9. Cindy-Lang Kubick, "Lincoln Woman Survived Refugee Boat Sinking," *Lincoln Journal Star,* January 28, 2006, final ed.

10. Ibid.

11. Ibid.

12. Author interview with Eva Dorn Rothschild, Ascona, Switzerland, April 16, 2012.

13. Milda Bendrich letter to Inge Roedecker, June 9, 1981, courtesy of Inge Bendrich Roedecker.

14. Author telephone interview with Inge Roedecker, March 9, 2012.

15. Kater, *Hitler Youth,* 88.

16. Rose Rezas Petrus testimony included in July 10, 2007, letter to author as well as clipping of: Robert Dolgan, "30 Years Can't Erase Vision of Ship Sinking," *Plain Dealer,* Cleveland, OH.

17. Author telephone conversation with Peter Petrus, Sept. 8, 2011.

18. Author interview with Rita Rowand, Washington, DC, January 29, 2012.

19. Kater, *Hitler Youth*. 44-45.

20. Inge Salk diary entry, diary courtesy of Rita Rowand.

21. Letter from Walter Salk to parents January 14, 1945, courtesy of Rita Rowand.

22. Author interview with Irene Tschinkur East and Ellen Tschinkur Maybee, Tecumseh, Ontario, December 4, 2012.

23. Author email with Irene East, March 29, 2012.

24. Author interview with Irene East and Ellen Maybee, Tecumseh, Ontario, December 4, 2012.

25. Ibid.

26. Author interview with Helga Reuter Knickerbocker, Las Vegas, NV, November 6, 2012.

27. Max Egremont, *Forgotten Land: Journeys Among the Ghosts of East Prussia* (New York: Farrar, Straus & Giroux, 2011), 40.

28. Author interview with Helga Reuter Knickerbocker, Las Vegas, NV, November 6, 2012.

CHAPTER TWO: HITLER'S HOSTAGES:
LIFE IN THE EASTERN TERRITORIES

1. Ursula Mahlendorf, *The Shame of Survival: Working Through a Nazi Childhood* (University Park: Pennsylvania State University Press, 2009), 75.

2. Author interview with Helga Reuter Knickerbocker, Las Vegas, NV, November 6, 2011.

3. Laurence Steinhardt to Cordell Hull, September 9, 1939. FRUS, 861.20/481, 779-780, National Archives and Records Administration (NARA), Washington, DC.

4. Gunther telegram to Secretary of State Cordell Hull, 9/16/39, Foreign Relations of the United States Diplomatic Papers, Record Group 59, Stack 250.740.0011 European War, 1939/332, NARA, Washington, DC.

5. Cordell Hull to Joseph Kennedy, September 1, 1939, FRUS, 740.00116 European War 1939/19a, 541-542. NARA, Washington, DC.

6. Michael Burleigh, *The Third Reich: A New History* (New York: Hill & Wang, Farrar, Straus & Giroux, 2000), 448-449.

7. "Baltic Germans Arrive in Danzig: More than 2,000 from Latvia and Estonia land over the weekend from 3 ships," *New York Times*. October 31, 1939, final ed.

8. Michael H. Kater, *Hitler Youth* (Cambridge: Harvard University Press, 2004), 34-35.

9. Kater, *Hitler Youth,* 14.

10. Author interview with Helga Reuter Knickerbocker, Las Vegas, NV, November 6, 2011.

11. Gunther to Cordell Hull, conveying a telegram from Ambassador Anthony J. Dresel Biddle Jr., FRUS, 740.00116 European War 1939/61, 554-555, NARA, Washington, DC.

12. Timothy Snyder, *Bloodlands: Europe between Hitler and Stalin* (New York: Basic Books, Perseus Book Group, 2010), 126.

13. Ruth Weintraub, video testimony, RG 50.155 #03 US Holocaust Memorial Museum Archives, Washington, DC.

14. Michael Burleigh, *Moral Combat: Good and Evil In World War Two* (New York: HarperCollins, 2011), 145.

15. Snyder, *Bloodlands,* 131.

16. Stanislaw Jaskolski, *Come with Me and Visit Hell,* trans. Jakub Przedzien-kowski, Kindle ed., http://www.amazon.com/Come-With-Visit-Hell-ebook /dp/B005CM1TZ6, last accessed April 17, 2012.

17. Marke Orski, *Des Francais au camp de concentration de Stutthof,* Gdansk: Muzeum Stutthof w Sztutowie: 1995. Note: Of the 13 Americans imprisoned in Stutthof, 5 were Jewish and 8 were US citizens of Polish origin.

18. Jaskolski, *Come with Me.*

19. Ibid.

20. Ibid.

21. Marian Kampinski, testimony, United States Holocaust Memorial Museum, Washington, DC.

22. Max Egremont, *Forgotten Land: Journeys Among the Ghosts of East Prussia* (New York: Farrar, Straus & Giroux, 2011), 272.

23. Helga Reuter Knickerbocker, phone interview with author, January 5, 2012.

24. This and subsequent recollections of Helga Reuter Knickerbocker from author's interview with Helga Reuter Knickerbocker, November 6, 2011, Las Vegas, NV, and email and phone correspondence.

25. Victor Schiff, "'Last Fortress' of the Nazis—In the Alps East of Switzerland Hitler's Henchmen are Expected to Make a Final Stand," *New York Times,* February 11, 1945, final ed.

26. The History Place, http://www.historyplace.com/worldwar2/hitleryouth/ hj-prelude.htm, last accessed May 4, 2012.

27. Edward A. Westermann, *Hitler's Police Battalions: Enforcing Racial War in the East* (Lawrence: University Press of Kansas, 2005), 129.

28. This and subsequent recollections of Irene Tschinkur East and Ellen Tschinkur Maybee from author's interview December 5-6, 2011, and email and phone correspondence.

29. Kater, *Hitler Youth,* 19.

30. This and subsequent recollections of Eva Dorn, from author's interview with Eva Dorn Rothschild, Ascona, Switzerland, April 15, 2012.

31. *Führer Conferences on Naval Affairs 1939-1945,* foreword by Jak P. Mailmann Showell (London, UK: Chatham Publishing, 2005) 172.

32. Andrew Nagorski, *The Greatest Battle; Stalin, Hitler and the Desperate Struggle for Moscow that Changed the Course of World War Two* (New York: Simon & Schuster, 2007), 91.

33. Mahlendorf, *The Shame of Survival,* 106.

34. Burleigh, *Moral Combat,* 240.

35. As quoted in Prit Buttar, *Battleground Prussia: The Assault on Germany's Eastern Front, 1944-1945* (Oxford, UK: Osprey Publishing, 2010), 77.

36. Alexander Solzhenitsyn, "Prussian Nights, A Poem," trans. by Robert Conquest (New York: Farrar, Straus and Giroux, 1974.)

37. Ibid.

38. Propaganda leaflet distributed to Red Army soldiers at time of East Prussian offensive.

39. Victor Schiff, "'Last Fortress' of the Nazis, *New York Times*, February 11, 1945, final ed.

40. David Welch. *The Third Reich: Politics and Propaganda*, 2nd ed. (Abingdon Oxon, Canada: Routledge, 1993), 138.

41. Bernt Engelmann, *In Hitler's Germany: Everyday Life in the Third Reich*, trans. Krishna Winston (New York: Pantheon Books, 1986), 284.

42. Submarine Gazette, IV, 9, February 26, 1944, Submarine Force Library and Museum, Groton, CT.

43. John Toland, *The Last 100 Days* (New York: Random House, 1976), 1.

44. Henrik Eberle and Matthias Uhl, eds., *The Hitler Book: The Secret Dossier Prepared for Stalin from the Interrogations of Hitler's Personal Aides* (New York: Public Affairs, 2005), 41.

45. Westermann, *Hitler's Police Battalions*, 222, 242-243.

46. Alexander Werth, *Russia at War: 1941-1945* (New York: E.P. Dutton, 1964), 701.

47. Dora Love, testimony of Dora Love on life at Stutthof, Shoah Resource Center, International School for Holocaust Studies Source, Yad Vashem Archives 0.3-7504

48. Toland, *The Last 100 Days*, 3.

49. Ibid., 3.

50. Record Group 226 OSS Box 136 A-1 Stockholm-MO-OP-5 Folder 2309, NARA, Washington, DC.

51. "There's No Stopping the Russians," *Submarine Gazette*, IV, 14, April 1, 1944, Box 157, Submarine Force Library & Museum, Naval Submarine Base, New London, CT.

52. Alfred-Maurice de Zayas, *Nemesis at Potsdam: The Anglo-Americans and the Expulsion of the Germans* (London, Boston: Routledge & Kegan Paul, 1977), 62.

53. As quoted in Mahlendorf, *The Shame of Survival*, 181.

54. From report on conditions in Denmark about November 15, 1944 to Headquarters, from Stockholm, December 8, 1944. Record Group 226 OSS E125 Box 13 Folder 210 Stockholm-SO-INT-2, NARA, Washington, DC.

55. "12-mile Gain in East; Russians Turn German Defense in North," *New York Times*, January 30, 1945, final ed.

CHAPTER THREE: OPERATION HANNIBAL AND THE CROWN OF THE FLEET, THE *WILHELM GUSTLOFF*

1. Karl Dönitz, *Memoirs: Ten Years and Twenty Days*, trans. R.H. Stevens with David Woodward (New York: Da Capo Press, 1997), 431.

2. Ibid., 433.

3. Ibid., 433.
4. Kurt Reitsch, attaché German embassy in Ankara, Turkey, writing to Admiral Conrad Englehardt, January 26, 1965. Ost-Dok. 4/21, Bundesarchiv, Lastenausgleichsarchiv, Bayreuth, Germany.
5. Dönitz, *Memoirs*, 466.
6. "Reich Besieged: Black Days for Hitler," *New York Times*, February 4, 1945, final ed.
7. Dönitz, *Memoirs*, 432-435.
8. Howard D. Grier, *Hitler, Dönitz and The Baltic Sea—The Third Reich's Last Hope 1944-1945* (Annapolis, MD: Naval Institute Press, 2007), 195.
9. Ibid., 196.
10. Excerpt from report #146, Dr. Med. Peter Siegel, Homburg-Saar, Univ.-Franenkink. Ost-Dok. 4/1 Bundesarchiv, Lastenausgleichsarchiv, Bayreuth, Germany.
11. Dönitz, *Memoirs*, 466.
12. "Student Admits to Killing Nazi Chief," *New York Times*, December 10, 1936, final ed.
13. "No Speedy Revenge Expected," *New York Times*, February 12, 1936, final ed.
14. David Bankier, *The Germans and the Final Solution: Public Opinion Under Nazism* (Cambridge, MA: Blackwell Publishers, 1992), 80.
15. "Nazi's Slayer Is Freed," *New York Times*, June 2, 1945, final ed.
16. Max Domarus, *Hitler: Speeches and Proclamations, vol. 2* (Wauconda, IL: Bolchazy-Carducci Publishers, 1992), 751.
17. "Hitler Takes Up Jew's Challenge. At Gustloff Funeral He Says They Have created a New Nazi Martyr," *New York Times*, February 13, 1936, final ed.
18. David Welch, *The Third Reich: Politics and Propaganda*, 2nd ed. (Oxon, Canada: Routledge, 1993), 69-70.
19. Bernt Englemann, *In Hitler's Germany: Everyday in the Third Reich*, trans. Krishna Winston (New York: Pantheon Books, 1986), 60-61.
20. Shelley Baranowski, *Strength Through Joy: Consumerism and Mass Tourism in the Third Reich* (New York: Cambridge University Press, 2004), 132.
21. Eiber Ludwig, ed. KZ-Aussenlager Blohm und Voss im Hamberger KZ-Gedenkstätte Neuengamme, Karin Schawe, site administrator, http://www.kz-gedenkstaette-neuengamme.de/index.php?id=940, last accessed March 5, 2012.
22. Baranowski, *Strength Through Joy*, 153.
23. Welch, *The Third Reich*, 114.
24. Ibid., 60.
25. "Nazis Launch Ocean Liner for Workers on Vacation," wireless to *New York Times*. May 6, 1937, final ed.
26. "Ship Captain Dies at Sea: Master of German Vacation Vessel Victim of Heart Disease," *New York Times*, April 24, 1938, final ed.
27. British Official Wireless—London—Aug 12, *Sydney Morning Herald*: August 13, 1938, p 11.

28. Germans From England—"JA" On a Special Trip Out to Sea," *Life Magazine,* May 2, 1938, vol. 4, no. 18, 20-21.

29. "Reich's Cruise Ships Held Potential Plane Carriers," special cable to *New York Times,* May 1, 1938, final ed.

30. Paul Vollrath, "Tragedy of the 'Wilhelm Gustloff," *Seabreezes: the Magazine of Ships and the Sea,* vol. 55, no. 424 (Liverpool, England), April 1981, 225.

31. Ibid., 226.

32. Ibid., 226.

33. Ibid., 226.

34. Ibid., 226.

35. Ibid., 227.

CHAPTER FOUR: "WE KNEW WE HAD TO GET OUT"

1. Author email with Horst Woit, April 30, 2008.

2. Author email with Horst Woit, July 30, 2007.

3. "Vain Efforts to Halt Soviet Advance, Germans Fortifying Berlin," *The Advocate,* January 27, 1945, final ed., http:/www.trove.nla.gov.au./ndp/del/article/68912009, last accessed June 12, 2012.

4. Author email with Irene Tschinkur East, July 2, 2012.

5. Ruth Weintraub testimony, US Holocaust Memorial Museum, Washington, DC, 76-77.

6. Author interview with Horst Woit, August 2007.

7. Prit Buttar, *Battleground Prussia: The Assault on Germany's Eastern Front: 1944-1945* (Oxford, UK: Osprey Publishing, 2010), 138-146; Eva Kretein, *Eva's War: A True Story of Survival* (Albuquerque, NM: Amador Publishers, 1990), 12-16.

8. Juergen Thorwald, *Defeat in the East* (New York: Bantam Books, 1980), 70.

9. "Russians Disdainful of Fawning Germans; East Prussians Quickly Shed Arrogance," *New York Times,* February 1, 1945, final ed.

10. James Charles Roy, *The Vanished Kingdom: Travels Through the History of Prussia (*New York: Basic Books, 2000), 235.

11. Henrik Eberle, and Matthias Uhl, eds., *The Hitler Book: The Secret Dossier Prepared for Stalin from the Interrogations of Hitler's Personal Aides* (New York: Public Affairs, 2005), 139.

12. Author telephone call with Horst Woit, March 7, 2012.

13. Ursula Mahlendorf, *The Shame of Survival: Working Through a Nazi Childhood* (University Park: Pennsylvania State University Press, 2009), 2.

14. Mahlendorf, *Shame,*103.

15. Author interview with Helga Reuter Knickerbocker, Las Vegas, NV, November 6, 2011.

16. *Life Magazine,* May 2, 1938, vol. 4, no. 18, 39.

17. Milda Bendrich letter to Inge Roedecker.

18. Author telephone interview with Inge Roedecker, March 9, 2012.

19. Stockholms-Tidningen newspaper, January 24, 1945, as quoted in Max Hastings, *Armageddon: The Battle for Germany 1944-1945* (New York: Macmillan, 2004), 318.

20. Record Group 226 OSS E125 Box 13 Folder 210 Stockholm-SO-INT-2, NARA, Washington, DC.
21. Record Group 226 OSS Field Station files Box 136 Folder 2305 A-1 Stockholm-MO-OP-1, NARA, Washington, DC.
22. Ibid.
23. Ibid.
24. As quoted in Thorwald, *Defeat in the East*, 14.
25. September 13, 1944, Record Group 226, Box 136, folder 2305 A-1 Stockholm-MO-OP-1, NARA, Washington, DC.
26. As quoted in Richard Bessel, *Germany 1945: From War to Peace* (New York: Harper Perennial, 2009), 73.
27. Eberle and Uhl, *The Hitler Book*,166.
28. Eberle, *The Hitler Book,* 181.
29. "Russians Sweep On–Break Obra River Line in 21-mile Smash into Reich," *New York Times,* January 31, 1945, final ed.
30. Ibid.
31. Max Hastings, *Armageddon: The Battle for Germany,* 318.
32. As quoted in Richard Bessel, *Germany 1945: From War to Peace,* 73.
33. Hastings, *Armageddon: The Battle for Germany,* 326.
34. Ian Kershaw, *The End: The Defiance and Destruction of Hitler's Germany: 1944-1945* (New York: Penguin Press, 2011), 179.
35. 740.001 European War 1939/12390: Telegram, 153, Chargé d'affairs Berlin, Leland B. Morris to Secretary of State Cordell Hull, June 23, 1941. NARA, Washington, DC.
36. Record Group 226 OSS Box 136 A-1 Stockholm-MO-OP-5 Folder 2309, NARA, Washington, DC.
37. Record Group 226 OSS Box 136 A-1 Stockholm-MO-OP-5 Folder 2309, NARA, Washington, DC.
38. Maria Soszynska, testimony US Holocaust Memorial Museum, Washington, DC.
39. Ruth Weintraub Kurt, video testimony, RG 50.155 #03 US Holocaust Memorial Museum Archives, Washington, DC.
40. Stanislaw Jaskolski, *Come with Me and Visit Hell,* trans. Jakub Przedzienkowski, published by Jakub Przedzienkowski, July 2010, available as ebook only, www.amazon.com/Come-With-Visit-Hell-ebook/dp/B005C M1TZ6.
41. W.H. Lawrence, "1,000 Poles slain as foe quit Lodz. Prisoners massacred methodically before dawn as Russians neared," *New York Times,* February 5, 1945, final ed.
42. Kershaw, *The End,* xvii.

CHAPTER FIVE: SAVING A SCUTTLED REPUTATION

1. Marcin Jamkowski, "Ghost Ship Found," *National Geographic,* February 2005, http://ngm.nationalgreographic.com/features/world/europe/balticsea /steuben/text?source-ge.
2. V.I. Dimitriev writing to Heinz Schön on the subject of the *S-13,* Ost-Dok. 4/64, 67. Bundesarchiv, Bayreuth, Germany.

3. Timothy Snyder. "Hitler vs. Stalin: Who Killed More?" *New York Times,* March 10, 2011.

4. Jamkowski, "Ghost Ship Found."

5. Martin J. Bollinger, *Stalin's Slave Ships: Kolyma, the Gulag Fleet, and the Role of the West* (Westport, CT: Praeger Press, 2003), 86.

6. Norman Polmar and Jurrien Noot, *Submarines of the Russian and Soviet Navies, 1718-1990* (Annapolis, MD: Naval Institute Press, 1991), 83.

7. V. I. Dimitriev writing to Schön "in order to choose a precious object for his attack" on the subject of the *S-13.*

8. Polmar and Noot, *Submarines,* 100, 108, 109.

9. Polmar and Noot, *Submarines,* 102, 109.

10. Record Group 226 OSS E125 Box 13, Folder 212 Stockholm-SO-INT-2. NARA, Washington, DC. Various dispatches including October 26, 1944, October 28, 1944, November 3, 1944, January 15, 1945 speak to the new U-boats.

11. Victor Korzh, *Red Star Under the Baltic: A First Hand Account of Life on Board a Soviet Submarine in World War Two,* trans. Clare Burstall and Vladimir Kisselnikov (South Yorkshire, England: Pen and Sword Maritime, Pen and Sword Books, 2004).

12. V.I. Dimitriev writing to Heinz Schön on the subject of the *S-13.*

13. Jamkowski, "Ghost Ship Found."

14. V. I. Dimitriev writing to Heinz Schön on the subject of the *S-13.*

15. Polmar and Noot, *Submarines,* 132.

16. Victor Korzh, *Red Star,* 31.

17. Polmar and Noot, *Submarines,*133.

18. Korzh, *Red Star,* 31.

19. "*Wilhelm Gustloff* German Hospital Ship Sunk," Mercantile Marine, https://sites.google.com/a/mercantilemarine.org/mercantile-marine/War-time-Stories/german, last accessed March 17, 2010.

20. Ibid.

21. USSR S-13 of the Soviet Navy–Submarine of the S (Stalinet) class–Allied Warships of WW2–uboat.net, http://uboat.net/allies/warships/ship/5098.html, last accessed February 12, 2012.

22. Ibid.

23. Korzh, *Red Star,* 69.

24. V.I. Dimitriev writing to Heinz Schön on the subject of the *S-13.*

25. Max Hastings, *Armageddon: The Battle for Germany 1944-1945* (New York: Macmillan, 2004), 328.

26. "Order of the People's Commissar of the USSR Navy, April 9, 1939, No. 0161 Moscow–Confidential/Declassified, 73, Submarine Force Library and Museum, Groton, CT.

27. Ibid., 7.

28. Ibid.

29. Testimony of Admiral Karl Dönitz during Nuremberg Trial Proceedings, May 9, 1946, http://avalon.law.yale.edu/imt/05-09-46.asp, last accessed May 17, 2012.

30. Ibid., 81.
31. Ibid., 81.
32. The words on the torpedoes were covered in Paul Vollrath's memoir, in V.I Dimitriev's letters, and other websites noted in the bibliography.
33. Polmar and Noot, *Submarines,* 92.
34. David Ritchie, *Shipwrecks: An Encylopedia of the World's Worst Disasters at Sea* (New York: FactsOnFile, Infobase Holdings Co., 1996), 208.
35. Ritchie, *Shipwrecks,* 208.

CHAPTER SIX: BATTLE FOR THE BALTIC

1. Dönitz, Karl Dönitz. *Memoirs: Ten Years and Twenty Days,* trans. R. H. Stevens with David Woodward (New York: Da Capo Press, 1997), 398-399.
2. Victor Korzh, *Red Star Under the Baltic: A First-hand account of Life on Board a Soviet Submarine in World War Two,* trans. Clare Burstall and Vladimir Kisselnikov (South Yorkshire, England: Pen & Sword Maritime, 2004), xxii.
3. *Führer Conferences on Naval Affairs 1939-1945,* foreword by Jak P. Mallmann Showell (London: Chatham Publishing, 2005; Greenhill Books, 2006), 39.
4. Spencer C. Tucker, ed., *Naval Warfare: An International Encyclopedia,* vol. 1 (Oxford, England: ABC-Clio, 2002), 324-325.
5. *Führer Conferences,* 39.
6. Peter Padfield, *War Beneath the Sea: Submarine Conflict During World War II* (New York: John Wiley & Sons, 1995), 3.
7. Tucker, *Naval Warfare,* xxxi.
8. *Führer Conferences,* 32.
9. Ibid., 22-24.
10. Vice Admiral Freidrich Ruge, *Der Seekrieg, The German Navy's Story 1939-1945,* (Annapolis, MD: US Naval Institute Press, 1957), 99-100.
11. Ibid.
12. Norman Polmar and Jurrien Noot, *Submarines of the Russian and Soviet Navies, 1718-1990* (Annapolis, MD: Naval Institute Press, 1991), 75.
13. Polmar and Noot, *Submarines,* 74.
14. Ibid., 98.
15. *Führer Conferences,* 143.
16. Ibid., 80.
17. Dönitz, *Memoirs,* 209.
18. *Führer Conferences,* 277.
19. Dönitz, *Memoirs,* 373.
20. Tillmann Tegeler, "The Expulsion of the German Speakers from Baltic Countries," 71-81, in Steffan Prauser and Arfon Rees, eds., *The Expulsion of 'German' Communities from Eastern Europe at the End of the Second World War* EUI working paper No. 2004/1. (European University Institute, Florence, Italy, Department of History and Civilization. http://cadmus.eui

.eu/bitstream/handle/1814/2599/HEC04-01.pdf;jsessionid=2560C0CC62
EDC882D47D022A3B59A335?sequence=1, last accessed June 13, 2012.

21. *Führer Conferences*, 236.

22. Polmar and Noot, *Submarines*, 98.

23. Ibid., 102, 236.

24. Dönitz, *Memoirs*,153.

25. US Ambassador to the Soviet Union Laurence A. Steinhardt, Moscow, to Sec. State Cordell Hull, October 4, 1939, NARA, Washington, DC.

26. Record Group 226 OSS E125 Box 13 Folder 218 Stockholm-SO-INT-2, September 29, 1944, NARA, Washington, DC.

27. Howard D. Grier, *Hitler, Dönitz and the Baltic Sea–The Third Reich's Last Hope 1944-1945* (Annapolis, MD: US Naval Institute Press, 2007), 10.

28. *Fürher Conferences*, 233.

29. Ibid., 222.

30. Polmar and Noot, *Submarines*, 103.

31. Ibid., 108.

32. *Führer Conferences*, 289.

33. Korzh, *Red Star*, 5.

34. Polmar and Noot, *Submarine*, 109.

35. *Submarine Gazette*, vol. IV, no. 5, January 29, 1944, Submarine Force Library and Museum, Groton, CT.

36. Ibid.

37. Polmar and Noot, *Submarines*, 108.

38. Record Group 226 OSS E125 Box 13 Folder 212 Stockholm-SO-INT-2, To – Digit London, dispatched 16.40, January 15, 1945, NARA, Washington, DC.

39. "Order of the People's Commissar of the USSR Navy, April 9, 1939, No. 0161 Moscow—Confidential/Declassified; Polmar and Noot, *Submarines*, 97.

40. Polmar and Noot, *Submarines*, 99.

41. Ibid.

42. Grier, *Hitler, Dönitz, and the Baltic Sea*, 11.

43. *Führer Conferences*, 176.

CHAPTER SEVEN: CHAOS ON DECK

1. Excerpt from report #146 by Dr. Med. Peter Siegel, Homburg-Saar, Univ.-Franenkink, Ost-Dok, 4/1 Bundesarchiv, Bayreuth, Germany.

2. This and subsequent recollections of Eva Dorn come from author's interview with Eva Dorn in Ascona, Switzerland April 16, 2012.

3. Paul Vollrath, "Tragedy of the 'Wilhelm Gustloff," *Seabreezes: the Magazine of Ships and the Sea*, April 1981, vol. 55, no. 424, Liverpool, England, 228-229.

4. Max Hastings, *Armageddon: The Battle for Germany 1944-1945* (New York: Macmillan, 2004), 328.

5. Richard J. Evans, *The Third Reich at War* (New York: Penguin Press, 2009), 455.

6. Rose Rezas Petrus testimony included in July 10, 2007, letter to author as well as clipping of: Robert Dolgan, "30 Years Can't Erase Vision of Ship Sinking," *Plain Dealer,* Cleveland, OH.

7. Ibid.

8. Vollrath, *Seabreezes,* 227.

9. Ibid., 227-228.

10. This and subsequent recollections from Horst Woit come from author's interview with Horst Woit in Kimberly, Ontario, August 2007, as well as email and telephone correspondence since 2007.

11. Eva Dorn interview with author, April 15, 2012, Ascona, Switzerland.

12. Hastings, *Armageddon,* 328.

13. Juergen Thorwald, *Defeat in the East: Russia Conquers–January to May 1945* (New York: Bantam Books,1980), 7, 8, 50. Also see Michael H. Kater, *Hitler Youth* (Cambridge: Harvard University Press, 2004).

14. Heinz Schön, *SOS Wilhelm Gustloff, Die größte Schiffskatastrophe der Geschichte* (Stuttgart: Motor buch Verlag, 1998), 6-11.

15. Ibid.

16. Vollrath, *Seabreezes,* 228.

17. Ibid.

18. Ibid.

19. This and subsequent recollections from Helga Reuter Knickerbocker are from author's interview with Helga Reuter Knickerbocker, November 6, 2012.

20. Author interview with Horst Woit, Kimberly, Ontario, August 2007.

21. This and subsequent reflections from Ellen Tschinkur Maybee from author's interview with Ellen Tschinkur Maybee, Tecumseh, Ontario, December 5-6, 2011.

22. Cindy Lange-Kubick, "Lincoln Woman Survived Refugee Boat Sinking, *Lincoln Journal Star,* January 28, 2006, final ed.

23. Testimony of Wilhelm Zahn to German naval board of inquiry, February 4, 1945, Ost-Dok, 4/64 Bundesarchiv, Beyreuth, Germany.

24. David Ritchie, *Shipwrecks: An Encyclopedia of the World's Worst Disasters at Sea* (New York: FactsOnFile, Infobase Holdings Co, 1996), 243.

25. Wilhelm Zahn to Naval Board of Inquiry, February 4, 1945, Ost-Dok. 4/64, Bundesarchiv, Bayreuth, Germany.

26. Testimony Harry Weller, captain and survivor, Ost-Dok 4/1, Bundesarchiv, Bayreuth, Germany.

27. Rose Rezas Petrus testimony in July 10, 2007 letter to author.

28. Vollrath, *Seabreezes,* 229.

29. Ibid.

30. Ibid.

31. Robert Jackson, *Battle of the Baltic: The Wars of 1918–1945* (South Yorkshire, England: Pen & Sword Maritime, Pen & Sword Books, 2007), 176.

32. V.I. Dimitriev writing to Heinz Schön on the subject of the *S-13,* Ost-Dok. 4/64, 67, Bundesarchiv, Bayreuth, Germany.

33. Vollrath, *Seabreezes,* 230.

CHAPTER EIGHT: PLUMMETING TO THE SEA FLOOR

1. This and subsequent recollections from Irene Tschinkur East from author's interview with Irene Tschinkur East, Tecumseh, Ontario, December 5-6, 2011, as well as email correspondence from December 2011 to present.

2. Adolf Hitler radio address to German Folk Project Muse, Johns Hopkins University Press in collaboration with Milton S. Eisenhower Library, http://muse.jhu.edu/books/9781603444415, last accessed March 7, 2012.

3. This and subsequent recollections from Helga Reuter Knickerbocker from author's interview with Helga Reuter Knickerbocker, Las Vegas, NV, November 6, 2011.

4. Vollrath, *Seabreezes*, 231.

5. Wilhelm Zahn to board of inquiry, February 4, 1945, Ost-Dok, 4/64 Bundesarchiv, Beyreuth, Germany.

6. Ibid.

7. Ibid.

8. This and subsequent recollections from Milda Bendrich's letter to her daughter Inge Roedecker, July 1981.

9. Rose Rezas Petrus testimony included in July 10, 2007, letter to author as well as clipping of: Robert Dolgan, "30 Years Can't Erase Vision of Ship Sinking," *Plain Dealer,* Cleveland, OH.

10. Ibid.

11. Vollrath, *Seabreezes*, 231.

12. Ibid.

13. Alfred Maurice de Zayas, *A Terrible Revenge: The Ethnic Cleansing of the East European Germans,* 2nd ed. (New York: Palgrave Macmillan, 1986).

14. Cindy Lange-Kubick, "Lincoln Woman Survived Refugee Boat Sinking," *Lincoln Journal Star,* January 28, 2006, final ed.

15. Vollrath, *Seabreezes*, 232.

16. Author interview with Inge Roedecker, March 9, 2012.

17. Ibid.

18. Rose Rezas Petrus testimony included in July 10, 2007 letter to author.

19. This and subsequent recollections from Eva Dorn Rothschild from author's interview with Eva Dorn, April 16, 2016, Ascona, Switzerland.

20. Vollrath, *Seabreezes*, 231.

21. Eva Dorn interview with author, April 16, 2012, Ascona, Switzerland.

22. Vollrath, *Seabreezes*, 232.

CHAPTER NINE: THE LITTLE RED SWEATER

1. Paul Vollrath, "The Tragedy of the *Wilhelm Gustloff*," *Seabreezes: the Magazine of Ships and the Sea,* April 1981, vol. 55, no. 424, 1981. 232.

2. Excerpt from report #146 by Dr. Med. Peter Siegel, Homburg-Saar, Univ.-Franenkink, Ost-Dok. 4/1, Bundesarchiv, Bayreuth, Germany.

3. This and subsequent recollections from Helga Reuter Knickerbocker are from author's interview with Helga Reuter Knickerbocker, Las Vegas, NV, November 6, 2011.

4. Capt. Heinz Vollmers of the MS *Gotenland* writing to Adm. Conrad Engle-hardt. 1945. Ost-Dok. 4/76, 124-125, Bundesarchiv, Bayreuth, Germany.

5. Excerpt from report #146 by Dr. Med. Peter Siegel, Homburg-Saar, Univ.-Franenkink, Ost-Dok. 4/1, Bundesarchiv, Bayreuth, Germany.

6. Letter from Maj. Erich Schirmack to Adm. Conrad Englehardt, October 27, 1965, Ost-Dok. 4/76, 127, Bundesarchiv, Bayreuth, Germany.

7. Heinz Schön correspondence, Ost-Dok. 4/64, Bundesarchiv, Bayreuth, Germany.

8. Paul Vollrath, *Seabreezes*, 234.

9. Ibid., 234.

10. Author interview with Horst Woit, Kimberly, Ontario, August 2007.

11. Heinz Schön correspondence, Ost-Dok. 4/64, Bundesarchiv, Bayreuth, Germany.

12. Rose Rezas Petrus testimony included in July 10, 2007, letter to author as well as clipping of: Robert Dolgan, "30 Years Can't Erase Vision of Ship Sinking," *Plain Dealer*, Cleveland, OH.

13. This and subsequent recollections from Irene Tschinkur East are from au-thor's interview with Irene Tschinkur East, Tecumseh, Ontario, December 5-6, 2011, and email correspondence thereafter.

14. Author telephone interview with Inge Bendrich Roedecker, March 9, 2012.

15. "Report about refugee transports out of Gotenhafen, January, February, March, 1945," Ost-Dok. 4/21, Bundesarchiv, Bayreuth, Germany.

16. "RAF Hits Dresden Heavy Night Blow: 1,400 Planes Also Attack Oil Plant Near Leipzig and Targets in Magdeburg, *New York Times*, February 14, 1945, final ed.

17. This and subsequent recollections from Eva Dorn Rothschild are from au-thor's interview with Eva Dorn Rothschild, Ascona, Switzerland, April 16, 2012.

CHAPTER TEN: THE FORGOTTEN STORY

1. Adm. Karl Dönitz, "Uber die Teilnalme des Ob.d.M. an der Führerlage," Jan. 31, 1945, 4 PM., Ost-Dok. 4/3, 149-150, Bundesarchiv, Bayreuth, Germany.

2. Heinz Schön addresses the problem of the numbers in his book *SOS Wil-helm Gustloff Die größte Schiffskatastrophe der Geschichte* (Stuttgart: Motor buch Verlag, 1998).

3. "German Liner Seen Sunk: Finnish Radio Says Only 1,000 of 8,700 Aboard Were Saved," *New York Times*, February 19, 1945, final ed.

4. "6,000 Died in Wartime Sinking," *New York Times*, January 31, 1955, final ed.

5. "Nachricthen Für Die Truppe," February 19, 1945, seite 4.

6. Ibid.

7. Karl Dönitz, *Memoirs: Ten Years and Twenty Days*, trans. R.H. Stevens, David Woodward (New York: Da Capo Press, 1997), 466.

8. Karl Dönitz, "Uber die Teilnalme des Ob.d.M. an der Führerlage," Bundes-sarchiv, Bayreuth, Germany.

9.   Dönitz, *Memoirs,* 153.

10. Wilhelm Zahn testimony before the board of inquiry, February 4, 1945, Ost-Dok. F-64, Bundesarchiv, Beyreuth, Germany.

11. Englehardt to Hering, November 24, 1964, Ost-Dok. 4/64, Bundesarchiv, Bayreuth, Germany.

12. Englehardt to Hering, November 17, 1965, Ost-Dok. 4/64, Bundesarchiv, Bayreuth, Germany.

13. Timothy Snyder, *Bloodlands: Europe between Hitler and Stalin* (New York: Basic Books, 2010), 318.

14. Felice Fey, email correspondence with author, October 17, 2011.

15. Alfred Maurice de Zayas, *Nemesis at Potsdam: The Anglo-Americans and the Expulsion of the Germans, Background, Execution, Consequences* (London: Routledge & Kegan Paul, 1977), 13.

16. "'World's Oldest' Shipwreck found in the Baltic Sea," Baltic News Network, July 16, 2011, http://bnn-news.com/world's-oldest-shipwreck-baltic-sea-32412, last accessed March 14, 2012.

17. Author interview with Mike Boring, telephone, January 17, 2012.

18. Ibid.

19. Christian Caryl, "Not Forever Amber: Treasure Hunters Seek a Golden Room," *US News & World Report,* July 4, 2000, http://www.usnews.com/usnews/doubleissue/mysteries/amber.htm, last accessed March 8, 2012.

20. Record Group 226 OSS E125 Box 135 Folder 216 Stockholm-SO-INT-2, October 26, 1944, NARA, Washington, DC.

21. Record Group 226 OSS E125, Box 13, Folder 212, Stockholm-SO-INT-2, To – Digit London, dispatched 16.40, January 15, 1945. NARA, Washington, DC.

22. *Battle Cry,* July 8, 1958.

23. Elisabeth Noelle Neumann, *The Spiral of Silence: Public Opinion, Our Social Skin* (Chicago: University of Chicago Press, 1984), 27.

24. Ibid., 29.

25. Henrik Eberle, Henrik and Matthias Uhl, eds., *The Hitler Book: The Secret Dossier Prepared for Stalin from the Interrogations of Hitler's Personal Aides* (New York: Public Affairs, 2005), xv.

26. Gertrud Mackprang Baer, "Germans Wrestle with the Culture of Memory," *The Toronto Star,* April 29, 2005, A25.

27. Ursula Mahlendorf, *The Shame of Survival, Working Through a Nazi Childhood* (University Park: Pennsylvania State University Press, 2009), 10.

28. As quoted in Neumann, *The Spiral of Silence,* 77.

CHAPTER ELEVEN: "WE HAD TO GET OVER IT"

1.   Rose Rezas Petrus testimony included in July 10, 2007, letter to author as well as clipping of: Robert Dolgan, "30 Years Can't Erase Vision of Ship Sinking," *Plain Dealer,* Cleveland, OH.

2.   Albert Schweitzer, "The Problem of Peace," Nobel Lecture, November 4, 1954, Oslo, Norway, http://www.nobelprize.org/nobel_prizes/peace/laureates/1952/schweitzer-lecture.html, last accessed May 17, 2012.

3. The 1945 Potsdam Conference (1945) allowed for the mass expulsion of the German population from Czechoslovakia and from the territories given over to Russian and Polish administration.

4. Marcin Jamkowski, "Ghost Ship Found," *National Geographic,* February 2005, http://ngm.nationalgreographic.com/features/world/europe/balticsea /steuben/text?source-ge; V. I. Dimitriev writing to Heinz Schön on the subject of the *S-13.* Ost-Dok. 4/64, 67, Bundesarchiv, Beyreuth, Germany.

5. Ibid.

6. Ibid.

7. Ibid.

8. Jury Lebedev, Deputy Director of the A.I. Marinesko Museum of the Russian Underwater Forces, as quoted in Sergey Glezerov, "The Heroic Deed of Marinesko and the Tragedy of the German *Gustloff,*" http://rusnavy. com/history/events/marinesko.htm?print=Y, last accessed September 7, 2012.

9. Author email correspondence with Horst Woit, May 8, 2008.

10. Ursula Mahlendorf, *The Shame of Survival. Working Through a Nazi Childhood* (University Park: Pennsylvania State University Press, 2009), 220.

11. Jefferson Caffery, Ambassador to France, to Cordell Hull, April 14, 1945, FRUS, 1945, vol. 3, 935, NARA, Washington, DC.

12. Author email correspondence with Horst Woit, September 26, 2011.

13. Simon Rees, *German POWs and the Art of Survival,* Weider History Group, Historynet.com, published online July 17, 2007.

14. Author email correspondence with Horst Woit, May 4, 2008.

15. This and subsequent recollections of Irene Tschinkur East come from author's interview with Irene Tschinkur East, Tecumseh, Ontario, December 5-6, 2011.

16. This and subsequent recollections of Helga Reuter Knickerbocker are from author's interview with Helga Reuter Knickerbocker, Las Vegas, November 6, 2011.

17. Author telephone interview with Inge Roedecker, March 9, 2012.

18. "Nine German Refugees Figure in Sea Drama. Over a Thousand Miles in 32-foot Yacht. Afraid of Another War. Exhausted on Arrival at Checkpoint," *Waterford News,* August 27, 1948, 6.

19. Ibid.

20. Ibid.

21. Elmear Ni Bhraonain, "Son charged with killing his mother bids a final farewell," *Irish Independent,* March 14, 2012, final ed.

22. Letter courtesy of Rita Rowand.

23. Salk confirmation courtesy of Rita Rowand.

24. Cindy Lange-Kubick, "Lincoln Woman Survived Refugee Boat Sinking," *Lincoln Journal Star,* January 28, 2006, final ed.

25. Obituary of Leonilla Zobs, *Lincoln Journal Star,* March 22, 2011, final ed.

BIBLIOGRAPHY

Applegate, Celia. *A Nation of Provincials: The German Idea of Heimat*. Berkeley: University of California Press, 1990.

Axell, Albert. *Russia's Heroes: 1941-1945*. New York: Carroll & Graf, 2001.

Baer, Gerturd Mackprang. *In the Shadow of Silence—From Hitler Youth to Allied Internment: A Young Woman's Story of Truth and Denial*. New York: HarperCollins, 2002.

Baer, Gertrud Mackprang. "Germans Wrestle with the Culture of Memory." *The Toronto Star*, April 29, 2005, p. A25.

Bankier, David. *The Germans and the Final Solution: Public Opinion Under Nazism*. Cambridge: Blackwell Publishers, 1992.

Baranowski, Shelley. *Strength Through Joy: Consumerism and Mass Tourism in the Third Reich*. New York: Cambridge University Press, 2004.

Bartov, Omer. *Hitler's Army: Soldiers, Nazis, and War in the Third Reich*. Oxford, England: Oxford University Press, 1942.

Bartov, Omer. *The Eastern Front: 1941-1945, German Troops and the Barbarization of Warfare*. New York: Palgrave Macmillan, 2001.

Bauer, Yehuda. "The Death Marches, January–May, 1945." *Modern Judaism* 3, no. 1 (1983): 1-21. doi:10.1093/mj/3.1.1.

Beevor, Antony. Berlin: *The Downfall, 1945*. London: Penguin, 2002.

Bessel, Richard. *Germany 1945: From War to Peace*. New York: Harper Perennial, 2009.

Bessel, Richard. *Nazism and War*. New York: Modern Library, 2006.

Bessel, Richard. *Political Violence and the Rise of Nazism: The Storm Troopers in Eastern Germany, 1925-1934*. New Haven: Yale University Press, 1984.

Bhraonain, Elmear Ni. "Son charged with killing his mother bids a final farewell." *Irish Independent*. March 14, 2012

Bruhns, Wibke. *My Father's Country. The Story of a German Family*. Translated by Shaun Whiteside. New York: Alfred A. Knopf, 2008.

Butler, Daniel Allen. *Warrior Queens: The Queen Mary and Queen Elizabeth in World War II*. South Yorkshire, UK: Leo Cooper/Pen & Sword Books, 2002.

Burleigh, Michael. *Moral Combat: Good and Evil in World War Two*. New York: HarperCollins, 2011.

Burleigh, Michael. *Germany Turns Eastwards: A Study of Ostforschung in the Third Reich*. Cambridge, UK: Cambridge University Press, 1988.

Burleigh, Michael. *The Third Reich: A New History*. New York: Hill and Wang/ Farrar, Straus & Giroux, 2000.

Buttar, Prit. *Battleground Prussia: The Assault on Germany's Eastern Front: 1944-1945*. Oxford, UK: Osprey Publishing, 2010.

Caryl, Christian. "Not Forever Amber: Treasure Hunters Seek a Golden Room." *US News & World Report*. July 4, 2000.

de Zayas, Alfred-Maurice. *A Terrible Revenge: The Ethnic Cleansing of the East European Germans*. 2nd edition. New York: Palgrave MacMillan, 1986.

de Zayas, Alfred-Maurice. *Nemesis at Potsdam: The Anglo-Americans and the Expulsion of the Germans. Background, Execution, Consequences*. London: Routledge & Kegan Paul, 1977.

Dönitz, Karl. *Memoirs: Ten Years and Twenty Days*. Translated by R.H. Stevens with David Woodward. New York: Da Capo Press, 1997.

Domarus, Ma. *Hitler. Speeches and Proclamations*. Vol. 2. Mundelin, IL: Bolchazy-Carducci Publishers, 1992.

Dönhoff, Marion. *Before the Storm: Memories of My Youth in Old Prussia*. Translated by J. Steinberg. New York: Knopf, 1990.

Drynko, Romuald. *Stutthof Museum Guide*. Sztutowo, Poland: Muzeum w Sztutowie, 1993.

Drywa, Danuta. *Zaglada Zydow w obozie koncentracyjnym Stutthof. The extermination of Jews in Stutthof concentration camp*. Gdansk, Poland: Stutthof Museum in Sztutowo, 2004.

Eberle, Henrik, and Matthias Uhl, eds. *The Hitler Book: The Secret Dossier Prepared for Stalin from the Interrogations of Hitler's Personal Aides*. New York: Public Affairs, 2005.

Egremont, Max. *Forgotton Land: Journeys Among the Ghosts of East Prussia*. New York: Farrar, Straus & Giroux, 2011.

Englemann, Bernt. *In Hitler's Germany: Everyday Life in the Third Reich*. Translated by Krishna Winston. New York: Pantheon Books, 1986.

Ehrenburg, Ilya. *The War 1941–45*. Translated by Tatiana Shebunina with Yvonne Knapp. London: MacGibbon & Kee, 1964.

Erickson, John. *The Road to Berlin: Stalin's War with Germany*. Vol. 2. New Haven: Yale University Press, 1999.

Evans, Richard J. *The Third Reich at War*. New York: Penguin Press, 2009.

Feig, Konnilyn G. *Hitler's Death Camps: The Sanity of Madness*. New York: Holmes & Meir, 1981.

Frankel-Zaltzman, Paula. "Haftling (prisoner) no. 94771," Experiences in German lagers (camps) 1941-1945. Lithuania: Dvinsk, Riga, Kaiserwald. Germany: Stutthof, Torun, Bromberg. Memoirs of Holocaust Survivors in

Canada, vol. 28. Montreal, Quebec: Concordia University Chair in Canadian Jewish Studies, Montreal Institute for Genocide and Human Rights Studies, 2003.

Fritxche, Peter. *Life and Death in the Third Reich*. Cambridge: Belknap Press/ Harvard University Press, 2008.

Führer Conferences on Naval Affairs 1939-1945. Foreword by Jak P Mallmann Showell. London, UK: Chatham Publishing, 2005.

Galles, Arie Alexander. "Fourteen Stations: (arbaesreh takhanot Kiddush Hashem): Auschwitz-Birkenau, Babi Yar, Buechenwald, Belze, Bergan-Belsen, Gross-Rosen, Dachau, Chelmo, Treblinka, Mauthausen, Majdanek, Sobibor, Rabensbruk [*sic*], Stutthof." Fourteen black and white drawings on paper by Arie Galles, accompanied by fourteen *gematria* poems by Jerome Rothenberg. A. Galles, 1993. In US Holocaust Memorial Museum, Washington, DC.

Glantz, David M. and Jonathan House. *When Titans Clashed: How the Red Army Stopped Hitler*. Lawrence: University Press of Kansas, 1995.

Sergey Glezerov. "The Heroic Deed of Marinesko and the Tragedy of the German "Gustloff." www.RusNavy.com.

Graf von Krockow, Christian. *Hour of the Women*. Translated by Krishna Winston. New York: HarperCollins, 1991. Originally published as *Die Stunde der Frauen: Bericht aus Pommern 1944 bis 1947 Nach einer Erzählung von Libussa Fritz- Krockow* (Stuttgart, Germany: Deutsche Verlags-Anstalt, 1988).

Grier, Howard D. *Hitler, Dönitz and the Baltic Sea–The Third Reich's Last Hope 1944-1945*. Annapolis, MD: Naval Institute Press, 2007.

Gröner, Erich. *German Warships: 1815–1945. Volume 1: Major Surface Warships*. Annapolis, Maryland: Naval Institute Press, 1990.

Hastings, Max. *Armageddon: The Battle for Germany 1944-1945*. New York: Macmillan, 2004.

Heineman, Elizabeth. "The Hour of the Women: Memories of Germany's 'Crisis Years' and West German National Identity." *American Historical Review* 101, no. 2 (April 1996): 354-395.

Hoffman, Eva. *Shtetl: The Life and Death of a Small Town and the World of Polish Jews*. New York: Public Affairs, 2007.

Jackson, Robert. *Battle of the Baltic: The Wars of 1918–1945*. South Yorkshire, England: Pen & Sword Maritime, 2007.

Jaskolski, Stanislaw. *"Come With Me and Visit Hell."* Translated by Jim Przedzienkowski. Published by Jakub Przedzienkowski, July 2010. Amazon Digital Services.

Kamusella, Thomasz. "The Expulsion of the Population Categorized as 'Germans' from the Post-1945 Poland." Ch. 2 in "The Expulsion of the 'German' Communities from Eastern Europe at the End of the Second World War." Steffen Prauser and Arfon Rees, eds. EUI working paper No. 2004/1. European University Institute, Florence, Italy.

Kater, Michael H. *Hitler Youth*. Cambridge: Harvard University Press, 2004.

Kershaw, Ian. *The End: The Defiance and Destruction of Hitler's Germany: 1944-1945*. New York: Penguin Press, 2011.

Klemperer, Victor. *The Klemperer Diaries: I Shall Bear Witness: 1933-1945*. New York: Modern Library, 1999.

Kretein, Eva. *Eva's War: A True Story of Survival*. Albuquerque, NM: Amador, 1990.

Kopelev, Lev. *To Be Preserved Forever*. Translated and edited by Anthony Austin. Philadelphia: J.B. Lippincott, 1977.

Korzh, Victor. *Red Star Under the Baltic: A firsthand account of Life on Board a Soviet Submarine in World War Two*. Translated by Clare Burstall and Vladimir Kisselnikov. P. South Yorkshire, England: Pen & Sword Maritime, 2004.

Kurth, K.O. *Documents of Humanity*. New York: Harper and Brothers, 1954.

Lane, Thomas. *Victims of Stalin and Hitler. The Exodous of Poles and Balts to Britain*. New York: Palgrave MacMillan, 2004.

Larsen, Erik. *In the Garden of Beasts: Love, Terror, and an American Family in Hitler's Berlin*. New York: Crown, 2011.

Lehndorff, Hans. *Token of a Covenant; Diary of an East Prussian Surgeon, 1945-47*. Translated by E. Mayer. Chicago: Henry Regnery, 1964.

Lemberg Eugen. "Der Wandel des politischen Denkens," in *Die Vertriebenen in Westdeutschland: ihre Eingliederung und ihr Einfluss auf Gesellschaft, Wirtschaft, Politik und Geistesleben*. 3 vols. Edited by Eugen Lemberg and Friedrich Edding. Kiel, Germany: Ferdinand Hirt, 1959.

Levine, Herbert S. *Hitler's Free City: A History of the Nazi Party in Danzig, 1925-1939*. Chicago: University of Chicago Press, 1930.

Lias, Godfrey. *I Survived*. London: Evan Bros., 1954.

Love, Dora. *After Stutthof Concentration Camp: What Hope?* Glasgow, Scotland: Clydeside Press, 2010.

Lucas, James. *War on the Eastern Front; 1941-1945. The German Soldier in Russia*. New York: Stein and Day, 1979.

Lukas, Richard. *Forgotten Holocaust: The Poles Under German Occupation, 1939–1944*. New York: Hippocrene Books, 1990.

Mahlendorf, Ursula. *The Shame of Survival: Working Through a Nazi Childhood*. University Park: Pennsylvania State University Press, 2009.

Maier, Charles. *The Unmasterable Past: History, Holocaust and the German National Identity*. Cambridge: Harvard University Press, 1988.

Mason, Tim. *Social Policy in the Third Reich: The Working Class and the National Community*. Oxford: Oxford University Press, 1993.

McDonald, James G. *Refugees and Rescue: The Diaries and Papers of James G. McDonald, 1935-1945*. Edited by Richard Breitman, Barbara McDonald Stewart, and Severin Hochberg. Bloomington: Indiana University Press, 2009.

Merridale, Catherine. *Ivan's War: Life and Death in the Red Army, 1939-1945*. New York: Metropolitan Books. Henry Holt, 2006.

Milgram, Stanley. *Obedience to Authority: An Experimental View*. New York: Harper Torch Books, Harper & Row, 1969.

Nagorski, Andrew. *The Greatest Battle: Stalin, Hitler and the Desperate Struggle for Moscow that Changed the Course of World War II*. New York: Simon & Schuster, 2007.

Naimark, Norman. *Fires of Hatred: Ethnic Cleansing in Twentieth-Century Europe*. Cambridge: Harvard University Press, 2001.

Naimark, Norman, *The Russians in Germany: A History of the Soviet Zone of Occupation, 1945-1949*. Cambridge: Belknap Press/Harvard University Press, 1995.

Neumann, Elisabeth Noelle. *The Spiral of Silence: Public Opinion, Our Social Skin*. Chicago: University of Chicago Press, 1984.

"Nine German Refugees Figure in Sea Drama. Over a Thousand Miles in 32-foot Yacht. Afraid of Another War. Exhausted on Arrival at Checkpoint." *Waterford News*, Ireland. August 27, 1948.

Nussenbaum, Isidor. "He's Not Coming Here Anymore; A Survivor's Story" University of Michigan, 2005.

Orski, Marek. *The Americans in KL Stutthof*, KL Stutthof Muzeum Stutthof w Sztutowie. Gdansk, Poland: Stutthof Museum, 1996.

Orski, Marek. *Des Francais Au Camp de Concentration de Stutthof*. Gdansk: Muzeum Stutthof w Sztutowie, 1995.

"Order of the People's Commissar of the USSR Navy," April 9, 1939, No. 0161 Moscow–Confidential/DeClassified. Submarine Force Museum, Groton, CT.

Padfield, Peter. *War Beneath the Sea: Submarine Conflict, 1939-1945*. London: Random House UK,1995.

Paine, Lincoln P. *Ships of the World: An Historical Encyclopedia*. Boston: Houghton Mifflin, 1997.

Persson, Hans-Ake. "Settling the Peace, the Cold War, and the Ethnic Cleansing of Germans in Central and Eastern Europe," November 5, 1998, at the Institut für Migrationsforschung und Interkulturelle Studien, Universität Osnabrück.

Pleshakov, Constantine. *Stalin's Last Folly: The Tragic First 10 Days of World War Two on the Eastern Front*. Boston: Houghton Mifflin, 2005.

Polmar, Norman & Jurrien Noot. *Submarines of the Russian and Soviet Navies, 1718-1990*. Annapolis, MD: Naval Institute Press, 1991.

Prince, Cathryn J. *Shot from the Sky: American POWs in Switzerland*. Annapolis, MD: Naval Institute Press, 2003.

Reichling, Gerhard, *Die deutschen Vertriebenen in Zahlen: Teil I, Umsiedler, Verschleppte, Vertriebene, Aussiedler, 1940-1985*. Bonn: Kulturstiftung der deutschen Vertriebenen, 1995.

Ritchie, David. Shipwrecks: *An Encyclopedia of the World's Worst Disasters at Sea*. New York: Facts On File, Infobase Holdings, 1996.

Rohwer, Jürgen. *Chronology of the War at Sea 1939-1945: The Naval History of World War Two*. 3rd revised ed. Annapolis, MD: Naval Institute Press, 2005.

Roy, James Charles. *The Vanished Kingdom: Travels Through the History of East Prussia*. New York: Basic Books, 2000.

Schechtman, Joseph B. *The Refugee in the World: Population and Displacement*. New York: A.S. Barnes, 1963.

Schön, Heinz. *SOS Wilhelm Gustloff, Die größte Schiffskatastrophe der Geschichte*. Stuttgart, Germany: Motor buch Verlag, 1998.

Schulze, Rainer. "The German Refugees and Expellees from the East and the Creation of a Western German Identity after World War II." In *Redrawing Nations: Ethnic Cleansing in East-Central Europe, 1944-1948*. Edited by Philipp Ther and Ana Siljak Lanham. New York, Oxford: Rowman & Littlefield, 2001.

Semmens, Kristin. *Seeing Hitler's Germany: Tourism in the Third Reich*. New York, Palgrave Macmillan, New York: 2005.

Shirer, William. *The Rise and Fall of the Third Reich: A History of Nazi Germany*. New York: Simon & Schuster, 1960.

Snyder, Timothy. *Bloodlands: Europe Between Hitler and Stalin*. New York: Basic Books, 2010.

Snyder, Timothy. "Hitler vs. Stalin: Who Killed More?" *New York Times*, March 10, 2011.

Stein, George H. *The Waffen SS: Hitler's Elite Guard at War*. Ithaca: Cornell University Press, 1984.

Sruoga, Balys. Dievu miskas. *Forest of the Gods: Memoirs*. Vilnius, Lithuania: Vaga, 1996.

Tegeler, Tillmann. "The Explusion of the German Speakers from Baltic Countries." Ch. 6 in "The Expulsion of the 'German' Communities from Eastern Europe at the End of the Second World War." Edited by Steffen Prauser and Arfon Rees. EUI working paper No. 2004/1. European University Institute, Florence, Italy.

Thacker, Toby. *Joseph Goebbels: Life and Death*. New York: Palgrave Macmillan, 2009.

Ther, Philipp, and Ana Siljak, eds. *Redrawing Nations: Ethnic Cleansing in East-Central Europe, 1944-1948*. New York, Oxford: Rowman & Littlefield, 2001.

Thorwald, Juergen. *Defeat in the East: Russia Conquers–January to May 1945*. Originally published as *Flight in Winter*. Translated and edited by Fred Wieck. New York: Bantam Books, 1980.

Toland, John. *The Last 100 Days*. New York: Bantam/Random House, 1976.

Tucker, Spencer C., ed. *Naval Warfare: An International Encyclopedia*. Vol.1. Oxford, England: ABC-Clio, 2002.

Vollrath, Paul. "Tragedy of the 'Wilhelm Gustloff.'" *Seabreezes: the Magazine of Ships and the Sea* 55, no. 424 (April 1981), Liverpool, England.

Wall, Robert. *Ocean Liners.* New York: D.P. Dutton, 1977.

Welch, David. *The Third Reich: Politics and Propaganda.* 2nd edition. Oxon, Canada: Routledge, 1993.

Weinberg, Gerhard. *A World At Arms: A Global History of World War Two.* Cambridge: Cambridge University Press, 1995.

Werth, Alexander. *Russia At War: 1941-1945.* New York: E.P. Dutton, 1964.

Westermann, Edward A. *Hitler's Police Battalions: Enforcing Racial War in the East.* Lawrence: University Press of Kansas, 2005.

Whitley, M. J. *German Destroyers of World War Two.* Annapolis, MD: Naval Institute Press, 1991.

Wojciechowska, Bogusia. *Waiting To Be Heard: The Polish Christian Experience Under Nazi and Stalinist Oppression 1939–1955.* Blooomington, Indiana: Author House, 2009.

"'World's Oldest Shipwreck Found in the Baltic Sea." Baltic News Network, July 16, 2011. http://bnn-news.com/world's-oldest-shipwreck-baltic-sea-32412, last accessed March 14, 2012.

Zelkovitz, Rose Pinkosovic. *From the Carpathian Mountains to the New Jersey Seashore: A Holocaust Survivor's Memoir.* United States Holocaust Memorial Museum, Washington, DC., 2004.

UNPUBLISHED SOURCES

Inge Salk Diary

Letter from Serafima Tschinkur to Otto and Felix von Lieven

Letter from Milda Bendrich to Inge Bendrich Roedecker

Inge Bendrich papers

Letter from Rose Rezas Petrus to author.

WEBSITES

The Soviet Submarine Force in World War Two. www.ww2f.com/eastern-europe. Last accessed April 4, 2011.

United States Holocaust Memorial Museum. http://www.ushmm.org/wlc/en/?ModuleId=10005143. Last accessed Dec. 22, 2011.

HistoryNet.com. http://www.historynet.com/soviet-prisoners-of-war-forgotten-nazi-victims-of-world-war-ii.htm.

ARCHIVES

National Archives and Records Administration, Washington, DC/College Park

Bayreuth Archives, Bayreuth, Germany

United States Holocaust Memorial Museum, Washington, DC

Submarine Force Library & Museum, Groton, Connecticut

INDEX